WORLD GEOGRAPHY
Case Studies

EDITED BY
Vincent Bunce

SERIES EDITOR
David Lambert

Published by the Press Syndicate of the University of Cambridge
The Pitt Building, Trumpington Street, Cambridge CB2 1RP
40 West 20th Street, New York, NY 10011-4211, USA
10 Stamford Road, Oakleigh, Melbourne 3166, Australia

© Cambridge University Press 1994

First published 1994

Printed in Great Britain at the University Press, Cambridge

A catalogue record for this book is available from the British Library

ISBN 0 521 45667 3

Designed and produced by Hart McLeod

Illustrated by Sheila Betts, Jeff Edwards, Steve Hawes, Peter Welford, John York

Acknowledgements
These case studies were originated as part of a project in the Geography Curriculum Development Unit (GCDU) at the Institute of Education, University of London. The editors would like to thank Ashley Kent and Frances Slater for the support they gave to the initiation and development of the project.

The authors and the publishers would like to thank the following for their advice and assistance: Jeanette Kayes, Case Study M; Tate & Lyle, Case Study N.

Photographs
5, University of Cambridge Committee for Aerial Photography; 6, Michael Brooke; 15 (*bckgrnd*), 17, 19, 21*t*, 35 (*bckgrnd*), 36*b*, 43*l*, *r*, Anne Longbottom; 27*t*, 94, Alan Doherty; 25 (*bckgrnd*), 29, 30*r*, Peter Hulme/Ecoscene; 30*l*, 61*l*, 92*l*, Wildlife Matters; 31, Lorne Gill/Scottish Natural Heritage; 45 (*bckgrnd*), 49, courtesy of Vauxhall Motors Ltd/photo: Altair Photo, Madrid; 46, courtesy of SEAT; 55 (*bckgrnd*), 75*tc*, Mick Rock/Cephas; 56*b*, Emma Lee/Life File; 60, Mark Hibbert/Life File; 61*r*, courtesy of IBM UK Ltd; 61*c*, 67*l*, 68*br*, 69*b*, 73 (*bckgrnd*), 75*r*, David Simson/das Photo; 65 (*bckgrnd*), 66*l*, Sally Morgan/Ecoscene; 75*l*, Agence Vu/Didier Lefevre; 77*tl*, Marc Morceau/La Photothèque EDF; 77*tr*, Bertrand Clech/La Photothèque EDF; 77*cr*, *bl*, Robert Harding Picture Library; 75*bc*, 80, Mike & Miriam Robinson; 77*br*, Y. Arthus Bertrand/Robert Harding Picture Library; 83 (*bckgrnd*), 88*t*, *b*, David Kampfner/Life File; 84, 141 (*bckgrnd*), 143*l*, 145*bl*, 148*bl*, 148*bc*, 148*br*, Jeremy Hartley/Panos Pictures; 91 (*bckgrnd*), Brown/Ecoscene; 92*r*, Eric Burt/Cephas; 103*t*, 121 (*bckgrnd*), 126, 143*r*, 148*tr*, Ron Giling/Panos Pictures; 101 (*bckgrnd*), 104, 107*t*, Bob Bradnock; 107*b*, Roderick Johnson/Images of India/Link Picture Library; 111 (*bckgrnd*), 112, 115, 116*t*, Bill Adams; 123*r*, Andrew Ward/Life File; 127, 129, Adrian Neville/Robert Harding Picture Library; 128*t*, D. Donne Bryant/DDB Stock Photo; 131 (*bckgrnd*), Maptec International Ltd/Science Photo Library; 133*t*, Paul Smith/Panos Pictures; 133*b*, courtesy of Tate & Lyle Sugars/photo by Alan W. Smith; 136*r*, D. Donne Bryant Stock Photos/Suzanne Murphy-Larronde; 148*tl*, Benoit Gysembergh/Camera Press; 151 (*bckgrnd*), 152, 154*b*, Jeremy Hoare/Life File; 153, Brian Heppell; 154*l*, Andreas Rubin/ Life File

Every effort has been made to reach the copyright holders; the publishers would be pleased to hear from anyone whose rights they have unknowingly infringed.

Notice to teachers
It is illegal to reproduce any part of this work in material form (including photocopying and electronic storage) except under the following circumstances:
(i) where you are abiding by a licence granted to your school or institution by the Copyright Licensing Agency;
(ii) where no such licence exists, or where you wish to exceed the terms of a licence, and you have gained the written permission of Cambridge University Press;
(iii) where you are allowed to reproduce without permission under the provisions of Chapter 3 of the Copyright, Designs and Patents Act 1988.

Contents

Introduction

Case Studies

UK local area, home and contrasting region

A The Cambridge Phenomenon   *Jenny Blumhof*   5
B King Coal is Dead – New Jobs for Wakefield   *Vincent Bunce*   15
C Changing Rural Land Use in the Flow Country   *Alan Doherty*   25
D Farming in the Yorkshire Dales: Issues and Conflicts   *Kerstin Jarman*   35

The European Union (Spain, France and Germany)

E Car Production in Spain   *John Huckle*   45
F The Farmers of Languedoc-Roussillon, and the EC Wine Lake   *Vincent Bunce*   55
G Cleaning-up the River Rhine   *Pauline de Wit van Schlie*   65
H The French Energy Dilemma   *Mike and Miriam Robinson*   73

CIS/former USSR and USA

I All Change for Farmers of the Former Soviet Union   *Vincent Bunce*   83
J Western USA's Water Crisis: The Case of Mono Lake   *Alan Doherty*   91

Economically developing countries

K Irrigating India   *Bob Bradnock*   101
L Sokoto River Project, Nigeria   *Bill Adams*   111
M The Mexican Oil Industry   *David Fox*   121

Enrichment case studies

N A Multinational Company: Tate & Lyle   *Neil Larkin*   131
O Subsistence Farming in Burkina Faso   *Tony Binns*   141
P The Rise and Rise of Taiwan and the East Asian NICs   *Brian Heppell*   151

Index   160

Introduction

To really understand *World Geography* it is necessary to examine a variety of patterns and processes – physical, human and environmental. Often these can be seen across the whole planet – when studying volcanic activity, population distribution or air pollution, for example. However, only by examining situations more locally can the impact of these patterns, and the processes which bring them about, be seen and understood. That is why this book concentrates on providing a variety of **case studies**. Each one examines a particular issue in some detail.

There are 16 case studies. Each is designed to help you understand certain aspects of world geography. Whether you are investigating the reasons for building a dam on a river in Nigeria, changing employment patterns in a British city, or the impact of the European Union on agriculture in southern France, certain elements of each case study remain the same:

- At the start of each case study you are given a **role**.
- Each case study is structured as an **enquiry**.
- There are **key questions** to guide your enquiry.
- A range of **resources** is included to help your investigation.
- You will have to consider how **people** control or are affected by the processes operating in each case study.

Your **role** is important because it gives you a **purpose** for studying the resources. It should also help you to really get involved in each case study. The **key questions** provide a structure which guide the subsequent enquiry you will undertake, and there are plenty of activities for you to do. Remember to check your progress regularly and make sure that the key understandings at the end of each case study are clear. Finally, *enjoy* these case studies!

Case Study A

The Cambridge Phenomenon

Cambridge is a city with two faces. It has a fascinating history dating back to Anglo-Saxon times and is home to a world-famous university. It is also at the forefront of a late 20th-century industrial initiative – the establishment of science parks. But what *are* science parks? Why is Cambridge such a good location for this new type of industrial activity?

> You are the Economic Development Officer of a city in northern England. Your city is interested in setting up a science park. You have been asked to find out as much as you can about science parks, so that you can report back to your city council about these new industrial areas.

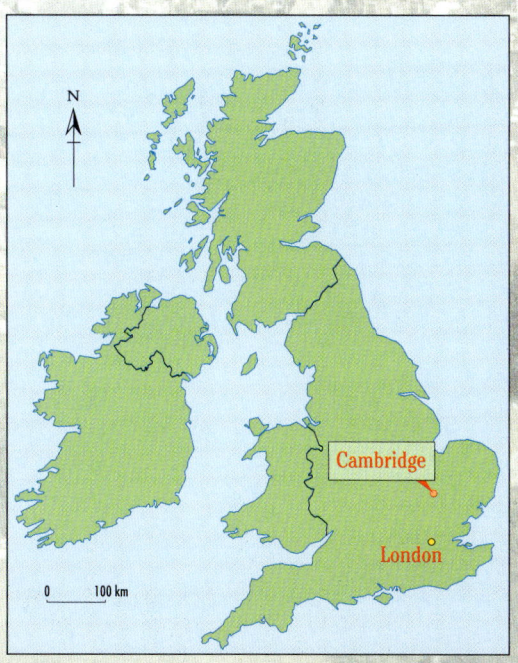

The position of Cambridge in the UK.

CASE STUDY A

The Cambridge Phenomenon

Key Question 1
What kind of industrial initiative is a science park?

The Two Faces of Cambridge

Resource A

Cambridge developed around a river crossing, and was an early trading centre. In the 12th century two monasteries were established, and the University developed from their schools. Today, the city attracts academics and tourists from many countries. It still retains its medieval atmosphere, with quaint narrow winding lanes, and some beautiful old buildings.

Old Cambridge.

Modern Cambridge.

The other face of Cambridge, its high-technology image, can be seen beside the modern roads which bypass the city to the north. A collection of futuristic metal, glass and concrete structures have been built in what looks like a green park. This is the Cambridge Science Park.

Resource B

Directory of Science Parks

The history of science parks

The 'science park' was an American idea which began life on the campus of Stanford University near San Francisco. Forty years ago, students leaving Stanford were encouraged to establish their own companies. One such student was Bill Hewlett. He worked in his garage with a fellow student called David Packard building audio oscillators. Hewlett Packard is now a huge worldwide company. A pattern of complex links between people, products and research is common in **high-technology industries** like Hewlett Packard and in science parks.

Science parks in the UK

In the mid-1960s the British government suggested that the universities should encourage the development of high-technology industries. Partly because of that, but also through the universities' own initiative, these industries have slowly developed all over Britain. In 1972 the first two science parks were established by Trinity College in Cambridge and by Heriot-Watt University in Edinburgh. Many cities in Britain now have a science park.

What exactly is a science park?

Many developments call themselves **science parks**. However, the UK Science Park Association (UKSPA) lists only 42 'true' science parks. According to the association, a 'true' science park is a collection of new factory buildings with operational links to a higher educational institution. The Cambridge Science Park's own definition adds a need for landscaped surroundings. They say that a science park is a collection of high-technology industries or research institutes in attractive, well-landscaped surroundings and developed to a low density.

Operational science parks in the UK, 1992.

Parks	42
Hectares	463
Buildings constructed	475,214 m²
under construction	33,457 m²
Tenants	1,092

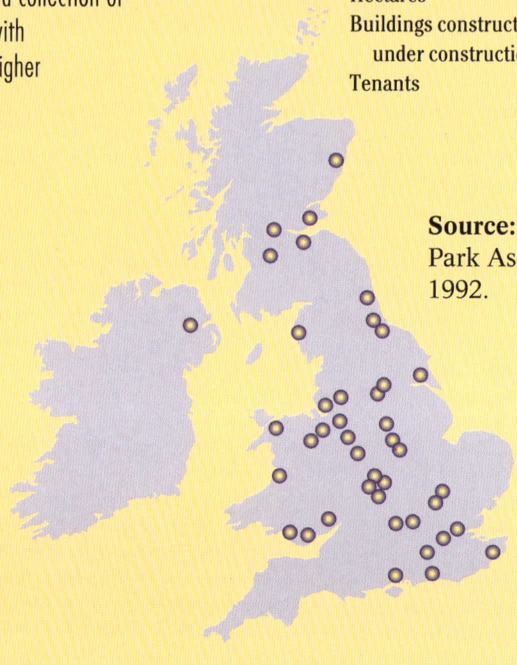

Source: UK Science Park Association, 1992.

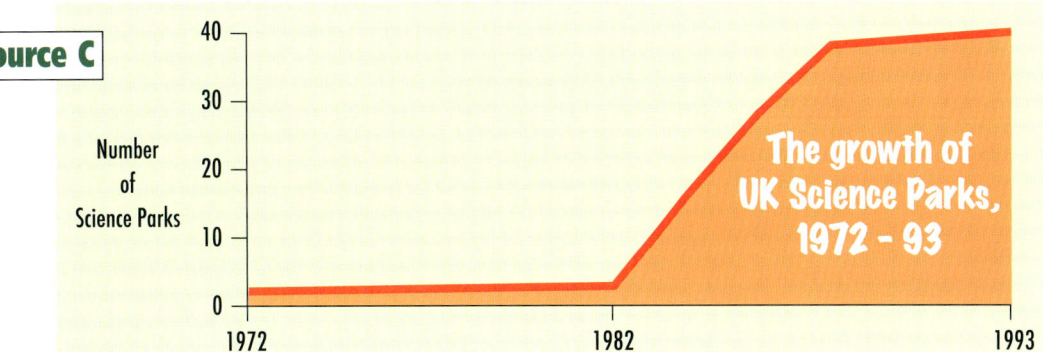

CASE STUDY A

The Cambridge Phenomenon

Resource D

Science Parks in the UK, 1992	Year of opening	Total area (ha)	Number of tenants
Aberdeen: Aberdeen Science & Technology Park	1988	24.3	26
Aberystwyth: Aberystwyth Science Park	1985	2.4	14
Antrim: Antrim Technology Park	1986	32.4	9
Ascot: Silwood Park	1987	3.2	15
Aston: Aston Science Park	1983	8.9	70
Bangor: Menai Technology Enterprise Centre	1987	0.8	5
Billingham: Belasis Hall Technology Park	1988	46.5	70
Birmingham: University of Birmingham Research Park	1986	3.2	19
Bradford: Listerhills Science Park	1983	7.1	30
Brighton: Sussex University Technology Park	1985	1.4	16
Brunel: Brunel University Science Park	1986	2.6	22
Cambridge:			
Cambridge Science Park	1972	52.6	85
St John's Innovation Park	1987	8.1	83
Canterbury: Kent Research and Development Centre	1986	4.0	7
Cardiff: Cardiff Business Technology Centre	1987	0.6	15
Cranfield: Cranfield Technology Park	1991	40.5	1
Deeside, Clwyd: Newtech Innovation Centre	1985	4.0	15
Durham: Durham Mountjoy Research Centre	1985	1.1	21
Edinburgh: Heriot-Watt University Research Park	1971	35.2	44
Glasgow/Strathclyde: West of Scotland Science Park	1983	24.9	20
Guildford: The Surrey Research Park	1984	28.3	56
Hull: Newlands Science Park	1984	1.2	15
Keele: Keele University Science Park Ltd	1987	6.1	22
Leeds: Springfield House, Leeds University	1983	0.8	7
Liverpool: Merseyside Innovation Centre	1982	0.8	11
London: South Bank Technopark	1985	0.7	43
Loughborough: Loughborough Technology Centre	1984	1.2	10
Manchester: Manchester Science Park	1984	6.3	19
Newcastle: Newcastle Technopole	1992	2.2	0
Newport: Imperial House, Newport, Gwent	1992	20.2	0
Nottingham: Highfields Science Park	1984	7.3	42
Oxford: The Oxford Science Park	1991	16.6	28
Reading: University of Reading Innovation Centre	1986	—	11
St Andrews: St Andrews Technology Centre	1984	0.3	6
Salford: Salford University Business Park	1988	4.0	37
Sheffield: Sheffield Science Park	1988	2.0	28
Southampton: Chilworth Research Centre	1985	10.5	26
Stirling: Stirling University Innovation Park	1986	5.7	20
Swansea: Swansea Innovation Centre	1986	1.4	19
Warwick: University of Warwick Science Park Ltd	1984	17.0	63
Whitehaven: Westlakes Science & Technology Park	1992	5.7	11
Wrexham: Wrexham Technology Park	1988	20.2	31

Source: UK Science Park Association.

Activities

When you have answered the following questions, write a preliminary report as the Economic Development Officer for your city council, giving the background to science parks.

1 Look at the right-hand photograph in Resource A. Describe this modern industrial scene. How are these industrial buildings different from factories in your own area?

2 The map (Resource B) shows the location of the science parks listed in Resource D. Copy the map, numbering the science park locations. Include the names of the science parks in a key, using an atlas and the list in Resource D to help you.

3 Describe the growth of science parks in the UK (Resource C), and explain why they are found where they are.

4 Copy and complete the following passage. Select the words you need from the word list below.

The idea of science parks came from the ▭. There was a call for ▭ between ▭ and ▭. Hewlett Packard was among the first ▭ companies in ▭ Valley, California. The science park movement started in the United Kingdom with the establishment by Trinity College Cambridge of a park in ▭ and by ▭ in Edinburgh in ▭.

> *industry   high-technology   Silicon*
> *USA   universities   co-operation*
> *Heriot-Watt University   1971   1972*

CASE STUDY A
The Cambridge Phenomenon

Key Question 2
Why locate a science park in Cambridge?

How did Cambridge's involvement with the science park begin?

In 1969 a Cambridge University Committee recommended that science-based industry in the city should be expanded. Such industry, which was small-scale and non-polluting, was unlikely to damage Cambridge's unique urban environment. Trinity College liked this idea, and owned some land on the outskirts of the city which was suitable for development.

Trinity College wanted to link the research done in the University to industries which could use this research directly. The Cambridge Science Park was opened in 1972.

In 1993 the Cambridge Science Park contained 80 companies covering a variety of high-technology activities. Some are recently established, small independent companies, while others are branches of larger corporations. High-technology companies often consist of just one or two people trying to exploit the commercial potential of a new scientific idea or technology. New companies form quickly as people change jobs, often to work on new projects.

What is 'Silicon Fen'?

Resource E

The Cambridge area, sometimes called 'Silicon* Fen', has become a centre for **quaternary industries**. By 1992 there were almost 850 firms involved in high-technology activity in Cambridgeshire, employing more than 23,400 people. This growth of high-technology industry has come to be known as the 'Cambridge Phenomenon'. There are only two other such high-technology concentrations in the country: Central Scotland's 'Silicon Glen' and the M4 corridor west of London.

* Computer chips are made from silicon.

Why did high-technology industry find Cambridge an attractive location?

The City of Cambridge has a number of locational advantages for high-technology industry:

✱ Cambridge has good communication links with London (M11) and the east coast ports (A45) as well as with the Midlands and the North. It is close to London's third airport at Stansted, and has good access via the M25 to larger airports at Heathrow and Gatwick. There is a regular and fast rail service between Cambridge and London.

✱ There is a good supply of high-quality labour in Cambridge, and the city is small enough for **entrepreneurs** to be in easy contact with each other, and to know quickly about the latest ventures.

✱ In the late 1970s a major bank decided to invest time and money to help people starting up high-technology enterprises. The city now has good supplies of **venture capital**, and has attracted many ancillary businesses such as patent agents, accountants, etc.

✱ Cambridge is fortunate in having a desirable and attractive environment for working and living. This is an increasingly important location factor when firms consider setting up or relocating.

✱ The final and perhaps most important advantage of Cambridge for high-technology industry is the University itself, which has a long record of technological excellence. In the 1960s it decided to encourage commercial activity by its staff, giving scientists a free hand to start business ventures, and now maintains strong links with many of the firms in the science park.

Resource F

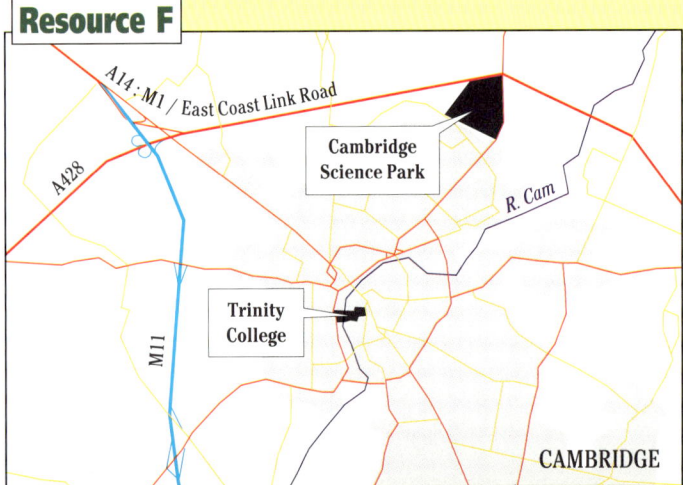

The location of the Cambridge Science Park.

Resource G

CASE STUDY A

The Cambridge Phenomenon

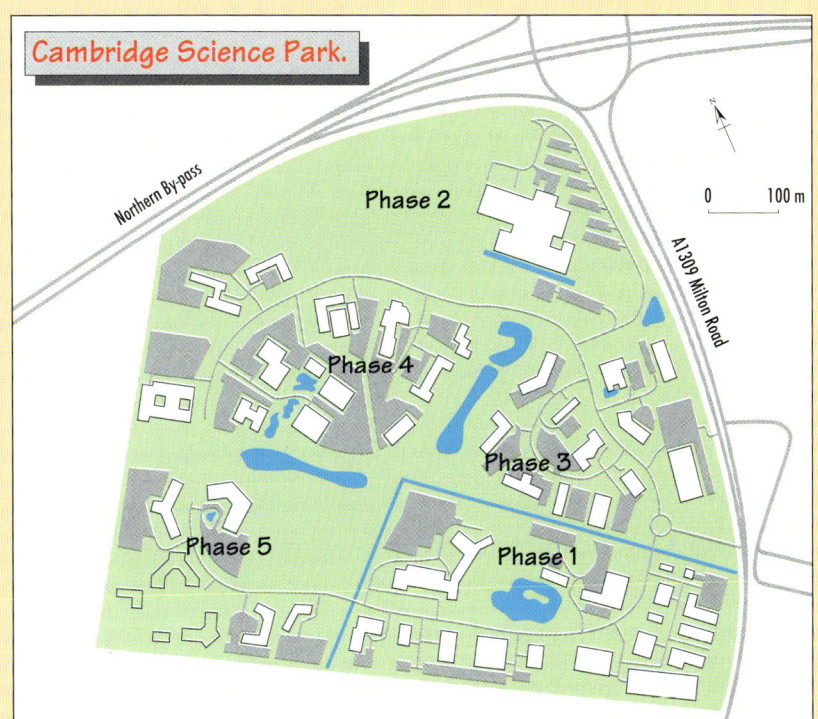

Cambridge Science Park.

Progress up to 1993 ...

- Site area
- No. of companies – 46
- Total occupied area – 86,183m^2
- Phases 1, 2 and 3 completed
- Phase 4 – two major buildings under construction

Features of the Cambridge Science Park

- Established in 1972 by Trinity College, the college where Isaac Newton and many other famous scientists studied and worked.
- Close links with the scientific excellence of Cambridge University.
- Low-density development in a park-like setting.
- Some 80 compatible neighbours also involved in high technology.
- High-quality, flexible buildings suited to office, laboratory or manufacturing use.

What is the Cambridge Phenomenon?

High technology in Cambridgeshire	Number of companies	Number employed	1992 company size								Total
			No. of employees	1–5	6–10	11–24	25–49	50–99	100–149	200–499	500+	
Established by 1974	61	1,750	No. of companies	369	154	147	89	46	20	15	6	____
Established by 1984	261	13,700	%									
Established by 1992	846	23,410										

Activities

The resources on these two pages indicate the advantages of Cambridge as a location for science-based industry. You believe that establishing a science park can benefit your home town or city considerably. Answer the questions below, then list as many reasons as you can why your own town or city council should set up a science park.

1 Look at Resource F carefully. Draw a sketch map showing the location of the Cambridge Science Park. Mark the main roads clearly.

2 Is there any evidence to suggest that the Cambridge Science Park is growing (Resource G)?

3 In small groups, discuss what sort of practical project work you could do on the Cambridge Science Park. Try to think of at least one hypothesis, question or idea which you could investigate.

4 Write a paragraph explaining some of the reasons for the growth of high-technology industry in the Cambridge area.

5 Examine Resource G carefully.
a What is the typical profile of a high-technology company, and what are its location requirements?
b Copy and complete the table of 'company size' by (i) calculating the number of high-technology firms in Cambridgeshire in 1992 and (ii) working out the percentage of companies in each size grouping. Put this figure in the final column of your table.
c What increase was there in the number of high-technology firms between 1984 and 1992?

CASE STUDY A

The Cambridge Phenomenon

Key Question 3
Is the development of high-technology industry in Cambridge good or bad?

As with all industrial growth, the development of high-technology and quaternary industries in the Cambridge Science Park can be said to pose problems and to offer possibilities.

Ms Liz Hudson
City Planning Department

James Weston
PR Associates

Resource H

Problems

1 Congestion The rapid development of high-technology industry has meant that the local people have had to cope with traffic congestion in and around the city, as well as a severe shortage of housing. To deal with these problems, the City Council is restricting development in the already crowded city centre, and is diverting new growth to the less-congested north and east of the city. It is also promoting the development of new villages as a way of housing the increasing population.

2 The skills and jobs mismatch A survey undertaken in 1986 showed that there were few job opportunities for semi-skilled or unskilled labour in the Cambridge area. High-technology firms require well-qualified staff and generally employ a high proportion of graduates.

Benefits

1 Employment High-tech industry has brought new jobs to the Cambridge City area. In 1993 the Cambridge Science Park provided 3,500 jobs. Already a second science park (the St John's Innovation Park) has been opened on a nearby 8-hectare site. And in the county of Cambridgeshire high-technology industry is an important employer.

2 Prosperity The rapid growth of the quaternary sector has brought new prosperity to the Cambridge area. Employment in high-technology firms accounts for almost 20% of jobs in the area. Many other companies have set up in and around Cambridge offering support services.

3 Innovation The combination of high-technology industries and higher education institutions like Cambridge University has led to many new inventions. Science parks demonstrate the many non-military and beneficial uses of science and technology. For example, Intervet (a Cambridge Science Park company) has developed three new poultry vaccines. Another company, Advanced Technologies, was in 1989 using 'state-of-the-art' genetic engineering to produce paper from fast-growing woods such as eucalyptus that will grow all over the world, even in very dry conditions.

On a national scale, the 'M11 corridor', which runs south from Cambridge to north London, is likely to become an important focus for future growth. It offers a pleasant environment, a skilled workforce, a successful tradition in high-technology industry and good communications.

CASE STUDY A: The Cambridge Phenomenon

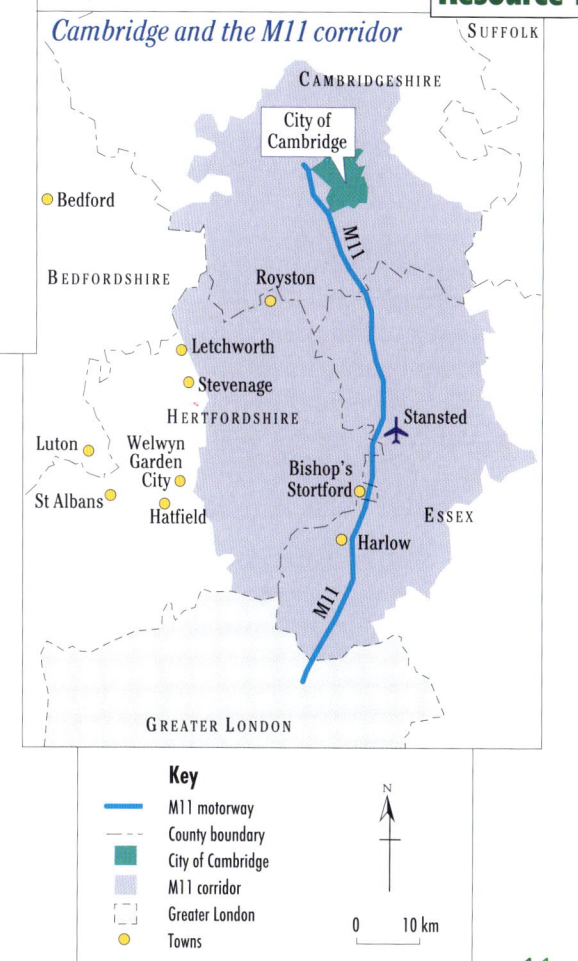

Resource I — Cambridge County Structure Plan

Key:
- Motorway
- Other trunk roads
- Main roads
- Railway
- Major centre
- Market town
- Rural growth point
- Centres designated for employment growth
- Areas of Green Belt, 'best landscape', important for nature conservation, Sites of Special Scientific Interest

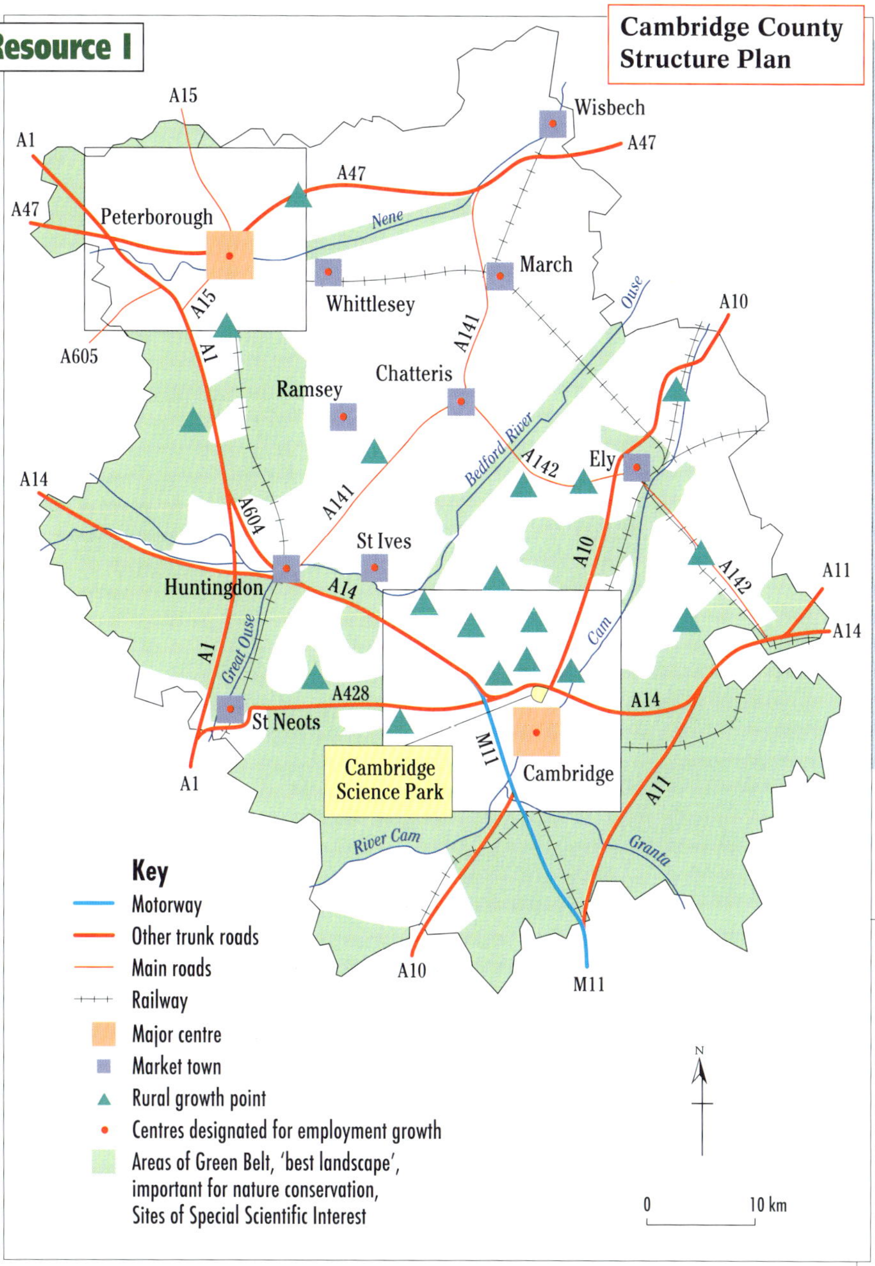

Source: Based on the Key Diagram of the Cambridgeshire Structure Plan Approved 1989.

Resource K — Occupational structure in the Cambridge area

Pie charts: High technology; Conventional industry.
- 'Blue-collar' jobs: Skilled manual/semi, unskilled
- 'White-collar' jobs: Managerial/professional/scientific/technical/clerical

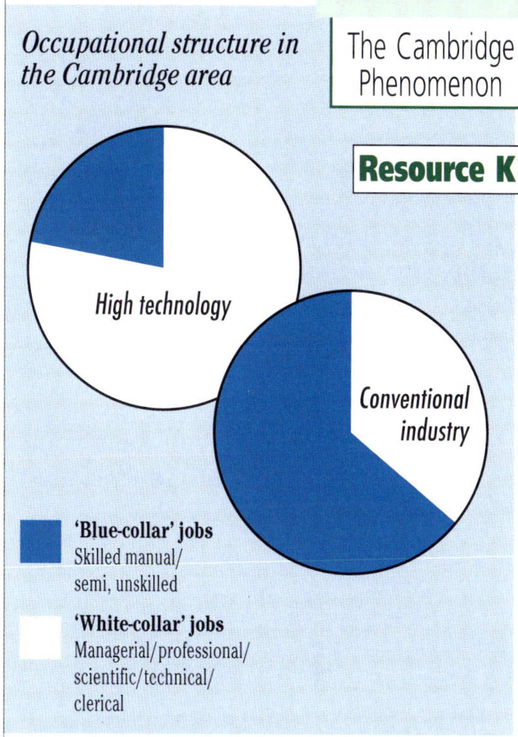

Source: Department of Land Economy, University of Cambridge.

Resource L — Cambridge and the M11 corridor

Key: M11 motorway; County boundary; City of Cambridge; M11 corridor; Greater London; Towns.

Resource J — High-technology employment in Cambridgeshire, 1988–92

Sector of industry	1988	1990	1992
Chemicals/biotechnology	3,251	2,993	3,095
Specialist mechanical engineering	920	1,066	1,078
Data-processing machinery	1,019	1,318	1,151
Electronics engineering	5,514	6,173	5,193
Instrument engineering	4,529	4,028	3,052
Computer services	3,093	3,804	3,769
Research & development	4,613	4,995	4,915
Total (incl. miscellaneous)	**23,980**	**25,548**	**23,410**

Source: Research Group, Cambs County Council.

CASE STUDY A

The Cambridge Phenomenon

Activities

While you are in Cambridge researching into science parks, you meet some local residents who claim that the science park has brought the City many problems. They also believe that trying to re-create the 'Cambridge Phenomenon' anywhere else would almost certainly fail. Answer the questions below to check your understanding of the resources on these pages, then write a letter to the residents group stating whether or not you now agree with the case they put to you.

1 In small groups, act out the discussion about the pros and cons of science parks shown in this case study.

2 Part of the Cambridge **Structure Plan** is shown in Resource I. Examine it carefully.
a In which locations is it proposed that employment growth should take place?
b Where is it suggested that employment growth should occur?
c What evidence is there on the map that Cambridge's environment is pleasant?

3 Why is it so important for people wanting a job in the high-technology sector to have training? (Resource K)

4 Look at the table on high-technology employment in Cambridge (Resource J).
a List the sectors of high-technology employment in rank order (starting with the largest) for (i) 1988 and (ii) 1992. Note any changes.
b Calculate the percentage of high-technology employment in each sector in 1992, and plot your results on a pie-chart.

5 If you were able to start up your own high-technology business, what would you like to research, develop and manufacture?

Further activities

Short-answer tasks

1 What does the term 'high-technology industry' mean? Give some examples.

2 Hewlett Packard is one company involved in high-technology industry. List four similar companies and identify one product manufactured by each.

3 Write out short definitions of **primary**, **secondary**, **tertiary** and **quaternary industries**.

4 Write a short article for a Cambridge newspaper informing the local people of the advantages and disadvantages of high-technology industry.

Find out about . . .

1 Find out about high-technology development in *either*:
a Scotland's 'Silicon Glen', *or*
b Silicon Valley in California, USA.

2 Try to find out something about the nearest science park to your school. How many companies operate in the science park, and what do they specialise in? Why did they choose to locate on this particular site?

Library and research tasks

1 Which sectors of industry (primary, secondary, etc) are the most important where you live? Have these changed in the last few years? Is there any quaternary industry locally? You might find some information by asking in your library, or writing to the local council.

2 Try to design your own science park. Remember the photographs and plans you have seen of the Cambridge Science Park. Either draw some sketches to show what your science park would look like, or make a plan of the site. Decide where in the UK you would locate your science park.

Assessment activity

The map below shows part of Britain's south coast, which has been a popular location for high-technology firms recently.

CASE STUDY A

The Cambridge Phenomenon

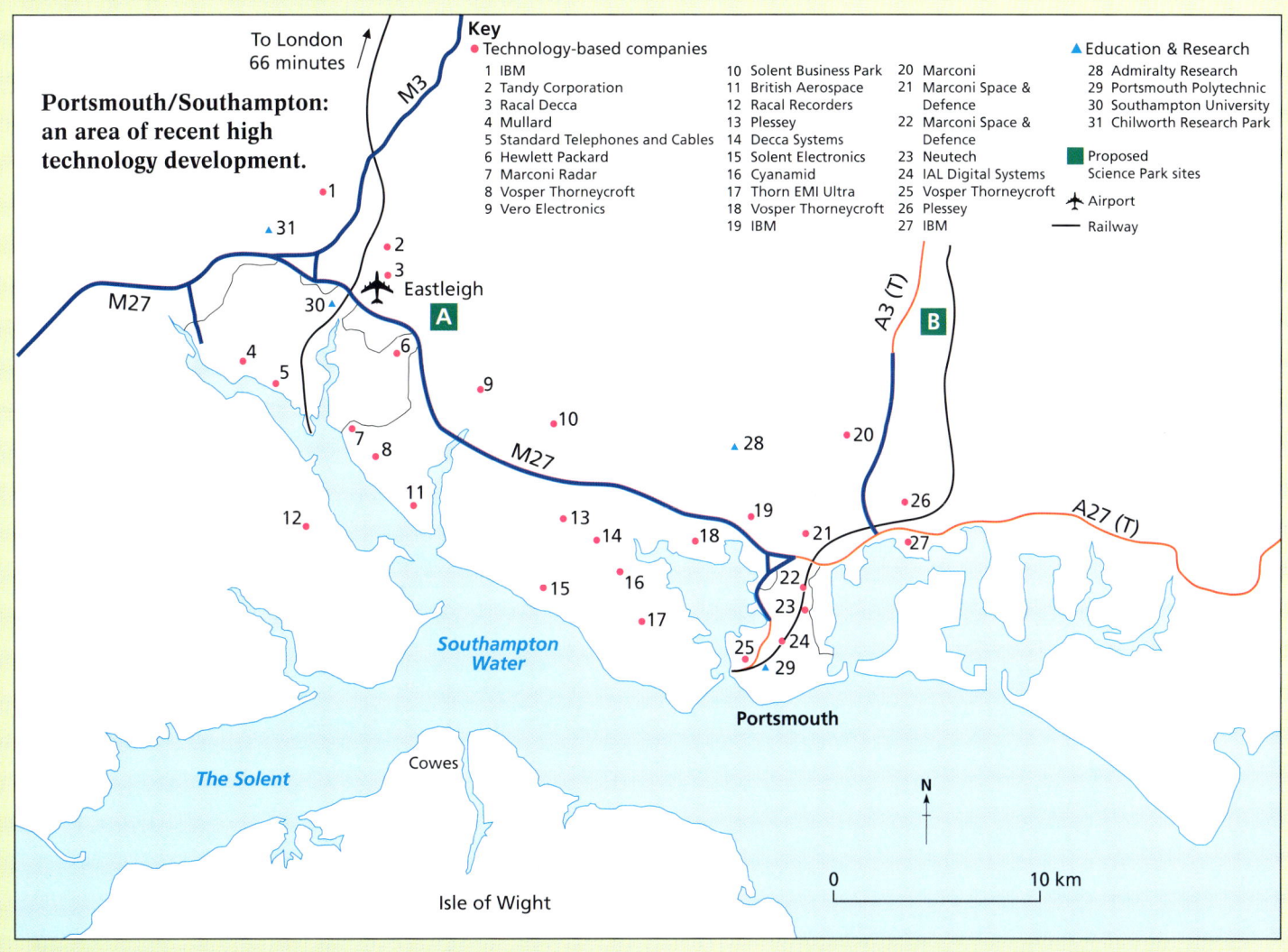

Portsmouth/Southampton: an area of recent high technology development.

Key
- Technology-based companies
  1. IBM
  2. Tandy Corporation
  3. Racal Decca
  4. Mullard
  5. Standard Telephones and Cables
  6. Hewlett Packard
  7. Marconi Radar
  8. Vosper Thorneycroft
  9. Vero Electronics
  10. Solent Business Park
  11. British Aerospace
  12. Racal Recorders
  13. Plessey
  14. Decca Systems
  15. Solent Electronics
  16. Cyanamid
  17. Thorn EMI Ultra
  18. Vosper Thorneycroft
  19. IBM
  20. Marconi
  21. Marconi Space & Defence
  22. Marconi Space & Defence
  23. Neutech
  24. IAL Digital Systems
  25. Vosper Thorneycroft
  26. Plessey
  27. IBM
- Education & Research
  28. Admiralty Research
  29. Portsmouth Polytechnic
  30. Southampton University
  31. Chilworth Research Park
- Proposed Science Park sites
- Airport
- Railway

1a Name *two* high-technology firms based in the area and a product manufactured by each one. (*3 marks*)
b Which *two* important educational institutions are found in the area? (2)
c Why are these important for high-technology industry? (1)
d Explain one other advantage of this area for the development of high-technology industry. (2)

2 Explain the differences between high-technology industry and conventional manufacturing industry. (2)

3a Explain in your own words what a science park is. (3)
b Two possible sites (A and B) for a science park are shown in the map above. Decide which location would be best for such a development, and explain why. (3)
c Give one reason why the local population might not wish to have a science park located nearby. (2)

4 Why are many local authorities interested in establishing a science park in their area? (2)

5 Using the information on the map above to help you, devise a poster showing the main benefits of the Portsmouth-Southampton area as a location for high-technology industry. (5)

Total 25 marks

Postscript

High-technology industries brought prosperity to Cambridge throughout the 1980s when the national economy was growing. In the early 1990s, however, the recession has affected Cambridge quite seriously, as the newspaper article (right) shows. Many companies, including the high-technology industries, have struggled to stay in business. A similar story can be found elsewhere. Many other cities across southern Britain can no longer be regarded as affluent places.

Source: Cambridge City Council.

Cambridge boom turns to gloom

David Brindle
Social Services Correspondent

The recession has brought "visible and widespread poverty" to Cambridge, the city synonymous with the boom of the late 1980s, a report by the city council said yesterday.

Unemployment, debt and homelessness have soared as the growth of the city's economy, led by hi-tech industry, has fallen back. Collapsing house prices have hit even the most affluent districts.

Almost one in six of Cambridge's population is now living in, or on the margins of, poverty compared to fewer than one in 10 two years ago.

In the late 1980s the city attracted the computer companies on which national economic growth was founded.

Unemployment is shown to have risen almost threefold in three years. Throughout the 1980s the city's jobless rate was below the national average; by early this year it was matching it. One in three unemployed people has been out of work for more than a year and nine people chase each job vacancy.

Overall, the report estimates that 18,560 people in the city, or 17 per cent of the population, are living in or on the margins of poverty.

Source: © *The Guardian*, 6 August 1993.

Key Terms

entrepreneurs people involved in taking the risks necessary to set up a business.

high-technology industry includes the manufacture of goods using or incorporating sophisticated machinery, eg electronics, aerospace and defence systems, computers and biotechnology. High-technology industry involves research and development as well as manufacture of new products.

quaternary industry (or **sector**) jobs that are concerned with research, with the assembly, processing and transmission of information, and with the administration and control of other industrial sectors.

science park a collection of high-technology industrial companies or research organisations located in attractive surroundings. The development is low in density, and situated near a major scientific university.

structure plan plans drawn up by county councils comprising written statements and maps. They show how the county council would like the land in their area to be used.

venture capital money made available (usually as a loan) for a specific industrial venture, which may carry some risks.

Key Understandings

- High-technology and quaternary industries often locate together near higher education establishments.

- The science park concept was first developed in the USA, before it came to the UK and Europe.

- A science park was established in Cambridge because the city offered research and scientific expertise, a skilled labour supply, good accessibility to markets and a pleasant living and working environment. The boom of high-technology industry in the area is known as the 'Cambridge Phenomenon'.

- Science parks may cause problems such as congestion, increased demands for housing, the development of attractive 'greenfield' sites, and a demand for very specific labour skills.

Case Study B

King Coal is Dead – New Jobs for Wakefield

Wakefield is a city in West Yorkshire. It has a population of 75,600 and is located midway between Leeds and Sheffield. The city and the area around it has for decades relied on coal and wool to provide jobs. Gradually, though, both these industries have declined. Like many other towns and cities, Wakefield is trying to attract new industries to provide jobs for local people.

Why has the city's employment structure changed, and what is being done to provide new jobs?

As part of your school's work experience programme, you are offered a one-week placement in the offices of the Wakefield Post, a Yorkshire newspaper. Your task is to investigate how the employment situation in Wakefield is changing, and in doing so to learn some of the skills of a journalist.

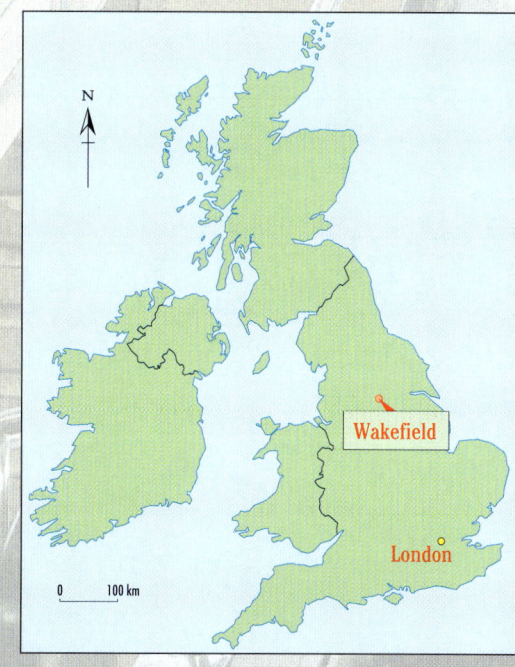

The position of Wakefield in the UK.

CASE STUDY B: New Jobs for Wakefield

Key Question 1
Is the employment structure of Wakefield changing?

Resource A

For many years woollen textiles and coalmining have been the major employers in the Wakefield area. Both now employ fewer people than ever before. The whole character of the area is changing as these old industries – which were the basis of Wakefield's growth – decline, and give way to newer ones.

Coalmining is a **primary industry**, as it is concerned with extracting a raw material from the earth. The woollen industry involves manufacturing wool into cloth, and so is a **secondary industry**. Coalmining employment declined gradually during the 1980s as one pit and then another closed down. The rate of change has now accelerated with the pit closure programme announced in 1992/93. Since 1981, some 15,000 jobs have been lost from the collieries around Wakefield. Only two collieries remain open in what was, just a decade ago, the heart of the Yorkshire coalfield, and their long-term future is in doubt.

Newer types of employment include jobs in light industry, commerce, distribution and tourism. The last three involve providing services, and so are called **tertiary industries**. Some people in Wakefield are today employed in **quaternary industries** – these are concerned with information handling. It is unclear, however, how many quaternary jobs there are.

Changes in **employment structure** mean different things to different people. It takes a long time for a new industrial structure to replace an old, declining one. As a result some school-leavers cannot get a job and many older people become unemployed and are made **redundant** as older industries shut down. However, there should eventually be a wider range of jobs for school-leavers to choose from (more diversification) than in the past.

The appearance of the environment gives clues that an area's industries are changing. Some of Wakefield's textile mills and coalmines are now derelict, but there are new workplaces including warehouses, offices and modern low-rise factory units.

Resource B

Glass-making industry collapses

Del Monte says 'Yes' to Wakefield

Coca-Cola opens bottling and canning plant

New distribution centre for ASDA

Pit closure programme shock - more jobs to go

"Wakefield 41" industrial estate opens

Recent industrial changes in the Wakefield area.

Resource C

Wakefield's changing employment structure.

1954 — 30,600 jobs

1990 — 109,600 jobs

Key
- Primary (blue)
- Secondary (red)
- Tertiary (yellow)

Resource D

An Economic Development Officer's view of job patterns in Wakefield.

> Up to 20 years ago, many school-leavers in Wakefield could expect to find jobs either in the coalmines or in mining engineering firms, or in local clothing and textile companies. Today there is a much wider choice. New industries and services are being attracted to the district, and Wakefield's employment structure is changing.

CASE STUDY B

New Jobs for Wakefield

Resource E

Wakefield's changing industrial landscapes.

(a) Caphouse Colliery, which was closed in the late 1980s.
(b) Site of demolished George Lee & Sons Whiteoak Mills.
(c) Wakefield's new 41 Business Park.
(d) Coca-Cola bottling plant.

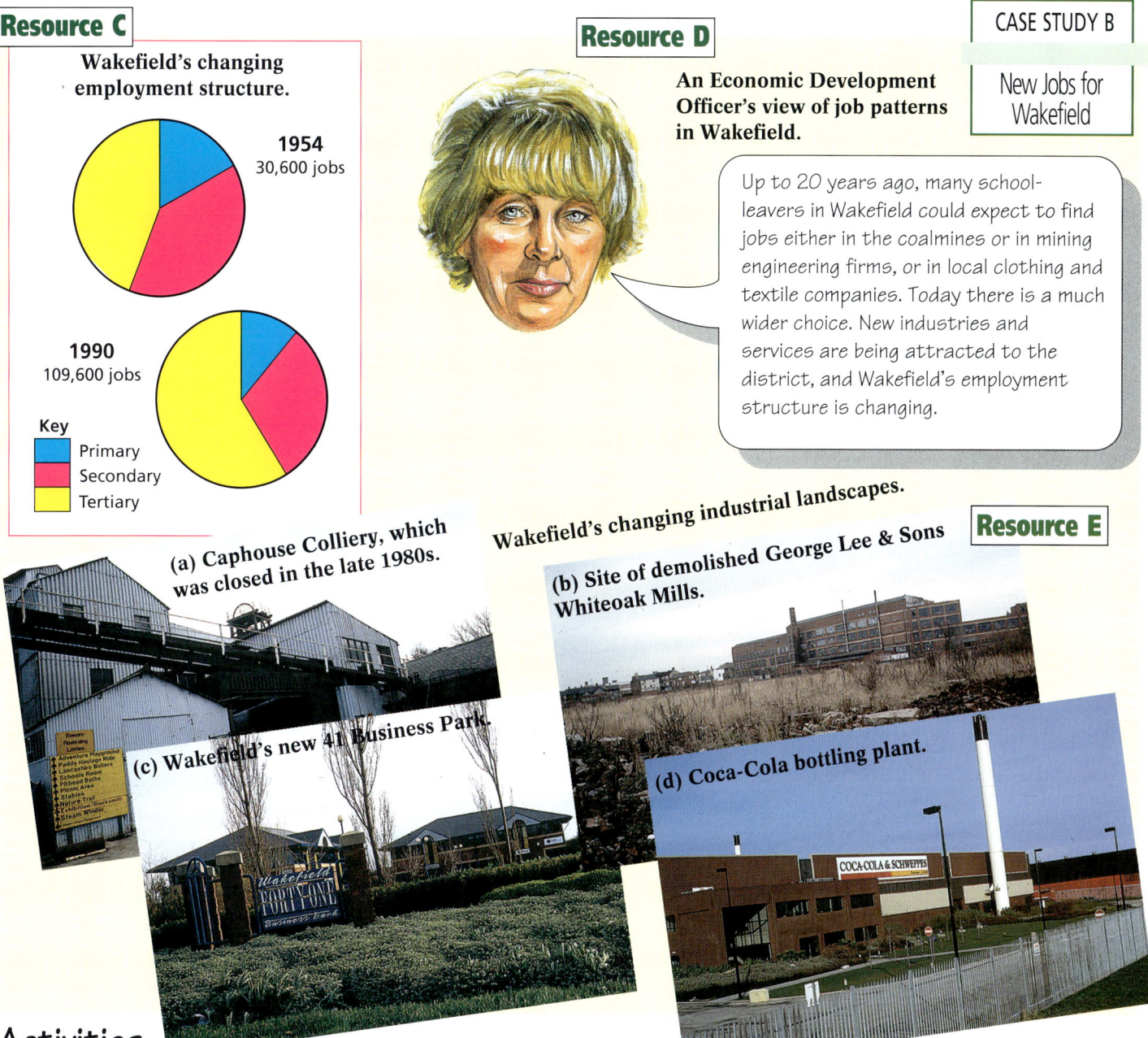

Activities

You are presented with the resources on these pages and asked to do research on industrial change in Wakefield for a newspaper article. Answer the questions below to check your understanding of the situation, then write a short report for the Editor. Include the main facts, identify the important issues and answer Key Question 1 on page 16.

1a Which two major industries helped Wakefield to grow?
b Are these two industries primary, secondary or tertiary?

2 From the headlines in Resource B and from what you have read, make two lists: one of industries that are declining, the other of industries that are growing. For each industry say whether it is primary, secondary or tertiary.

3 Study the pie-charts (Resource C) carefully.
a Describe the changes that took place in the city's employment structure between 1954 and 1990.
b Calculate the numbers of primary jobs, secondary jobs and tertiary jobs available in Wakefield in 1990.

4 Look at Resource E which shows some of the industrial environments around Wakefield.
a Which photographs show declining industries?
b Do you think that new industries improve the appearance of the environment or not? Explain your answer.

CASE STUDY B

New Jobs for Wakefield

Key Question 2
What are the causes and effects of Wakefield's changing employment structure?

Consultant's report

Resource F

A major decline in the number of jobs provided in the Wakefield area by British Coal is causing serious problems:

- There were 20 working pits in the Wakefield area in 1979, but only 8 remained in 1987.
- In the first three months of 1988, collieries at Ferrymoor Riddings, South Kirkby and Woolley were closed with 1,900 job losses, leaving just five working pits.
- The closure of Royston Drift in 1989 and Denby Grange in 1991 left three working collieries.
- The pit closure programme put forward by British Coal in 1993 closed Sharlston and left only the Prince of Wales and Frickley collieries producing coal; even their long-term future is not guaranteed.

Mining employment in the Wakefield area, 1979–93

	1979	1984	1987	1990	1993
Number of working collieries	20	16	8	4	2
Number of jobs	16,900	15,061	6,096	3,684	1,751

Causes

Mining employment has declined for many reasons. Coalmining is a strategic industry, so governments have traditionally had strong feelings about how coal production should be organised. In 1947 the industry was nationalised. Low investment, outdated equipment and increased competition from other fuels all caused difficulties.

In 1974 a miners' strike resulted in the Tory government losing power. Since then tension has increased between miners, British Coal, and the government. The need for increased profits meant that only modern pits with thick coal seams survived. Pressure on electricity generators to produce electricity in the cheapest and cleanest way possible has led to National Power and PowerGen placing fewer orders for coal and turning to gas and nuclear power to generate electricity. The 'dash for gas' in the 1980s resulted from the attractive price of gas and its clean image.

These and other economic factors have contributed to job losses in Wakefield's coalmines. Many miners feel that their industry has been reduced in size because the government favours nuclear energy, even though this may be more expensive and dangerous than coal.

Effects

The massive reduction of around 70% in mining employment in the Wakefield area since 1979 has had a knock-on effect on other industries, especially engineering. Textiles have also continued to decline. Taken together, these changes have hit the city hard. The rate of unemployment rose to almost 15% between 1984 and 1987. In late 1992, unemployment stood at 10.5% for the Wakefield area. This was still above the national average.

Industrial change on this scale has many effects. The worst are felt by individuals and families and by the community as a whole. Those miners who lose their jobs are unlikely to find new jobs in mining. They must either retrain to acquire new skills or face long-term unemployment. As more and more people lose their jobs, there is less money to spend and local shops and businesses begin to suffer. Some people may even move away. Empty collieries and factories are likely to become derelict, houses look run down and businesses close. However, fewer coalmines means less noise, fumes and dust in the air.

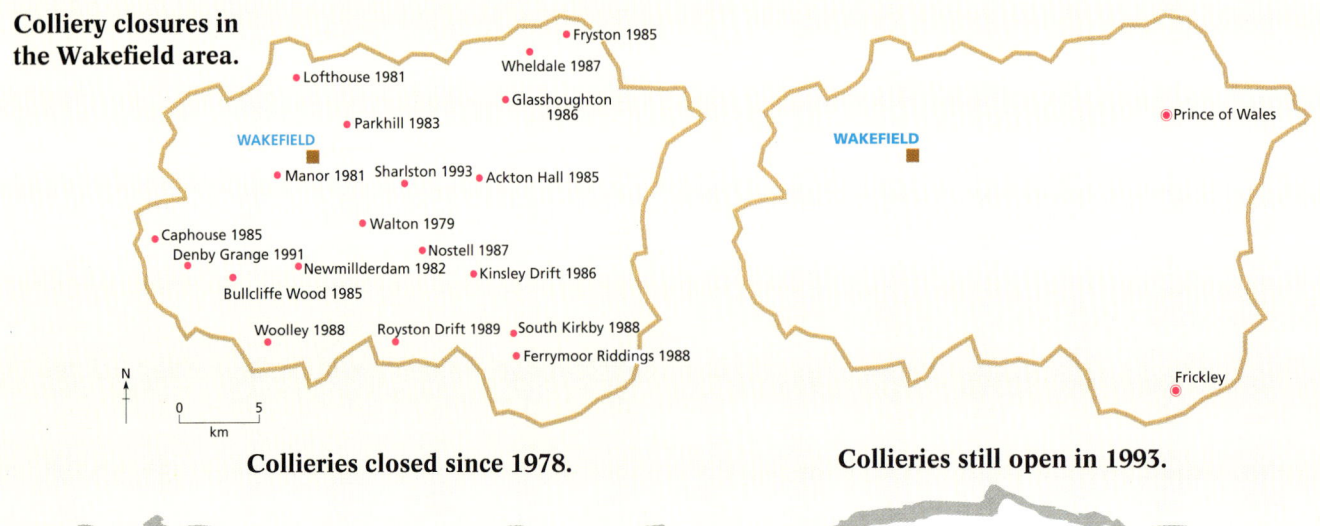

Colliery closures in the Wakefield area.

Collieries closed since 1978.

Collieries still open in 1993.

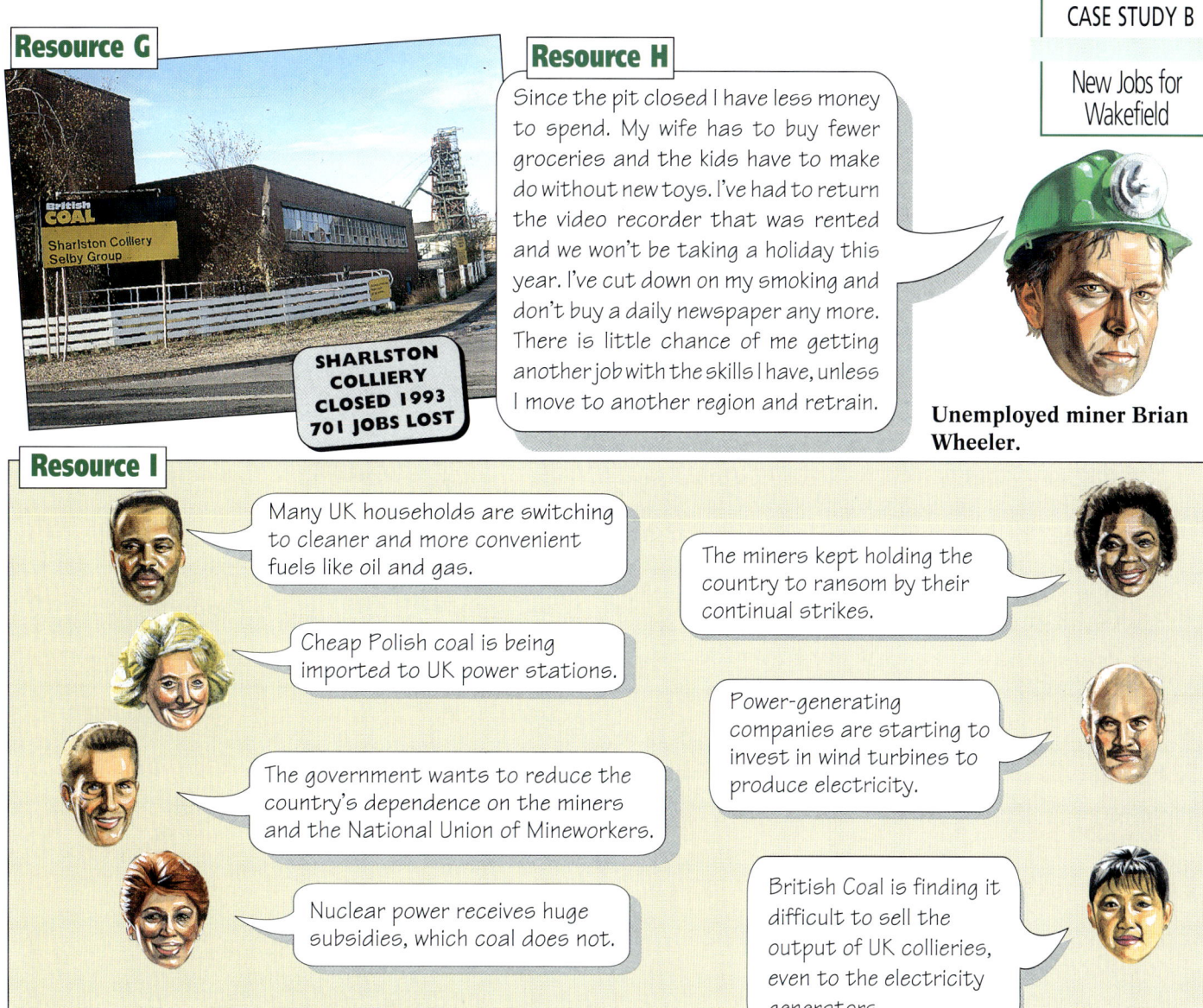

Activities

You must submit a short article (250 words) to the Editor which explains the causes and effects of employment changes in the coal industry. Answer the questions below, then draft your article with a suitable headline. You may include one illustration.

1 Refer to the Consultant's Report (Resource F):
a How many mining jobs were lost in the Wakefield area between 1979 and 1988?
b Which two local collieries are still open?
c Draw a line graph to show how mining employment has changed since 1979. (Vertical scale for graph 1 cm = 2,000 jobs.)

2 Less coal is needed today. In small groups, try to explain why this is the case. Which do you think is the most important factor influencing the demand for coal (Resource I)? Are there others that are not shown?

3a Which local shops may be affected as a result of the changed lifestyle of people like Brian Wheeler (Resource H) who lose their jobs with British Coal?
b What can people like Brian Wheeler, made redundant through no fault of their own, do to get a new job?
c How would you feel if you were part of Brian Wheeler's family? Imagine you are one of his children: write a diary entry for the day your father comes home from the colliery for the last time.

4 How might a new school-leaver be affected by changes in Wakefield's employment structure?

CASE STUDY B

New Jobs for Wakefield

Key Question 3
How is Wakefield trying to attract new types of work?

Resource J

New jobs for the city!
by Sam Wilson

The decline in Wakefield's traditional industries since the 1960s and 1970s has caused many problems. Unemployment rates became so high that action was needed. To prevent a serious **spiral of decline**, the local council established an 'Economic Development Department' to attract new types of jobs to the city.

A plan was devised and this has brought a variety of new industries to the city. This **diversification** means that Wakefield will not be so seriously affected in future if one industry begins to decline.

A good location remains one of our key assets. The city has good road, rail and air transport links. Modern light industries, especially those concerned with assembly and distribution, are being attracted to this sort of **accessible** location.

- The sportswear and sport equipment company Dunlop Slazenger is based here.
- Asda Stores has just built a major regional distribution centre providing 350 jobs.
- The largest canning and bottling plant for soft drinks in Europe has been built by Coca-Cola and Schweppes at Junction 41 of the M1. From here, soft drinks will be distributed all over northern England.
- Approval was given in 1992 for the development of 'Wakefield Europort', a Channel Tunnel railfreight terminal and industrial village.

Wakefield must compete with towns all over Britain which are trying to attract industry, and so the local authority is encouraging tourists and providing better town centre amenities. 'The Ridings', a major regional shopping centre, was opened near the cathedral in 1983. Visitors are also attracted by the beauty of the nearby Yorkshire Dales and Peak District National Parks. Wakefield's location makes it an ideal touring centre for visitors.

Resource K

Wakefield Council's six 'Ideas for Action'

★ To attract new industry
★ To encourage the development of small- and medium-sized firms
★ To improve labour mobility
★ To develop service industries including tourism
★ To promote the use of new technology
★ To improve the physical environment

Source: City of Wakefield Metropolitan District Council.

Wakefield's good transport links.

Resource L

Source: Economic Development Dept, City of Wakefield.

Resource M

The Ridings Centre, Wakefield.

Resource N

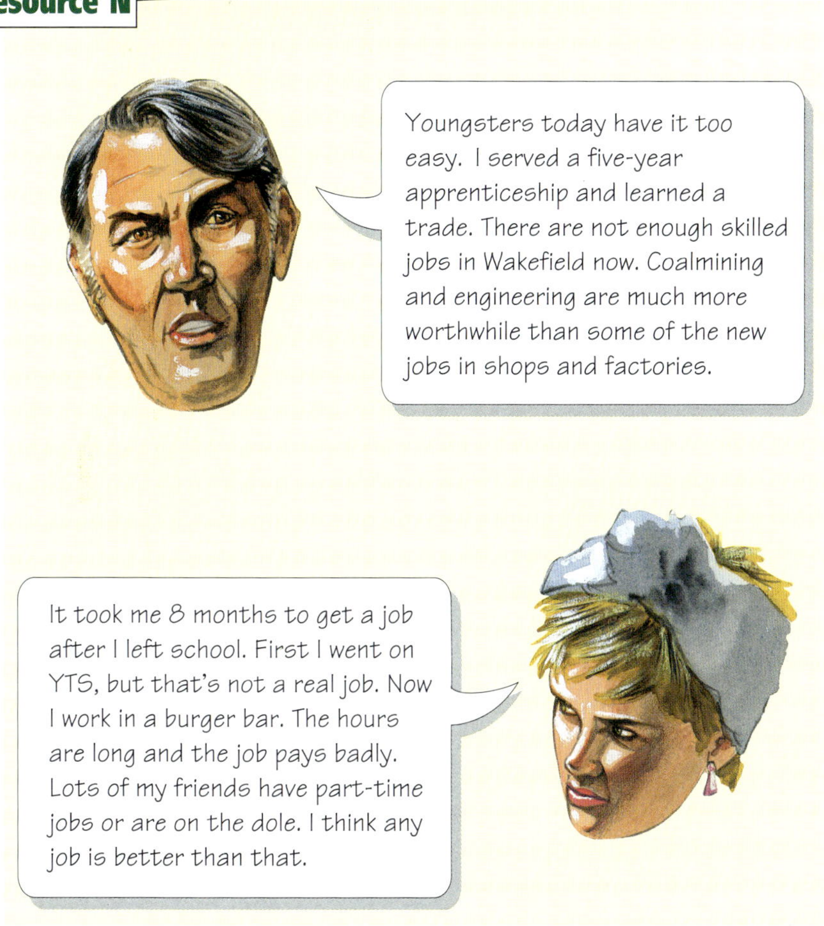

Youngsters today have it too easy. I served a five-year apprenticeship and learned a trade. There are not enough skilled jobs in Wakefield now. Coalmining and engineering are much more worthwhile than some of the new jobs in shops and factories.

It took me 8 months to get a job after I left school. First I went on YTS, but that's not a real job. Now I work in a burger bar. The hours are long and the job pays badly. Lots of my friends have part-time jobs or are on the dole. I think any job is better than that.

Contrasting views on the job situation.

CASE STUDY B

New Jobs for Wakefield

Activities

The *Wakefield Post* decides to mount an advertising campaign to attract people and business to the city. It is intending to publish a special supplement which will be distributed all over the country. You are asked to design a poster for the centre-spread of the paper to illustrate the advantages of working and living in Wakefield. The aim is to persuade new industries to locate near the city. Answer the questions below, then try to design a large poster.

1 Complete the following passage. The words below the passage should help you:
Wakefield is located in ▓▓▓▓▓▓▓. The area is within easy reach of the ▓▓▓▓▓▓▓ National Park. Wakefield is easy to get to and from. This sort of location is described as being ▓▓▓▓▓▓▓. It has attracted firms like ▓▓▓▓▓▓▓ and Asda Stores.

> *North Yorkshire/West Yorkshire*
> *remote/accessible*
> *Yorkshire Dales/Dartmoor*
> *Pepsi Cola/Dunlop Slazenger*

2 Choose two of the Council's six 'Ideas for Action' (Resource K) and list some of the things that could be done to help each one succeed.

3 Use the map in Resource L for this activity.
a List the main transport advantages of Wakefield's location.
b Using an atlas, draw your own map of this part of northern England.
c What differences do you notice between the map in Resource L and your map?
d Do you think the map in Resource L was drawn for any particular reason?

4 What are the benefits of a modern enclosed shopping centre like 'The Ridings' (Resource M)? Are there any disadvantages?

5 Some people have criticised the sort of jobs being attracted to Wakefield (Resource N). Which view do you most agree with? Explain your answer.

CASE STUDY B

New Jobs for Wakefield

Further activities

Short-answer tasks

1 Which types of employment are increasing in Wakefield? Give examples.

2 What does 'made redundant' mean?

3 Look at the advertisement below, which was placed in the *Financial Times* by Wakefield Council's Economic Development Department.
a Which of the city's advantages do you think the Department is trying to draw attention to?
b Is there anything about Wakefield which might put off industries looking to relocate in or near the city?

Find out about . . .

1 Find out about the Yorkshire woollen industry. Compile a short report explaining the location, development and changes in the industry. Include a map.

2 See if you can now make a list of reasons which may have contributed to the decline of the Yorkshire woollen industry. Look back at Resource 1 which dealt with the coal industry – it may help you.

3 *Developing the Wakefield area*
a A number of projects have been suggested to help provide new jobs in the area. These are listed below, with their approximate costs. You are asked to write a special article in the newspaper to advise the local council on how to spend a special grant of £15 million which may be offered to help regenerate the area.

Possible project	£ million
Constructing a road/rail/canal freight terminal	15.0
Road improvements linked to industrial estates	7.7
Re-opening old railway lines	1.8
Developing tourist attractions	6.4
Building a technology park	4.5
Reclaiming derelict land at old collieries	15.0
Developing industrial land in the urban area	10.6

Which project (or projects) would you fund? List the reasons why you think your chosen project(s) would help to provide new jobs.
b Can you think of any other useful ways of attracting new jobs to the Wakefield area?

WHY WAKEFIELD Mr Igarashi?

CONTACT THE INWARD INVESTMENT TEAM

We'll tell you why Wakefield beat tough competition from other areas of the UK and Europe when the Pioneer Electronic Corporation of Japan chose Wakefield for its first audio visual equipment factory in the UK.

The Inward Investment Team,
Economic Development Department,
PO Box 92, 22 Cheapside,
Wakefield WF1 1XS.
Telephone 0924 295837
Facsimile 0924 295803

Photographer: Richard Rayner

Source: Economic Development Dept, City of Wakefield.

CASE STUDY B
New Jobs for Wakefield

GOVERNMENT GIVES GO-AHEAD TO WAKEFIELD EUROPORT

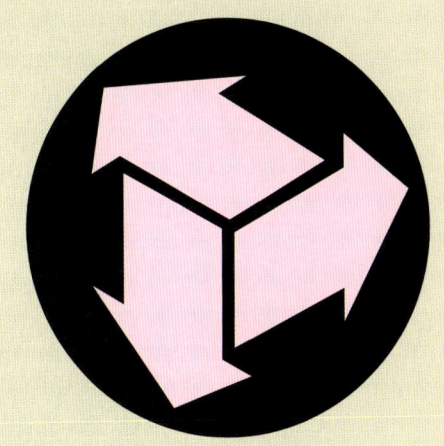

The long awaited result of the Public Inquiry into the proposed Channel Tunnel railfreight village and terminal at Normanton was announced on 28th October.

The Government has given approval for the project to proceed, which means that Wakefield Europort can now become a reality.

Wakefield Europort will offer businesses the opportunity to locate in a quality environment, alongside the M62 motorway and with a direct rail link to Europe via the Channel Tunnel. Wakefield will become a key part of a 150,000 mile railway network stretching across the continent. The regular daily service will bring quick, reliable and economically attractive access to the European market-place.

By the time it has been completed, the development should bring over 5,000 new jobs into the Wakefield District. However, Wakefield Europort should act as a catalyst for further industrial development and inward investment into the area, bringing even more employment opportunities in the future.

Councillor Graham Phelps, Chairman of Wakefield's Employment and Economic Development Committee, welcomed the news: "With the threat to many local jobs from the proposed closures in the mining industry, the development of Wakefield Europort is more important than ever. It will be a major boost to the District, assisting in our efforts to regenerate the local economy and bringing much needed jobs to the area."

Source: Economic Development Dept, City of Wakefield.

CASE STUDY B

New Jobs for Wakefield

Library and research tasks

1 Find out the current unemployment rate for your area, and for Wakefield. Compare these rates with the rate for Wakefield in October 1992 (10.5%). Is unemployment in your area increasing or decreasing?

2 From resources in your school or local library, try to find out about:
a changes in UK coalmining (technology, employment, output, number of collieries, etc)
b the decline in UK coalmining during the 1980s and the 1990s, especially the pit closure programme proposed in 1992/93.

3 Using library books, an atlas and holiday brochures, plan a five-day holiday for two foreign tourists staying in the city of Wakefield. They want to spend one day in the city itself and four days touring the area by car. Draw up an itinerary for the couple, including a map showing the places you have suggested they visit.

For discussion

Many towns and cities in the United Kingdom have an Economic Development Department like the one in Wakefield. Its objectives are twofold:

1 to persuade employers to relocate in their district

2 to attract grants from the UK government and the European Community in Brussels.

To achieve each of these objectives, written submissions must be made describing the area. With reference either to Wakefield or to another area you have studied, discuss in small groups how these written submissions might differ.

What points need to be made to grant-giving authorities to persuade them that the area in question needs special support? What points are focused on in attracting new industries to the area?

Key Terms

accessible easy to get to and from.

diversification increasing the variety of types of work available in an area.

employment structure the balance between different types of work in an area.

primary industry jobs that involve extracting natural resources, like those in mining, fishing, farming and forestry.

quaternary industry jobs that involve the assembly, processing and transmission of information, and the control of other enterprises.

redundant being without employment, having lost a job.

secondary industry jobs that involve manufacturing (making) things, usually in a factory.

spiral of decline a gradual deterioration in an area's economy, environment and quality of life, often following the closure of an important industry.

tertiary industry jobs that involve providing a service for others.

Key Understandings

- An area's employment structure may change over time, altering its whole environment, economy and character.

- Industries grow and develop in a specific location for particular reasons.

- In an area where an industry declines and eventually closes, there is likely to be unemployment, and a spiral of decline that affects the whole character of the area.

- Many towns and cities are now actively encouraging new industries to locate near them by diversifying their employment and by advertising the advantages of their locations.

Case Study C

Changing Rural Land Use in the Flow Country

The term 'flow' is a northern expression for any flat, deep, wet peatland or bog. The largest area of peatland or blanket bog in Britain lies in Caithness and Sutherland in northern Scotland. The area, almost 4,000 square kilometres, has come to be known as the **Flow Country**, and although it is remote, it has become the focus of some controversy.

> Your family has owned land in this area for many generations. About 30 years ago your father left the Flow Country and moved to where you now live. One day he surprises everyone by announcing suddenly that he wants to move the whole family back to the area when he retires. You find some information left on the table at home – the resources in this case study – and decide to investigate what is going on in the Flow Country for yourself.

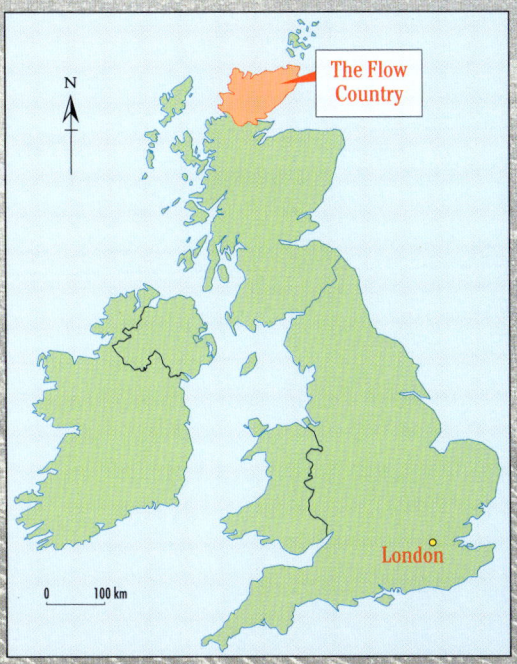

The Flow Country in north-east Scotland.

CASE STUDY C

The Flow Country

Key Question 1
Which physical and human factors have influenced primary activities in the Flow Country?

All Change in the Flow Country

Resource A

Malcolm Morrison is the last crofter in Strath Halladale in eastern Sutherland. He moved there from Glasgow in 1984 to help his grandmother run the **croft**. Once, there were nine tenanted crofts in the valley – now there is one. This rural depopulation is not new. During the late 18th century the price of wool soared. The landlords introduced huge flocks of sheep, which displaced the native population in a largely forced **migration** called the Highland Clearances. From the 1870s onwards, deer-stalking replaced sheep-farming in many areas, leading to another round of evictions and migration. The Crofters' Act of 1886 ended the conflict, by promising **security of tenure** and fair rents to the crofters.

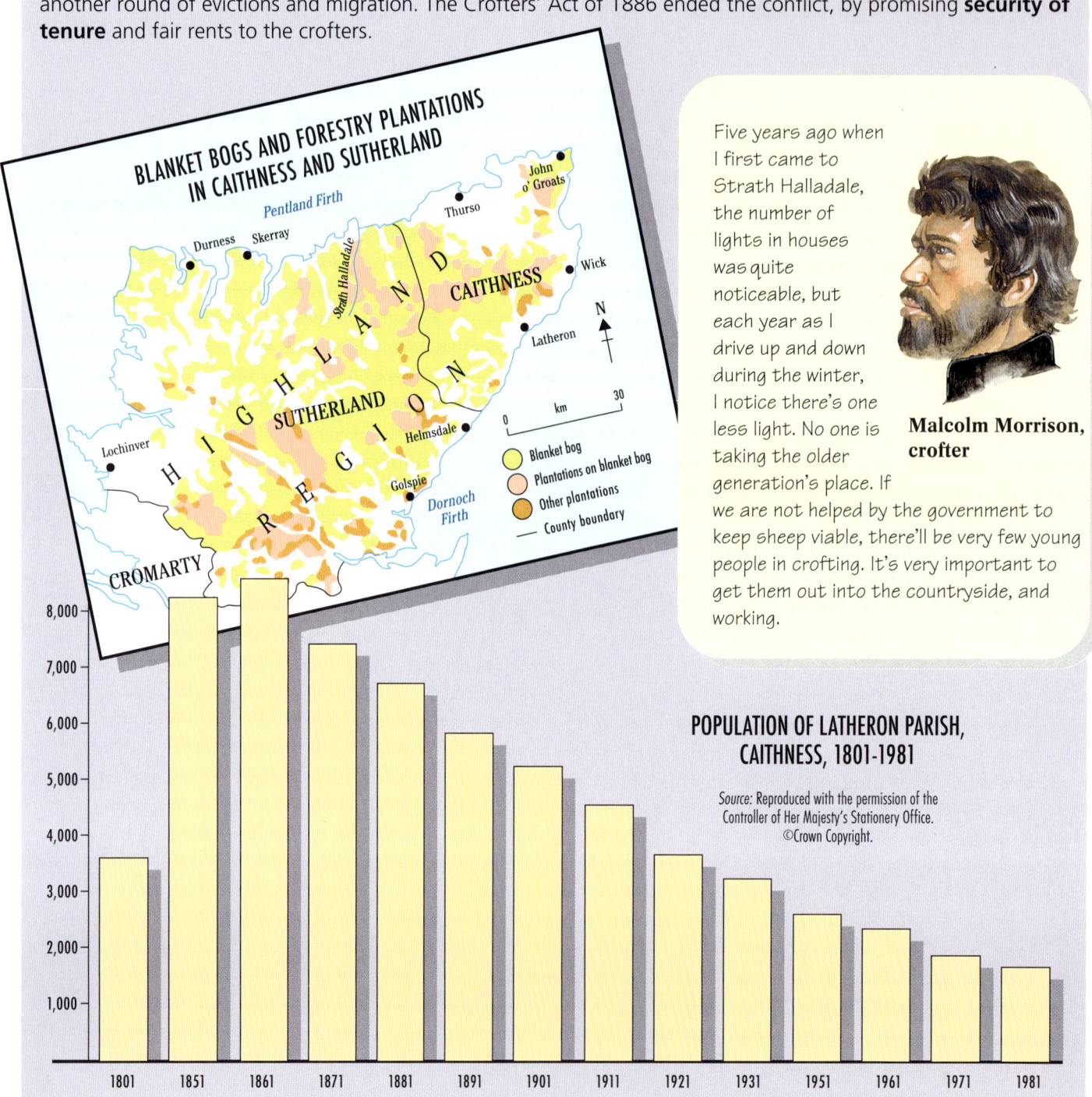

Five years ago when I first came to Strath Halladale, the number of lights in houses was quite noticeable, but each year as I drive up and down during the winter, I notice there's one less light. No one is taking the older generation's place. If we are not helped by the government to keep sheep viable, there'll be very few young people in crofting. It's very important to get them out into the countryside, and working.

Malcolm Morrison, crofter

POPULATION OF LATHERON PARISH, CAITHNESS, 1801-1981

Source: Reproduced with the permission of the Controller of Her Majesty's Stationery Office. ©Crown Copyright.

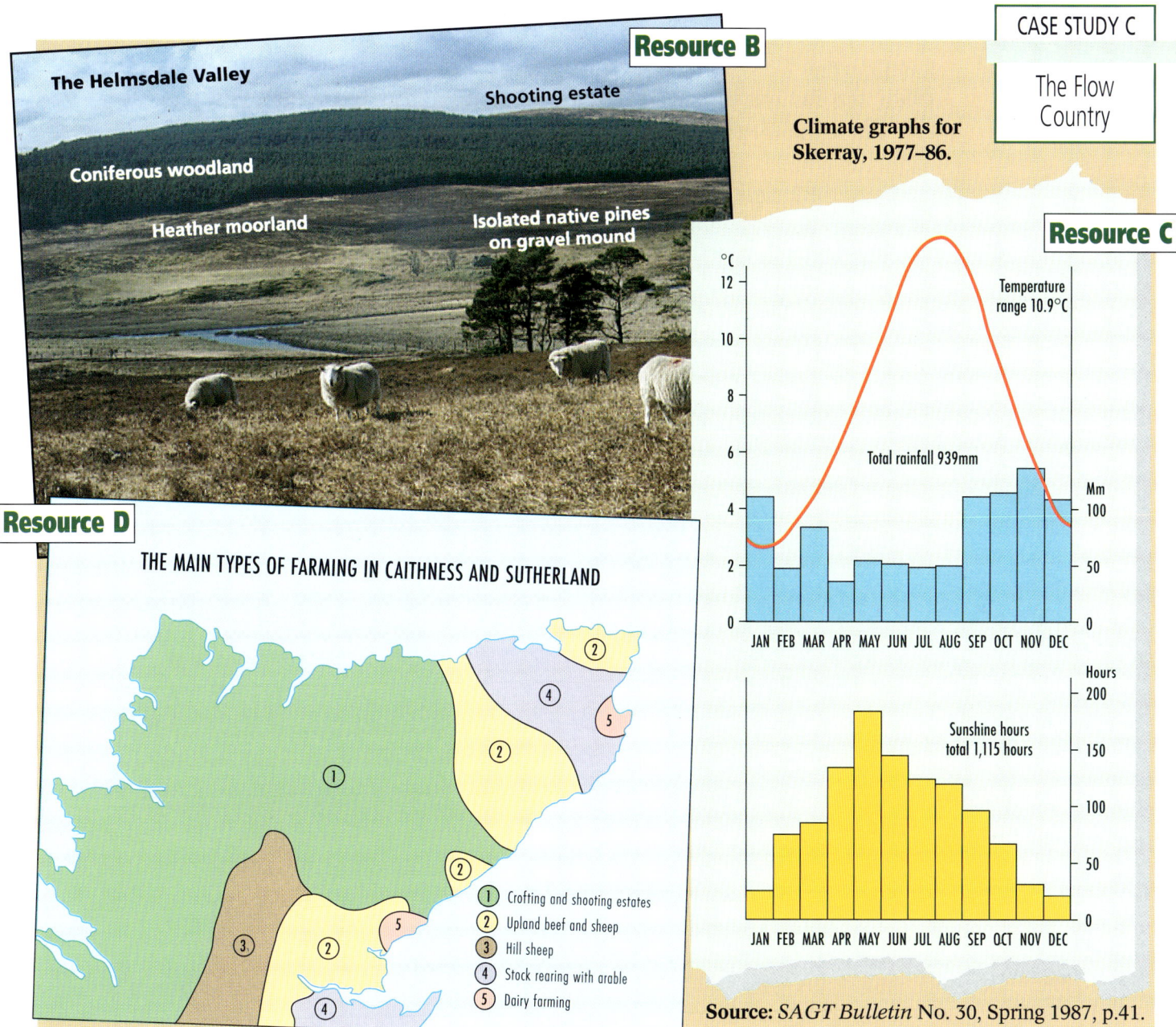

Activities

Your father decides to move to Strath Halladale at the start of next year, but gives you the option of completing your schooling before joining the family. Study the resources here so that you can answer the questions below. Then suggest the advantages and disadvantages of living in this part of Scotland, and explain whether you would like to move there or not.

1a Where are the other main areas of blanket peat bog in Britain? Use an atlas to find and name these areas.
b Which two animals could be found in the Flow Country in the last century?

2 How could the government help crofters like Malcolm Morrison?

3 Use the graph in Resource A for this activity.
a Estimate the population of Latheron parish in 1981.
b Describe the main population trends in Latheron parish over the last 200 years.
c Try to explain these trends in terms of changes in land use.
d Why are there no census details for 1941?

4 Peat is composed of layers of vegetation which have failed to decompose owing to a lack of oxygen. It is widely used by gardeners, and yet the Flow Country peat is obviously of little agricultural value. Refer to the climate graphs (Resource C) to help you explain the area's physical limitations.

CASE STUDY C
The Flow Country

Key Question 2
What are the major competing demands for the use of the rural landscape in the Flow Country?

On 23 July 1987 there were two separate press conferences about land use in the Flow Country, one in London, the other in Inverness. Although the conferences were on the same theme, widely different viewpoints were expressed.

Resource E

Press Release

In LONDON, the Nature Conservancy Council (NCC) and the Royal Society for the Protection of Birds (RSPB) presented a report called 'Birds, Bogs and Forestry: the Peatlands of Caithness and Sutherland'. This report outlined the importance of the area's peatland landscape, and may be summarised as follows.

1 The tundra-like appearance of the Flow Country is not due to the historical clearance of natural forests by people. It is a natural landscape formed in response to the cool, wet and windy climate of Scotland since the Ice Age.

2 The pools of water formed on the flatter areas of peatland are particularly important. They contain specially adapted mosses, which provide essential feeding **habitats** for wetland birds such as the golden plover, dunlin, greenshank and Arctic skua.

3 For trees to grow, the land must be ploughed and drained. This disturbs the water table and surface drainage patterns, which can lead to gullying on the hillsides, and shrinkage and erosion of the peatlands. Eventually the ground vegetation disappears completely as it is shaded out by the trees' branches.

4 Planting coniferous trees is therefore destroying the natural habitat of the 'flows'. Since 1919, 67,000 hectares of peatland have been lost to forestry (most of it since 1981).

5 The peatlands are also under threat from plans to remove peat for use as a fuel and in gardening.

Conclusion
There has been so much damage to the Flow Country environment that no more coniferous trees should be planted.

PRESS RELEASE

Highlands and Islands Development Board

In INVERNESS, the Highlands and Islands Development Board (HIDB) and the Highland Regional Council joined forces to defend the expansion of forestry, claiming that the NCC report threatened to end all forestry development in two Scottish districts. Their main arguments were as follows:

1. The Flow Country is the most northerly district on the UK mainland.
- It is a remote area 1,100 km from London.
- It has a small population which has been getting smaller for 120 years.
- Unemployment is high: 20% in Sutherland and 13% in Caithness.

2. Forestry is not new. Commercial forestry started in the 19th century and the Forestry Commission has been planting in this area since 1919.

3. A relatively low percentage of land is planted with trees - 8.1% in 1986 compared with 10% in the Highland region.

4. The Forestry Commission has created 101 full-time jobs in Caithness and Sutherland.
- Private forestry firms have created 51 full-time jobs since 1980 together with 153 jobs for fencing, ploughing and harvesting contractors.
- 70% of seasonal jobs are taken by local residents. Additional jobs will be created in processing and transport as the forests mature.

5. If no new planting is done, 1,000 jobs in planting and harvesting and 1,000 jobs in sawmilling and processing will be lost.

Conclusion
The Flow Country is a vast area. It should be possible to balance the need for nature **conservation** with the need for jobs in the area.

CASE STUDY C

The Flow Country

Resource F Blanket bog: peat is 94% water by volume.

Resource G

Raptors, eg Hen harrier
Moorland birds, eg Meadow pipit
Rare mainland colonies, eg Arctic skua
Rare open-country birds, eg Ptarmigan
Waders, eg Greenshank
Waterbirds, eg Red-throated diver
Reeds
Sphagnum moss

The Flow Country habitat at risk.

Resource H

With planting
With no more planting

Caithness and Sutherland: annual tree harvesting programme.
Source: *SAGT Bulletin* No. 31, Autumn 1987, p.52.

CASE STUDY C

The Flow Country

Different types of coniferous forestry plantation.

Resource I

(a) Blanket coverage.

(b) Plantations with some clearings – the soil and vegetation within these clearings will gradually change because they have been cut off from the extensive areas of bog land.

Activities

1 When a new development affects a community, a public meeting is often held to pass on information to the local people and to allow them to express their opinions.

   As a class, act out a public meeting in a rural parish hall in Caithness. Organise yourselves into small groups to represent the views of the NCC, the RSPB, the HIDB and the Highland Regional Council. The speakers will come from these groups. Other class members should adopt the roles of local large landowners, tenant crofters (who don't own any of the trees on the land that they rent), local forestry workers, birdwatchers, anglers, a local hotel owner, hillwalkers, etc. Work out a point of view for each group or individual before you begin the 'meeting'.

2 Which of the two press conferences, the one in London or the one in Inverness, do you think received the greater newspaper and TV coverage? Why would one receive more media attention than the other? What do you think were the consequences of this?

3 The value of landscapes varies according to the point of view of the person making the evaluation. Place the landscapes shown in Resources F and I in order of preference if you were
   - a tourist
   - a forestry worker
   - a forestry owner
   - a birdwatcher
   - a landowner
   - a sheep farmer.

   Construct a table to show your opinions and discuss the results with others in the class.

4 Why will the number of jobs in forestry in Caithness and Sutherland continue to rise until about the year 2030, whether or not more trees are planted?

Key Question 3
Can a successful land use strategy be devised for the Flow Country?

CASE STUDY C

The Flow Country

Resource J

A Welcome on the Hillside!

'A hard-won compromise' between development and conservation in the environmentally-sensitive Flow Country of Caithness and Sutherland was widely welcomed yesterday.

Conflicting interests in the row over forestry developments in the area have reached agreement – thanks to a working party set up by the Highland Regional Council 18 months ago. It included representatives from the Council, the Highlands and Islands Development Board, the Countryside Commission for Scotland, and the Nature Conservancy Council. The Forestry Commission was also involved as advisers, and the Scottish Development Department as observers.

The working party's report will now be sent to the Scottish Secretary. It recognises the scientific importance of factors such as nature conservation, agriculture and crofting, deer management, landscape, recreation and archaeology.

HIDB Chairman Sir Robert Cowan yesterday welcomed the report as a 'hard-won compromise', which would protect both jobs and wildlife. He said, 'This agreed strategy will allow the forestry industry to continue planting in a controlled and sustained way, which could create several hundred jobs in an area of limited alternative employment.'

The new planting areas represent a change in land use of only about 5%, but would create a viable forestry industry and downstream timber activities in the least environmentally sensitive areas.

'This is a substantial improvement on the position we were

More forests like this?

substantial parts of the peatlands of Caithness and Sutherland, but recommends an extra 39,000 hectares of tree-planting over the next 20 years, to create a total forest area of 100,000 hectares.

The report also divides the Flow Country into four categories where planting would be 'unsuitable', 'undesirable', 'possible' or 'preferable'. This classification takes account

facing last year, with the NCC calling for a total ban on forestry that could have seen the immediate loss of 200 jobs and financial loss to the area of around £25 million a year', said Sir Robert. With the impending run-down of Dounreay nuclear power station, every job in this area is vital.

The Chairman of the NCC, Sir William Wilkinson, said the working party had grappled with a seemingly intractable set of problems, but had produced a report that should allow all parties to go forward in a constructive manner.

CASE STUDY C

The Flow Country

Resource K

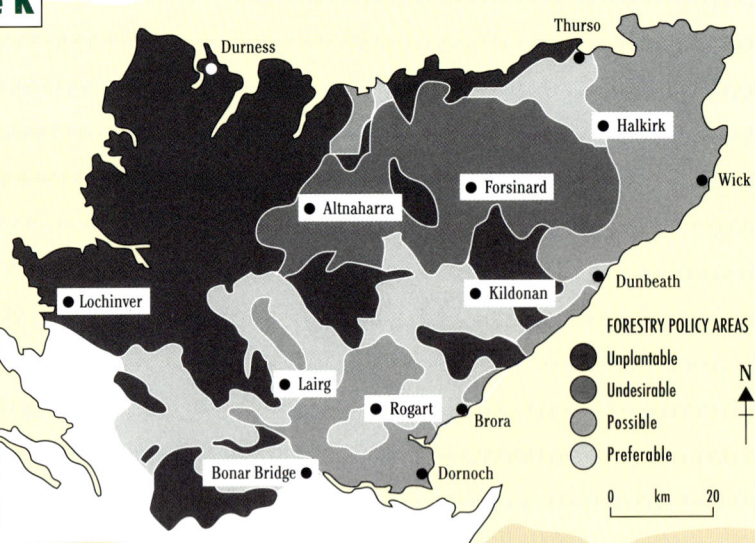

The working party identified four forestry policy areas.

Resource L

John McCormick, journalist and angler.

The only concession being made by this supposedly 'green' government is to agree that 'bits' of the Flow Country should be preserved, adding up to 15-20% of the total. Also at risk from the activities of the tree farmers is the outstanding quality of salmon, sea trout and brown trout fishing in Flow Country lochs and streams. Waters once clear as crystal are now the colour of brown-windsor soup – caused, I believe, by silt washed down from the deep forestry ploughing.

We feel it's a reasonable compromise. Some of the detail we're not happy with, but we can now continue to get on with the work in hand – subject, of course, to rigorous planting procedures.

Roz Lloyd, Fountain Forestry.

Charles Innes, local landowner.

Far from enjoying the bareness of the landscape, the inhabitants of Caithness have for generations bemoaned the lack of trees, and have tried to grow timber for shelter, use or amenity – proper land use in the Highlands has to mean mixed land use. There's a place for forestry here now – and in the future.

Caithness and Sutherland are still places of outstanding, wild beauty, softened perhaps here and there by forestry and made slightly more accessible by the forestry roads. The trout and salmon angling are still of the highest quality and give returns which are as good as ever.

I still think a lot of these trees are growing for the wrong reasons. They're the wrong trees, in the wrong place, growing for the wrong reasons. The Flow Country has been wrecked. Large areas are totally different to what they were before. Fortunately a big area will be safeguarded for the future – that's a major step forward for conservation.

Rachel Taylor, RSPB.

CASE STUDY C

The Flow Country

Activities

Imagine that you are the manager of a large (50,000 hectares) Highland estate. You are instructed to design a *land use strategy* that will allow for 20% of the estate to be forested over the next 20 years. Present forestry cover on the estate is minimal. Land use on the estate is as shown below.

Work through the following activities before you devise your strategy for the estate.

1 Compare the 'undesirable' area shown in Resource K on page 32 with the existing forests shown on the map in Resource A (page 26).

2 Why are the foresters so keen to bring the minimum forested area in the Flow Country up to 100,000 hectares?

3 What is meant by 'downstream timber activities'?

4 Has everyone been satisfied by the compromise that was worked out?

Now prepare your land use strategy, dealing with each land type in turn. Remember that your costs for planting will increase with altitude and distance from the road. Consider the size and shape of your forestry plantations.

Include sketches with your plan, and give reasons for the decisions you have made.

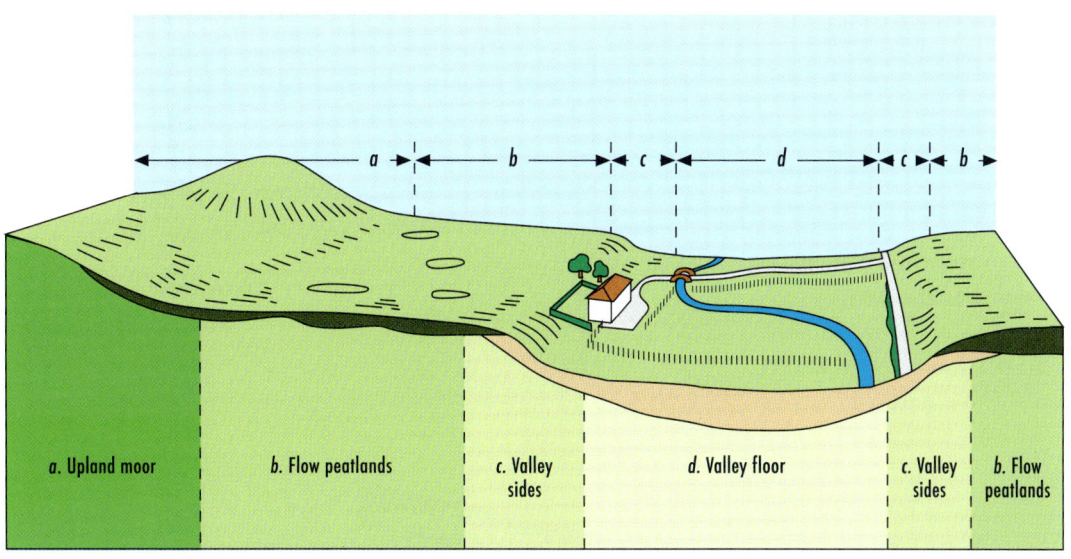

Block diagram of a Flow Country estate.

% of total estate	Land type
45%	**a. Upland moor** Up to 600 metres in altitude, with a thin rocky/peaty soil, used at present for deer and grouse shooting, and for rough summer grazing for sheep. Trees can grow here, but they are difficult to establish on the windswept summits.
40%	**b. Flow peatlands** Undulating peatlands at present used for poor, rough grazing for sheep.
5%	**c. Valley sides** Moderate slopes.
10%	**d. Valley floor** Improved pasture.

Two tenant crofters remain of an original ten crofters.

Further activities

Short-answer tasks

1 Farmland in the Flow Country is often described as 'marginal'. What does this mean?

2 What have been the main causes of rural depopulation in the Flow Country?

3 List the different ways in which peat has been or could be used in the Highlands.

4 Describe the vegetation and wildlife changes that take place when the Flow Country is deep ploughed for forestry.

5 Make a list of those people who are in favour of increased forestry and another list of those who are against it. For each person or group write one sentence summing up their point of view.

6 Describe the position of the crofters in any land use strategy for the Flow Country.

CASE STUDY C

The Flow Country

Find out about . . .

1 Major technological improvements have enabled foresters to extend their activities onto poorer land and increase their productivity. Find out about the machines and techniques that have made this possible.

2 Follow this up by outlining the problems that foresters have come across in extending the forested area, eg low fertility, and pests such as the pine beauty moth. How have the foresters tried to overcome these problems?

3 How are foresters attempting to design forests that are more pleasing to the eye, and which attract a wider range of wildlife, than the solid stands of conifers to be seen in many parts of Britain? Make a drawing of an 'ideal' forest.

4 In what ways are existing forests being adapted to meet increased demands for leisure and recreation?

5 Where are the major forested areas in Britain? On a blank map of the UK, mark on and name the major forests of Britain. Comment on their distribution.

Library and research tasks

1 Using an Ordnance Survey 1:50,000 map of your local area, complete a woodland survey of the area around your home. Draw a sketch map of the area, showing the following woodland categories:
- plantations
- shelter belts
- public parks
- parkland (scattered trees in pastureland)
- sound barriers (eg beside motorways)
- visual barriers (eg to hide a quarry).

2 Using a larger-scale map of your local area, find an area which, in your opinion, would benefit from tree planting. Give reasons for your choice and prepare 'before' and 'after' sketches.

3 A major problem facing commercial forestry today is *acid rain*. Using library books, prepare a short report on acid rain, outlining some of the causes, symptoms of damage to trees, and ways in which the problem can be prevented.

Key Terms

conservation protecting and preserving natural resources and the environment.

croft a small farm in the Highlands of Scotland, consisting of a small piece of land and farmhouse together with grazing rights on nearby hill pastures for sheep or cattle.

Flow Country name commonly given to the peaty bogland areas of Caithness and Sutherland in Scotland.

habitat natural environment which is the home of a range of plants and animals.

migration the movement of people (or animals) from one area to another.

security of tenure the guaranteed right to live on a particular piece of land.

Key Understandings

- The landscape and economic activity of most areas has been influenced by physical, human and historical factors.

- There are different points of view about how land in different places should be used and developed.

- Forestry has gradually become a more important land use in parts of upland Britain, with consequences for wildlife and people.

- In planning future land use, compromises are often reached which do not meet the interests of all groups and individuals.

Case Study D

Farming in the Yorkshire Dales: Issues and Conflicts

The Yorkshire Dales is an area in northern England where farming has gone on since ancient times. Recently agriculture has been in decline. Sheep and cattle are reared here as the conditions are largely unsuitable for arable farming. The land is difficult to farm or 'marginal' even for animal farming. The agricultural policies of the European Community (which changed its name to the European Union, or EU, in 1993) have provided **subsidies** for the farmers, but have also limited some of their activities by imposing **quotas**. The environment here has changed as a result of political factors, and today is still threatened.

You are a farmer from Vermont, a state in New England in the north-eastern USA. Vermont is best known for dairying. Agriculture in New England has been affected in recent years by international competition. The landscape is hilly, so the land is marginal for farming over wide areas. You have been chosen by the local farmers' union to visit the United Kingdom. You will be the guest of the Yorkshire National Farmers Union (NFU) and will examine all kinds of farming in the Dales, as well as learning about the European Community and its agricultural policies.

At the end of your visit you are expected to provide a detailed report for your fellow farmers in New England. You are also asked to write a short note for the US government Department of Agriculture in Washington DC, explaining the benefits and disadvantages of the European agricultural policy for farmers and the environment in Europe.

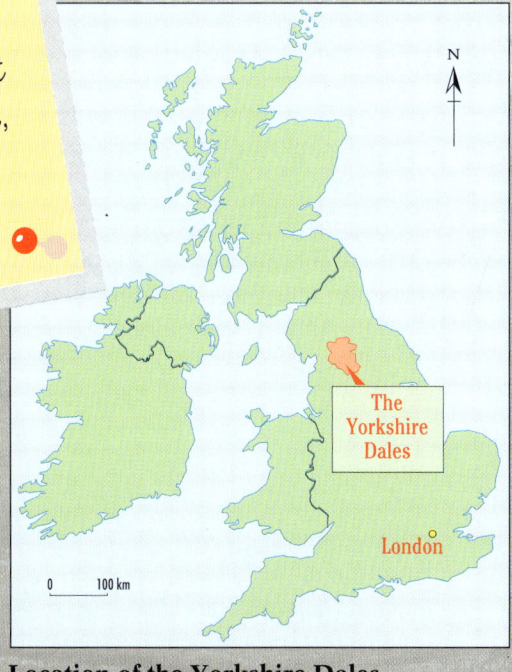

Location of the Yorkshire Dales.

CASE STUDY D
Yorkshire Dales Marginal Farming

Key Question 1
Why is hill farming in the Yorkshire Dales described as marginal?

Resource A

Farming in the Dales

The Yorkshire Dales are part of the Pennine hills of northern England. Farming in this difficult environment is hard. Winters are cold and wet, and summers often cool and wet. Hill or sheep farming is the only type of agriculture that suits this climate. Farming is only just possible here, economically and physically, and so the farms are described as on the margin, or **marginal**. The hill farms in the Dales contrast with the lowland farming areas of East Anglia, for example, where the climate is milder. Marginal farming occurs in highland areas elsewhere in Europe.

Outrake Foot Farm in Dentdale is typical of farms in the area. It lies in a glaciated valley and is surrounded by high hills. Only a few crops including hay and silage will grow here, and these must be sheltered near the river in the valley bottom. The rest of the land is used to keep sheep. They can survive quite well on the exposed pastureland and can cope with the wet, cold winters. Some cattle are also kept, but they have to be grazed on better pasture in the lower valley fields in summer, and in winter are generally kept inside and fed on silage.

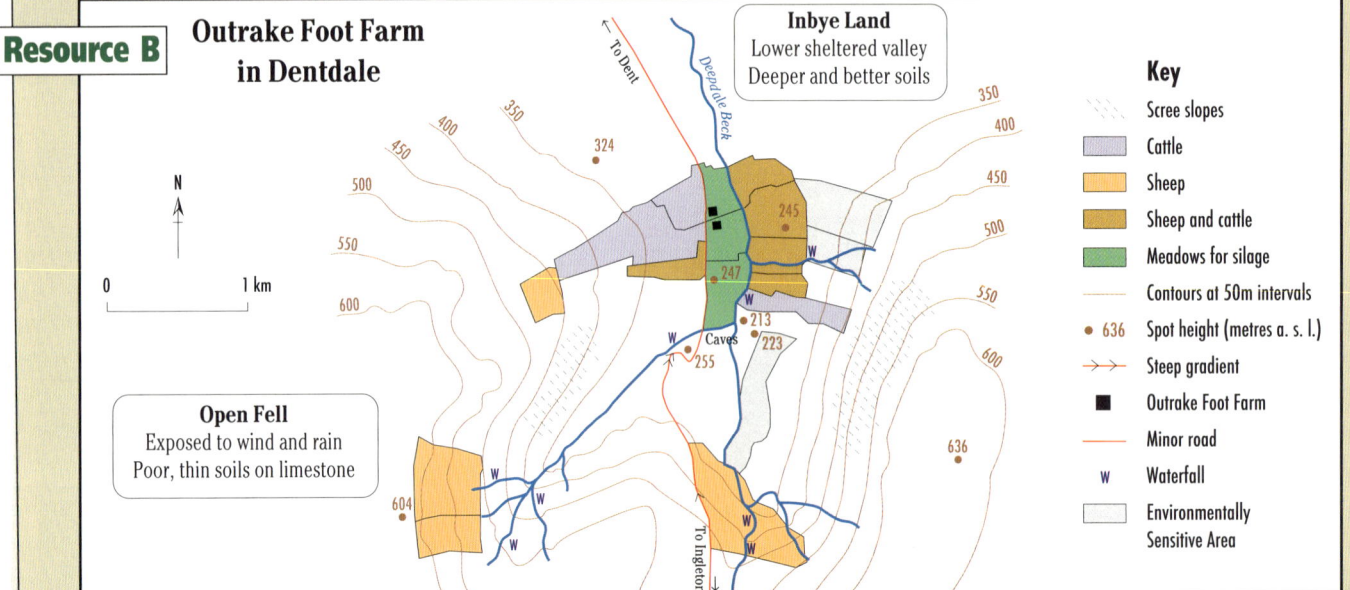

Resource B

The farm is a business and so must make a profit. The farmer aims to breed enough livestock to gain good prices in the spring and autumn sales. This can be difficult when a bad spell of winter snow may kill the flock. The farmer at Outrake Foot Farm also keeps some dairy cattle as he can sell milk at the cheese factory in Hawes, about 16 kilometres away. The profit the farmer makes helps pay the labourers and buy new machinery. However, in marginal farming areas the farmer cannot make enough profit to survive in business. He is competing with lowland farmers who are also producing lamb, beef and milk in better conditions. As a result, hill farmers get a subsidy from the European Commission, through its **Common Agricultural Policy** (CAP). This helps pay the additional costs of farming in marginal areas.

The features of a limestone dale.

Resource C

Resource D

CASE STUDY D
Yorkshire Dales Marginal Farming

Systems diagram : Outrake Foot Farm

INPUTS

Physical
eg land, climate, soils
162 hectares plus fell land

Stock
400 Leicester and Dalesbred sheep
16 Friesian cows
17 calves
1 bull
10 rams

Machinery
eg tractors, milking equipment

Labour
2 men, 1 woman

Feed and fertiliser
Silage and cattle cake
Manure and nitrates

Grants
eg EC grant towards new lambing shed
18 pence milk subsidy

PROCESSES

November
Breeding and take sheep onto fell

February–March
Feeding hay and cake to sheep on fell

April
Lambing

May–June
Cut silage and shear sheep

August
Worming and dosing

September–October
Sheep and cattle sales

Daily tasks
Milking and testing milk; collection by tanker

OUTPUTS

Sheep
To lowland farmers to fatten; also to Hawes market

Milk
53,000 litres of milk to Kendal depot, then to cheese factory

Beef
eg £131 per kilo for prime animals at Hawes market

Silage
Manure
Hay

← New machinery

	Jan	Feb	Mar	Apr	May	Jun	Jul	Aug	Sep	Oct	Nov	Dec
Temperature °C	4.8	5.0	5.6	9.0	11.4	15.5	16.2	15.7	13.9	10.1	7.8	5.9
Rainfall mm	87.2	24.4	127.2	150.4	68.8	130.1	220.2	385.5	260.0	110.7	120.9	201.4

Resource E

Climate data for Outrake Foot Farm.

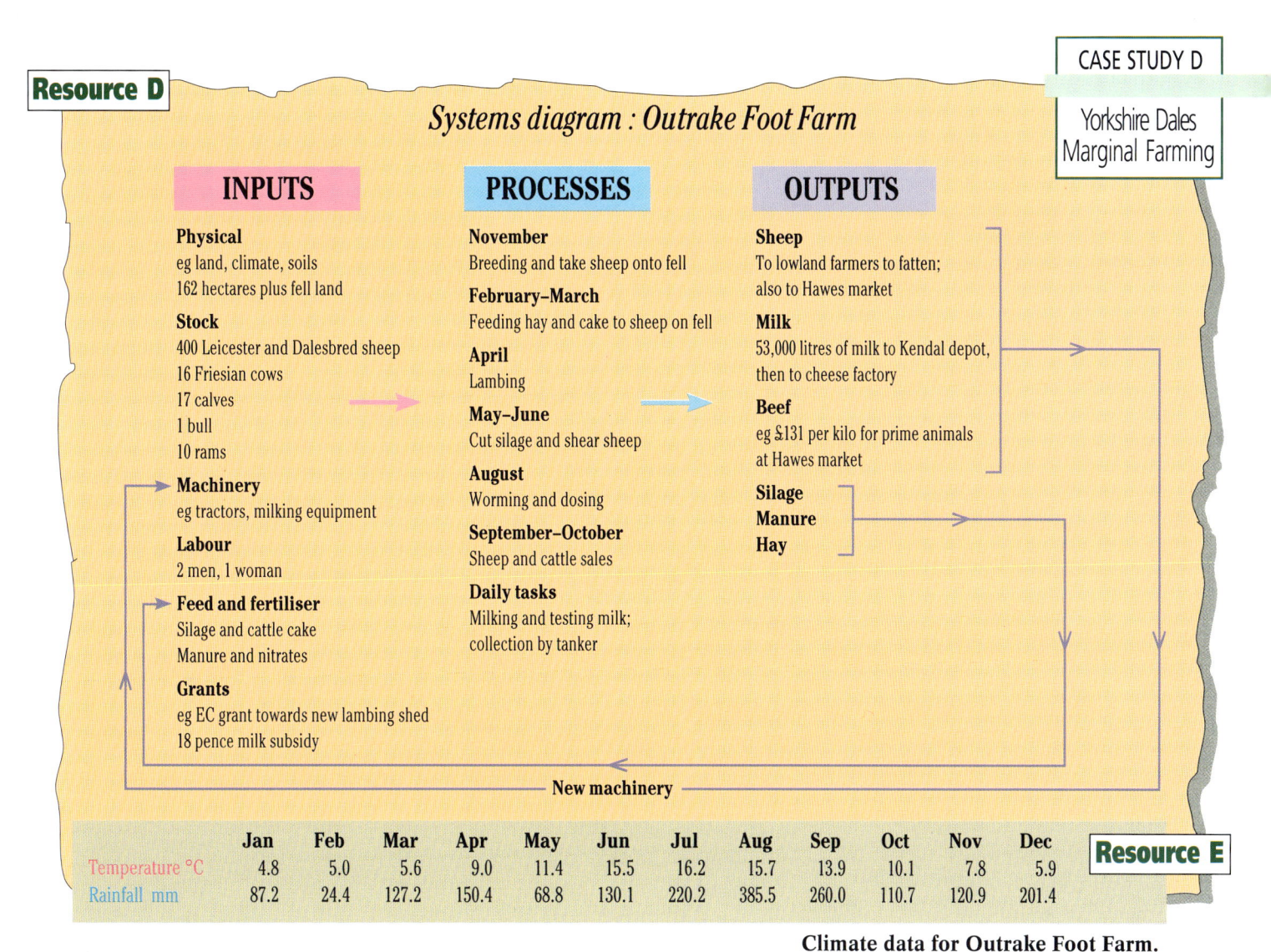

Activities

Study the dossier of resources on these two pages which have been collected by the National Farmers Union (NFU) in Yorkshire. They look closely at one hill farm – Outrake Foot Farm. Remember that you are visiting the area to learn about its farming. What impression do you get of the area and its farming from these resources? Write a summary which describes farming in the Dales for your fellow farmers back home in New England. First, answer the following questions.

1a What information in the dossier of resources suggests that Dentdale is not an easy area to farm? Look particularly at the map.
b The average hill farm in the Dales has an area of 160 hectares. The average size of farms in the UK is 60 hectares. Why do you think hill farms are much larger?
c Show the information in Resource E in a diagram (climate graph). The rainfall data should be shown as a bar graph and the temperature data as a line graph.

d Which description from those below best describes the climate shown by your graph?

warm and dry   *warm and wet*   *cool and wet*

Explain your choice of description clearly, and with reference to the climate graph.

2 From your answers to **1a**, **b** and **d**, explain why the term 'marginal farming' is used to describe the type of farming in Dentdale.

3a What is a subsidy?
b Who gives the subsidy to hill farmers in Europe?
c Imagine you are a hill farmer who has just survived a poor summer and bad winter. You see a letter in the local paper from a taxpayer who claims that subsidies cost too much. Write a letter in return to the local newspaper explaining why a subsidy is vital for you.

CASE STUDY D

Yorkshire Dales Marginal Farming

Key Question 2
How do political forces affect the rural landscape?

Resource F

Farming in Europe has changed dramatically in the last four decades

Growing more food

Most governments have encouraged their farmers to grow more food. This has meant introducing farm machinery; using chemical fertilisers; and implementing modern farming methods. As a result, rural landscapes all over Europe have changed.

The European Community

When Britain entered the European Community (EC) in 1972, farming was guided by the EC's Common Agricultural Policy (CAP). In part this meant that where the price of a farm product like wheat fell below a certain point, the EC bought up the surplus at a pre-set price. Farmers liked this as they knew in advance exactly what minimum price they would receive. Production was concentrated on products with high **intervention prices**, where their profits were greatest. Other farmers expanded their farms to bring more land into production – this often meant draining marshland, removing hedgerows to create larger fields, or ploughing up meadows to grow arable crops like wheat and barley which fetched high prices. Large-scale farming was seen to be efficient, and a heavy use of chemical fertilisers meant that yields rose. However, there was a cost to the environment.

The cost of the CAP

In 1993 the EC spent half its total budget on support for agriculture. This amounts to around US $50 billion. A further $80 billion was spent on prices which are higher than needed. This is the equivalent of £250 for every man, woman and child in the UK. The result of the massive support system is that:

- the EC is now self-sufficient in some foodstuffs like dairy products and beef
- vast surpluses of other products like cereals and butter are being created which are expensive to store, and which are often destroyed
- there is an elaborate system of support prices designed to encourage production, and quotas to restrict production
- farmers are now being asked to take land out of production altogether.

Marginal farming areas and the EC

The agricultural policy of the EC has had an important effect in the Yorkshire Dales and in other marginal farming areas. Marginal farms cannot easily increase their production either by using chemical fertilisers or creating new farmland. Since 1984, there have been quotas on milk. There are upper limits designed to restrict production and reduce the surpluses. To remain competitive, many marginal farms have amalgamated to form larger farms. Old barns and farmhouses have been abandoned and the number of farm workers has declined. Farmers in areas like Dentdale have had to find other ways of making a profit in order to stay in business. Many of them combine tourism and farming, and old farm buildings are being converted into holiday homes.

Resource G

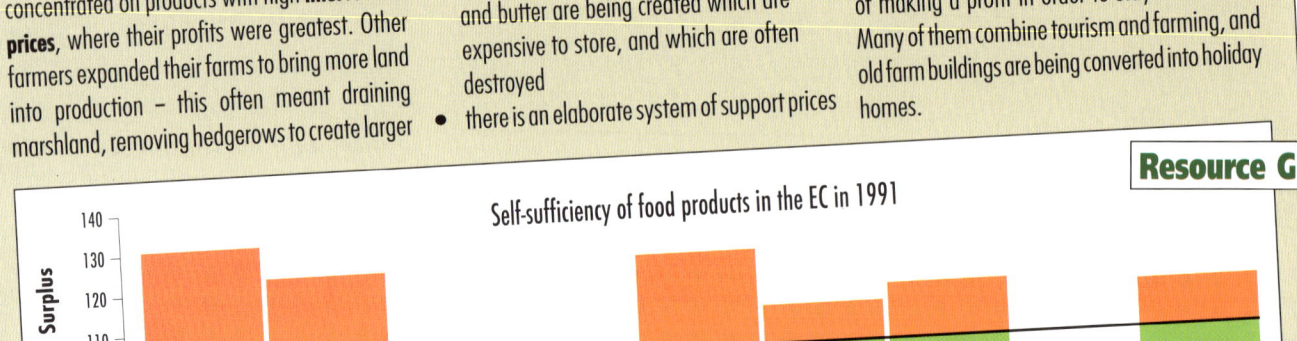

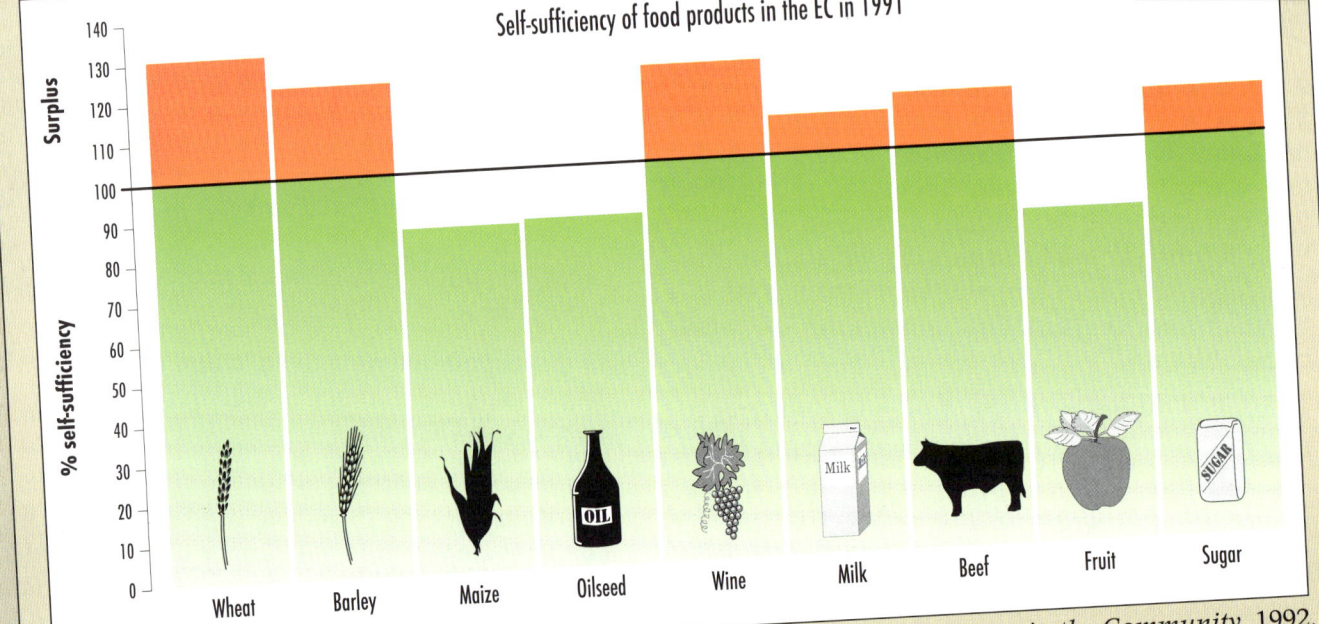

Self-sufficiency of food products in the EC in 1991

[Bar chart showing % self-sufficiency with surplus shown above 100% line for: Wheat (~132), Barley (~126), Maize (~90), Oilseed (~92), Wine (~132), Milk (~120), Beef (~125), Fruit (~97), Sugar (~127)]

Source: European Commission, *The Agricultural Situation in the Community*, 1992.

Resource H

How will the farmer decide to diversify?

ORGANIC FARMING
- Demand for 'natural' food is increasing
- Takes time to convert farm; may lose money

FORESTRY eg pines, oaks
- Demand for softwood increasing; profit in 30 years
- Pines make soil acidic; little wildlife encouraged in pine forests
- Hardwoods like oak take a long time to give a profit, eg 100 years
- Woods can be used for recreation

Thoughts:
- Has my farm the right climate, soils, relief?
- Have I the skills?
- Have I the right equipment?
- Is there a market?
- Have I got the labour?
- How much will it cost?
- Do I need advice?

ALTERNATIVE LIVESTOCK
- Deer farming
- Snail farming
- Trout farming
- Goats

ALTERNATIVE CROPS
- Viticulture (grapes)
- Lupins for animal feed

TOURISM
- Increasing demand for farm holidays
- People more mobile – increase in visitors to rural areas
- Can be seasonal profits only

Resource I

CASE STUDY D
Yorkshire Dales Marginal Farming

HIGH HALL RARE BREEDS FARM

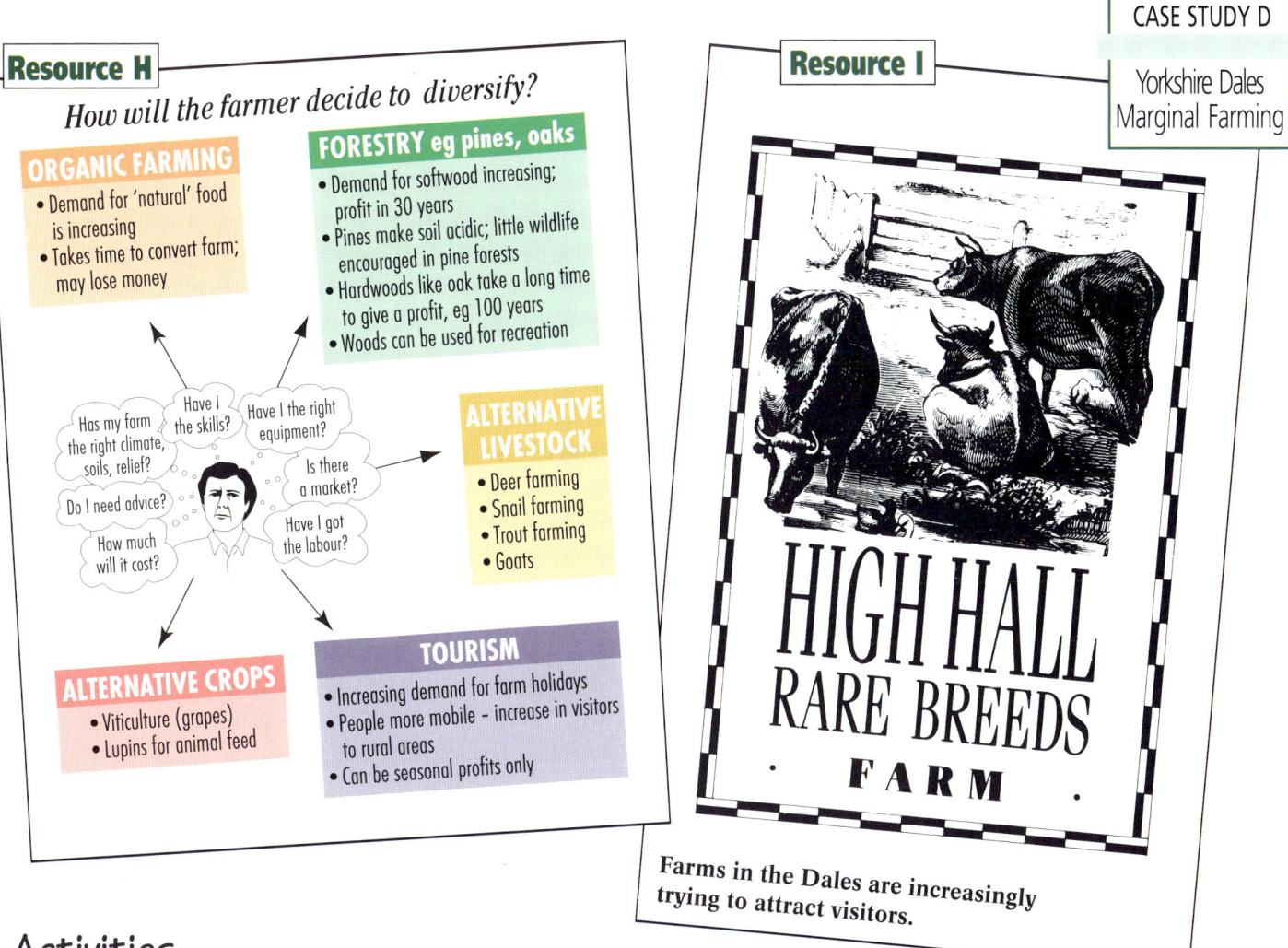

Farms in the Dales are increasingly trying to attract visitors.

Activities

1 Complete the following passage choosing from the words listed below it.

The Common Agricultural Policy or CAP has encouraged _____ of farm products in the EC. There are now food _____ of products like beef and _____. These are _____ to store. The EC has introduced _____ which set limits on how much milk can be produced.

> costly   surpluses   butter
> overproduction   quotas

2 Study the graph (Resource G) carefully.
a Which products were being overproduced in the EC?
b Which product had the largest surplus? Does this suggest anything to you about the level of the support price set for this product?

3 Study the resources on these pages before answering this question.
a What is meant by **diversification** in farming? Give an example of diversification in the Yorkshire Dales.
b List three important factors a farmer must think about before he can decide how he will diversify his farm (Resource H).
c Suggest one way of diversifying away from farming which will be least harmful to the environment.

4a List all the different ways you can think of in which farmers could earn money from tourism.
b 'The Yorkshire Dales' is a National Park. Why might Park authorities be concerned about the expansion of tourist facilities in their area?

Are there any lessons to be learned from the Common Agricultural Policy? When you have answered the questions above, remember that you were asked to write a short note to the US government explaining the benefits and disadvantages of the CAP for farmers and for the environment. In a small group, try to draft a letter (on one side of A4 paper) addressed to the Department of Agriculture in Washington DC.

CASE STUDY D
Yorkshire Dales Marginal Farming

Key Question 3
How can farming practices help protect the environment?

Save Our Dales Campaign

By the late 1980s the European Community and the UK government were becoming concerned about the cost of producing and storing food surpluses. One solution was to reduce the amount of land used for farming. Two schemes in particular have been put forward:

1 **Environmentally Sensitive Areas (ESAs)**
2 **The Set-aside Scheme**

Environmentally Sensitive Areas

Dentdale in the Yorkshire Dales has one of the UK's rarest and most fragile wildlife habitats. As hill farming uses few modern methods, machines or chemicals, these unique wildlife sites have survived, especially many traditional hay and water meadows. In recent years, though, farmers have been under pressure to intensify their production in order to produce more sheep for market. Some hay meadows have been drained, and others spoilt by chemical fertilisers. Wild flowers and habitats have been damaged or even destroyed by these actions.

In 1985, the EC agreed to provide funds to allow areas with important biological habitats or landscapes to be protected. Farmers would be paid to farm these 'environmentally sensitive areas' (ESAs) in a traditional way, and would be encouraged to improve them, perhaps by using less fertiliser, or leaving fields unploughed. The Pennine Dales was one of just 10 ESAs identified by the UK government in 1987, although by 1993 the number had almost doubled to 19. Farmers now maintain the traditional stone walls and barns that help make the landscape attractive to visitors. They also fence off woodland from grazing sheep so that the trees have a chance to regenerate. The scheme is voluntary but provides some additional income for farmers and reduces the pressure to intensify production.

Set-aside Scheme

In 1988, a voluntary set-aside scheme was set up to reduce cereal surpluses in the EC. A farmer joining the scheme must agree not to use 20% of his land for farming before being paid £200 for each hectare taken out of production. The land can either be left fallow, converted to woodland or used for non-agricultural purposes. Initially only about 2,000 farmers registered for the scheme, though many more farmers said they might join the scheme later.

A reform of the CAP in 1992 meant that farmers had to reduce their land use area by 15% in order to qualify for EC support. Other financial incentives are now available if farmers do other things with their land, for example developing recreational uses or tree planting.

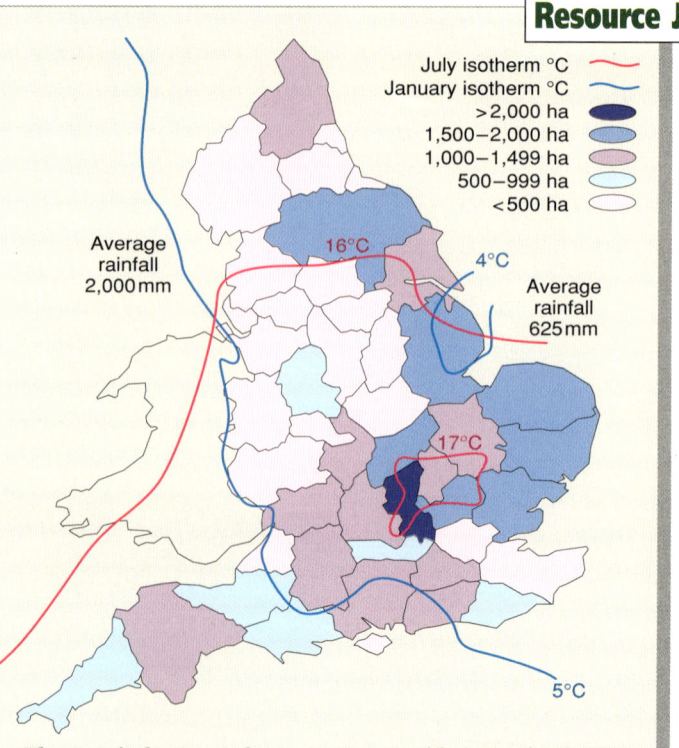

Resource J

July isotherm °C
January isotherm °C
> 2,000 ha
1,500–2,000 ha
1,000–1,499 ha
500–999 ha
< 500 ha

Average rainfall 2,000 mm
16°C
4°C
Average rainfall 625 mm
17°C
5°C

The area in hectares given over to set-aside in England, 1989.

How things will change

Under the reforms proposed by the EC in 1992, the form of support for farmers will change. The price Brussels offers to farmers will fall, but farmers will have their income topped up by around £188 per hectare, provided they take 15% of their land out of production, under a scheme known as 'set-aside'. Probable result: more big farms, more golf courses, more uncultivated land.

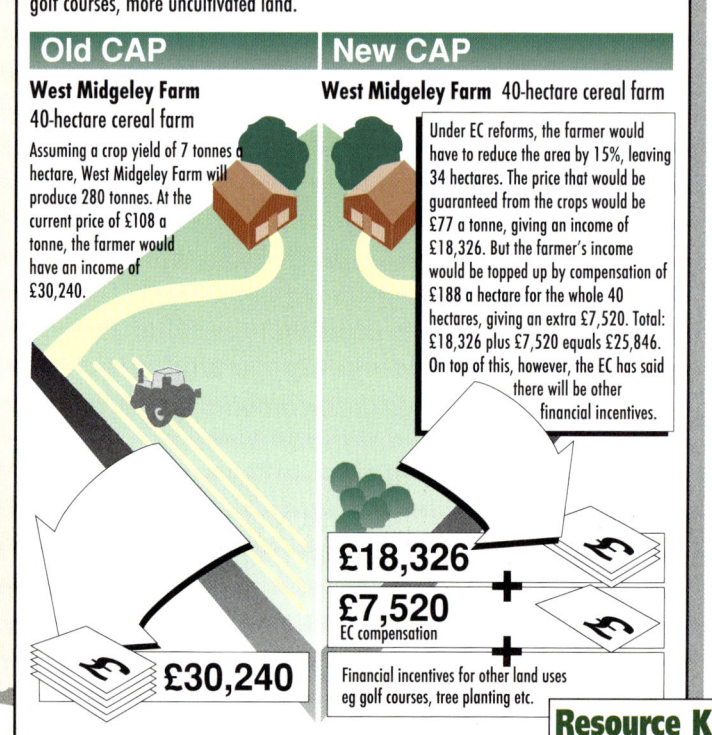

Old CAP
West Midgeley Farm
40-hectare cereal farm

Assuming a crop yield of 7 tonnes a hectare, West Midgeley Farm will produce 280 tonnes. At the current price of £108 a tonne, the farmer would have an income of £30,240.

£30,240

New CAP
West Midgeley Farm 40-hectare cereal farm

Under EC reforms, the farmer would have to reduce the area by 15%, leaving 34 hectares. The price that would be guaranteed from the crops would be £77 a tonne, giving an income of £18,326. But the farmer's income would be topped up by compensation of £188 a hectare for the whole 40 hectares, giving an extra £7,520. Total: £18,326 plus £7,520 equals £25,846. On top of this, however, the EC has said there will be other financial incentives.

£18,326
+
£7,520
EC compensation
+
Financial incentives for other land uses eg golf courses, tree planting etc.

Resource K

Resource L

Future Dales landscapes ... there *is* a choice

1 The intensive landscape

In this scene, little public money is available to subsidise Dales farming. The small farms are amalgamated to create large ranches, and modern technology is introduced.

Large sheds and wire fences would replace the barns and dry-stone walls. Heather moorland would disappear as a result of overgrazing, and mixed woodland would be replaced by coniferous woodland.

2 The sporting landscape

The landscape is turned into large estates for grouse and pheasant shooting, deer hunting and outdoor recreation. There would be many jobs on the estates and in tourism but few people would farm.

Large new woodlands would provide cover for wildlife and game as well as a profit from timber. The heather moorland would be retained for grouse shooting.

3 The abandoned landscape

If upland farming subsidies are taken away, farmers are left to compete with better farms in the lowland areas. Some farmers remain on the better land in the Dales with small flocks, but outlying meadows and moorland are abandoned to scrub and thistles.

To survive, farmers would turn to tourism or forestry. Barns and dry-stone walls would fall into ruin.

4 The conserved landscape

This scene could result if public money is given to farmers who continue to rear livestock *and* at the same time show they are conserving the landscape.

There would be more heather moorland and hay meadows (yellow patches) than today. Mixed woodlands, barns and dry-stone walls would be well maintained. Farmers could supplement their income from farm-based tourism.

Source: © Yorkshire Dales National Park Committee 1989.

CASE STUDY D

Yorkshire Dales Marginal Farming

Activities

While you are in the UK you notice that efforts are being made to lower farm output by reducing the area that is cultivated. You find this interesting, as in your district of Vermont farmers are simply going out of business, which is not always the fairest way to lower farm output.

When you have studied the resources on the last two pages, write a postcard to your family in the USA. Explain briefly what measures are being introduced in the UK to restore the rural environment. Remember that the whole system of support for agriculture may seem very strange to them.

1 Study the map in Resource J carefully.
a If arable crops like wheat and barley need warm, dry summers, which area (east or west) will be most suitable for their cultivation?
b Which area of Britain (east or west) appears to have 'set aside' most farmland?
c From your answers to **a** and **b** above, explain whether or not you think the set-aside scheme is likely to help reduce the grain 'mountains' (surpluses) in Europe.
d Which areas of Britain have the lowest take-up of the set-aside scheme? Can you suggest reasons for this?

2 Study Resource K.
a What effect will the changes to the Common Agricultural Policy have on (i) a farmer's income, (ii) grain surpluses, (iii) the landscape?
b Can you suggest any further changes to EC Agricultural Policy which might benefit the environment?

3 For this activity you will need to work in pairs. Study Resource L and read the description of each possible future landscape carefully.
a Make a copy of the table below, and using a scale of 1 to 10, decide in your pair what score each Dales landscape should get for each factor listed (1 is a low score and 10 is a high score). Total your marks at the end. Which landscape did you rate with the highest score? Why?
b How do your results compare with those of other pairs in your class?
c Discuss as a class which landscape is best for:
• maintaining the wildlife in the Dales
• providing the most profitable farming
• providing the best tourist environment.
d Write a letter to a local newspaper explaining which type of landscape you would like to see in the Dales.

Factor	Dales landscape			
	1	2	3	4
Meadows for wild flowers				
Traditional barns, buildings and walls				
Maintains small family-run farms				
Provides jobs for local people				
Provides a profit without government grants				
Maintains mixed woodland and abundant wildlife				
Total =				

Further activities

CASE STUDY D

Yorkshire Dales Marginal Farming

Short-answer tasks

1 Name three foods which are in surplus in the European Community.

2 How does the set-aside scheme aim to reduce food surpluses?

3 What evidence do the photographs below provide of farm diversification? What problems could arise if too many visitors went to the area on holiday, or for a day out?

4 Some supermarkets now sell fruit and vegetables grown by 'organic' methods. What does this mean? How does organic produce differ from that grown by other methods?

Signs of diversification in Wharfedale.

Find out about . . .

1 Write a short comparison between a marginal farm in another European country and a marginal hill farm in Britain. You could choose fiord farming in Norway or pastoral farming in southern Italy, for example.

2 Explain how the physical environment in the UK favours different crops. Do you think that physical or political factors are the most important in helping a farmer to decide what to farm?

CASE STUDY D

Yorkshire Dales Marginal Farming

Library and research tasks

1 The graph and table below show some statistics about agriculture in the European Community. Using any other resources and books you can find, attempt to explain the following.

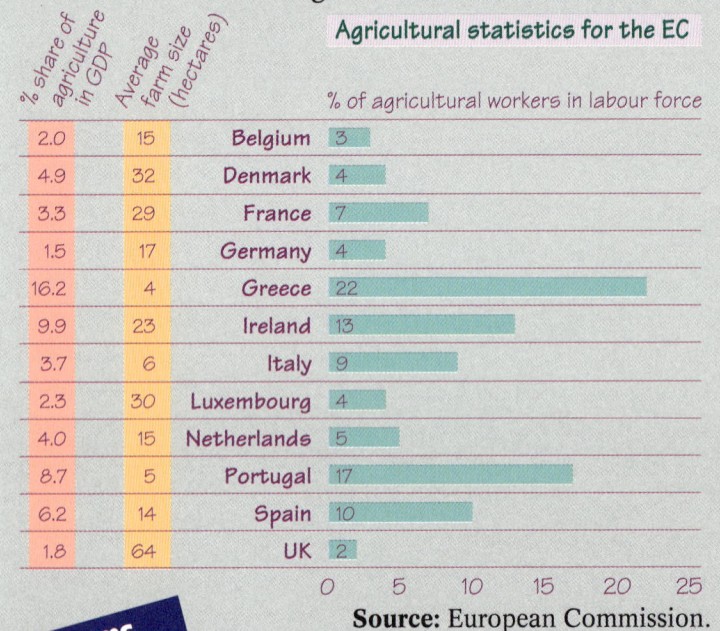

Agricultural statistics for the EC

% share of agriculture in GDP	Average farm size (hectares)	Country	% of agricultural workers in labour force
2.0	15	Belgium	3
4.9	32	Denmark	4
3.3	29	France	7
1.5	17	Germany	4
16.2	4	Greece	22
9.9	23	Ireland	13
3.7	6	Italy	9
2.3	30	Luxembourg	4
4.0	15	Netherlands	5
8.7	5	Portugal	17
6.2	14	Spain	10
1.8	64	UK	2

Source: European Commission.

a Why does the number of people working in agriculture vary between the 12 EC countries?

b Is there any correlation between average farm size and the number of agricultural workers?

c Draw a graph with *average farm size* (*x* axis) plotted against *percentage share of agriculture* (*y* axis) in GDP. Does your graph suggest any link between the two sets of data?

2 Find out how large the EC's surpluses currently are. How does the situation differ from the one shown in Resource G?

3 If you live in an agricultural area, find out how a farm near your home or school has changed over the last 30 years. You should consider the following:
- size
- number of employees
- the nature of the inputs
- farm equipment used
- type of crops grown and yields
- any non-farm sources of income.

Key Terms

CAP the European Community's Common Agricultural Policy.

diversification a farmer decides to develop land uses in addition to farming in order to make a profit and stay in business.

ESA Environmentally Sensitive Area – land that is farmed in a traditional way to reduce the risk to wildlife and to maintain the attractive landscape.

intervention price a guaranteed price given by the government or the European Community to the farmer for a farm product, eg wheat.

marginal farm where the physical conditions (climate and soils) only just make farming economically possible.

quota the amount of farm product that an individual farmer is allowed to produce. Currently there are quotas controlling milk production.

set-aside land which a farmer agrees not to use for farming and for which in return the farmer is paid compensation by the government.

subsidy money given to farmers by the government or the EC to help them stay in business.

Key Understandings

- A combination of physical, economic and political factors helps to determine the land use patterns in different areas.

- The climate and landscape of the Yorkshire Dales favour hill farming. As a result of physical limitations, farming here is difficult and is described as 'marginal'.

- The European Community's Common Agricultural Policy (CAP) has influenced farming landscapes and practices all over the UK, often with unfortunate effects on the rural environment.

- New policies recognise that the rural environment needs special protection, and provide incentives for farmers who agree to take land out of production, or to use more traditional methods which cause less damage to the environment and its habitats.

Case Study E

Car Production in Spain

You are to adopt the role of consumer. This may seem more straightforward than several of the other roles in this book, because almost certainly you are already a consumer, directly or indirectly, of motor vehicles. It is unlikely, though, that you have ever bought one. So to help you into the role we begin to look at the topic through the eyes of Sally. She has just got her first job as a surveyor with a large building company. The company asks her to choose a company car so that she can travel from one building site to another. She is able to choose one of the following three models:

- Seat Ibiza 1.2XL
- Vauxhall Nova 1.2L
- Ford Fiesta 1.1L.

Which should Sally choose?

The motor vehicle industry is one of the most important manufacturing industries of the 20th century. Motor vehicles transport people and goods all over the world. Millions of families depend upon the industry directly for jobs. The economy of whole nations depends upon the health of the industry, yet its control is in the hands of just a few companies. These companies are so big and powerful that they can earn more money in a year than many whole countries.

Spain freed itself from Fascism in the 1970s, and soon after joining the European Community it became an alternative location for the expanding car industry.

Spain's position in Europe.

CASE STUDY E

Car Production in Spain

Key Question 1
What factors should you consider when buying a new car?

The first thing Sally does is to buy a copy of *What Car?* The information in this magazine allows her to compare the performance of the three cars and judge which is the best value. They are all three-door hatchbacks, with five gears and a fitted radio. But the Fiesta has the best fuel consumption, the Nova is the cheapest to insure, and the Ibiza has the fastest acceleration. The cars are similar in lots of ways but the Ibiza is slightly larger and around £500 cheaper than the other two. All Nova 1.2Ls, Ibiza 1.2XLs, and some Fiesta 1.1Ls, are imported from Spain.

The next thing Sally does is to turn to the review pages of *What Car?* The guest drivers who were asked to try out the Ibiza 1.2XL had some reservations about it. Some of their comments can be found below.

The Ibiza 1.2XL.

Source: *What Car?*, September 1989.

Resource A

Some views on the Ibiza 1.2XL

I liked the handling but found the ride lumpy. I also liked the gearbox feel too, and the heating and ventilation. But there's not enough room in the rear.

Keith Walker, 42, builder

Smart interior design. But disappointing overall. Performance is sluggish, it feels heavy to drive and is noisy.

Kerrie Cooke, 20, advertising executive

A bit bland. Didn't like the speedo having km/h instead of mph as prominent figures. Quite pleasantly styled exterior.

Patsie Lake, 48, administrative manager

CASE STUDY E
Car Production in Spain

Just as Sally is about to order a Vauxhall Nova, her friend Susan shows her a copy of another magazine, *The Ethical Consumer*. This includes a report on the major car companies and their record on issues like trade with South Africa, the pollution of the environment, and the manufacture of weapons. Resource B is a summary of *The Ethical Consumer*'s report on five companies. The red squares and triangles show where independent researchers have raised questions about the companies' involvement in an issue. Squares indicate greater involvement than triangles.

Susan knows that Sally is an active peace campaigner, a potential **ethical consumer**. She suggests that if Sally really wants to make the world a more peaceful place, she should choose the Ibiza rather than the Nova or Fiesta. Volkswagen, who own SEAT, are not as involved with armaments as Ford who make Fiestas, or General Motors who own Vauxhall and make Novas.

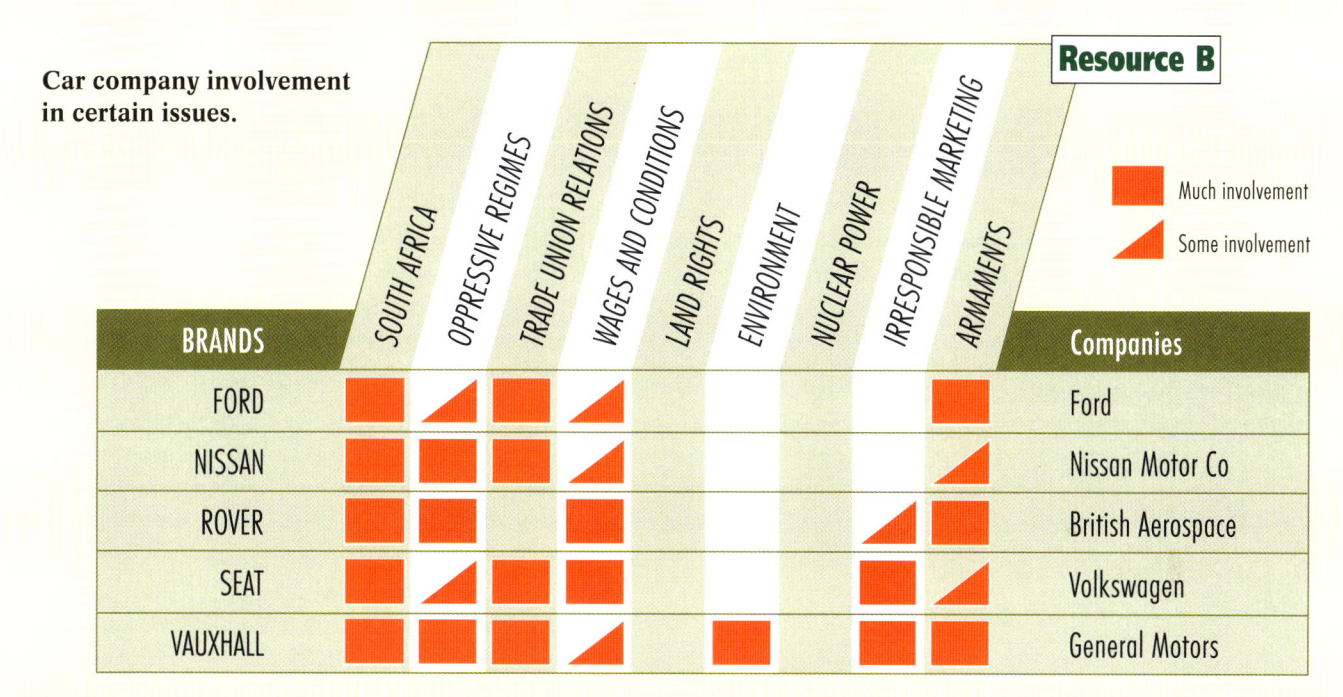

Resource B

Car company involvement in certain issues.

■ Much involvement
◢ Some involvement

BRANDS	SOUTH AFRICA	OPPRESSIVE REGIMES	TRADE UNION RELATIONS	WAGES AND CONDITIONS	LAND RIGHTS	ENVIRONMENT	NUCLEAR POWER	IRRESPONSIBLE MARKETING	ARMAMENTS	Companies
FORD	■	◢	■	◢					■	Ford
NISSAN	■	■	■	◢					◢	Nissan Motor Co
ROVER	■	■	■					◢	■	British Aerospace
SEAT	■	◢	■	■				■	◢	Volkswagen
VAUXHALL	■	■	■	◢		■		■	■	General Motors

Source: *Ethical Consumer*, Issue 3, July/August 1989.

Activities

Now imagine it is not Sally who is choosing a new car, but you. You have to select a new, small hatchback from all the models available.

1 First make a list of all things that your ideal car would have. Then collect brochures from garages and reports from motoring magazines like *What Car?* Which car best fits your ideal? Did you change your ideas about your ideal car as you found out more about the cars available?

2 Why do you think so many small hatchbacks have Spanish names? Make a list of all these names and find out how many of the cars are actually made in Spain and imported into Britain. Do you think it is a good idea to buy a Spanish car rather than one made in Britain?

3 Buying something is like voting for the company that made it. Look at Resource B. Which of the five companies would you most like to vote for by buying one of their cars? Which of the issues at the top of the diagram most influenced your choice?

CASE STUDY E

Car Production in Spain

Key Question 2
What factors do large companies consider when deciding where to build a car factory in Europe?

We have considered the factors which influenced Sally when she bought her car. Now we will turn our attention to the companies that make cars. Why did Ford, General Motors, and Volkswagen decide to build small cars in Spain, and export so many of them to Britain and to other parts of Europe (Resource C)? To answer that question we need to understand the changing nature of the European car industry.

Spanish car production.

(a) By numbers of units, 1992

General Motors	375,000
SEAT-Volkswagen	530,000
Ford	300,000
Total including others*	1,794,763

* Peugeot, Citroën, Renault

(b) By value (billions of $ US)

	Domestic production	% exported
1988	10.00	33
1989	10.82	35
1990	11.93	37
1991	12.51	43
1992	13.13	48

From our Industrial Correspondent

Resource C

More cars are made and sold in Europe than in any other continent – about 12.5 million. Most are still made by companies that began in Europe, like Volkswagen, Peugeot, Fiat, Renault and Rover. But a growing number are made by American and Japanese companies which have set up factories in Europe.

The large American and Japanese car companies are looking for a share of the profits which can be made from producing and selling cars in the large European market. In the past 25 years, Ford and General Motors have greatly expanded their European operations and they now have factories in many locations, including Spain. In 1976, Ford began to produce Fiestas from its new factory near Valencia. The Fiesta was the first 'European car'; assembled from parts made throughout Europe and designed to be sold in many European countries.

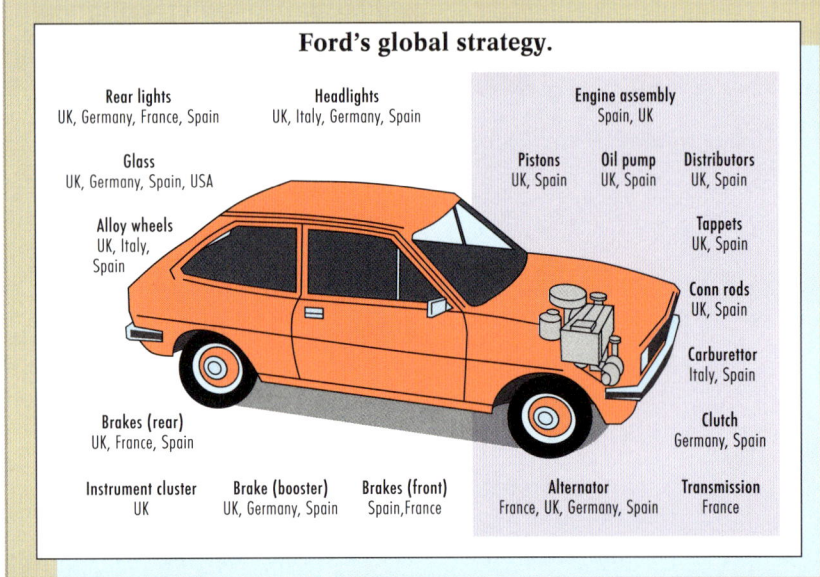

Ford's global strategy.

- Rear lights: UK, Germany, France, Spain
- Headlights: UK, Italy, Germany, Spain
- Engine assembly: Spain, UK
- Glass: UK, Germany, Spain, USA
- Pistons: UK, Spain
- Oil pump: UK, Spain
- Distributors: UK, Spain
- Alloy wheels: UK, Italy, Spain
- Tappets: UK, Spain
- Conn rods: UK, Spain
- Carburettor: Italy, Spain
- Brakes (rear): UK, France, Spain
- Clutch: Germany, Spain
- Instrument cluster: UK
- Brake (booster): UK, Germany, Spain
- Brakes (front): Spain, France
- Alternator: France, UK, Germany, Spain
- Transmission: France

By 1980, the European car industry was in a crisis. There were more cars being produced than could be sold. The carmakers' profits had been falling and they were losing business to rising Japanese imports. They had to find new ways of reducing their costs and making their cars more competitive.

To do this they introduced new models and materials, new technologies and work methods, and new joint ventures with other companies. They closed factories in countries where costs were high, and opened new factories where costs were lower. These changes resulted in more 'European cars' like the Fiesta and more new car factories in Spain.

New factories were built in Spain because car workers were cheap to employ. The Spanish government provided financial help to set up new factories and insisted that most of the cars were exported to earn foreign exchange. There was also a rapidly growing market for cars within the country and imports were kept out by high duties. Spain joined the EC in 1984 and by 1987 it had overtaken Britain as a car producer. As a member of the EC, the cars made there can be sold freely throughout the Community. The graph shows that by the late 1980s, Europe's car industry was growing again.

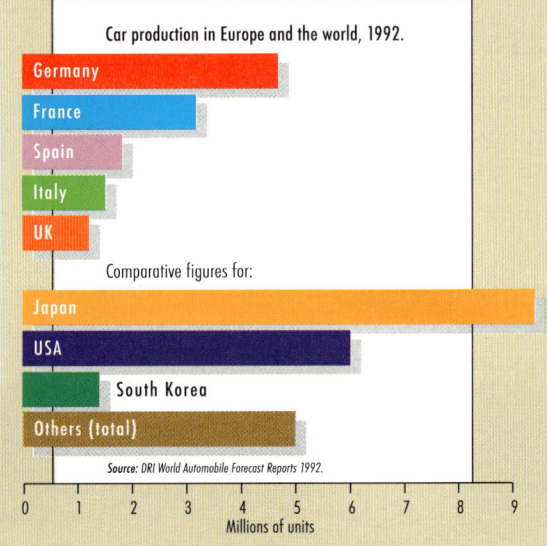

Car production in Europe and the world, 1992.

- Germany
- France
- Spain
- Italy
- UK

Comparative figures for:
- Japan
- USA
- South Korea
- Others (total)

0 1 2 3 4 5 6 7 8 9
Millions of units

Source: DRI World Automobile Forecast Reports 1992.

Source: © *The Economist*, 15 October 1988.

Resource D

General Motors in Europe

CASE STUDY E

Car Production in Spain

General Motors (GM) is the largest manufacturing company in the world. With its headquarters in Detroit USA, it has factories in more than 30 countries. It employs over 750,000 people and makes one-fifth of all the world's cars.

GM has made and sold cars in Europe since the 1920s. It now has factories in nine European countries including Britain and Spain. In 1992, GM did $28.8 billion of business in Europe and recorded profits of $1.2 billion.

GM's car factories in Britain are at Luton and Ellesmere Port. At Figueruelas (near Zaragoza) in Spain, it has built one of the world's most technologically advanced car factories. This employs 10,000 workers building the Opel Corsa (Vauxhall Nova) and Opel Kadett. They can produce 85 cars per hour on three shifts, or 332,000 cars each year. GM also makes car components at five other factories in Spain.

Aerial view of GM's plant at Figueruelas.

Activities

1 Use the figures in the table on page 48 to work out what percentage of cars built in Spain are exported. Show your results in the form of diagrams.

2 Why do you think GM changes the name of the Opel Corsa to Vauxhall Nova when it is imported into Britain (Resource D)?

3 Suggest reasons why the various parts of the Fiesta (Resource C) are made in several countries.

4 Look at the graph showing car production in Europe (Resource C). Which countries have been most successful in increasing their output? Which have been least successful? How may the policies of governments help to explain the variation in performances of different countries?

49

CASE STUDY E

Car Production in Spain

Key Question 3
How can trade unionists influence the plans of large companies like General Motors?

Resource E

Many workers in European car factories were hard-hit by the changes introduced by their employers in the 1980s. Restoring a company's competitiveness and profit levels often meant making workers redundant, and increasing the work rate for those who remained. It also meant holding down wages and using new technologies and work methods to reduce **trade union** power. This was often done with the help of governments which introduced new laws to limit trade union activity.

While employment in motor vehicle manufacture fell by 14% in the European Community between 1977 and 1985, some countries and workers were harder hit than others. Britain lost 220,000 jobs in the industry between 1980 and 1982 (half the EC total), while Spain continued to gain jobs. Workers at the Vauxhall plant in Luton realised that car imports from Spain were threatening their jobs. In 1984 they took action with other workers to stop imports of Novas built in Spain.

Resource G

Resource F

The Nova Ban

Until the mid-1970s, Vauxhall Motors, GM's British subsidiary, was a major manufacturer and exporter of passenger and commercial vehicles. But within a few years its European dealer network and design facilities were run down. Vauxhall was restricted to producing for the British market. In a major re-organisation, 17,000 jobs were lost at its three main plants.

After the import of 45,000 Cavaliers from Europe, the trade unions saw only one solution. A major campaign was launched bringing together all Vauxhall unions and involving trade unionists in the ports. Its target was to ban the import of the Spanish-made Nova.

After ships containing the blacked cars were turned away from the ports, GM soon came to the negotiating table. The unions won restrictions on imports, and 1,000 new jobs at Luton.

Source: GM *Workers' Voice*, 1985.

The 1985 Nova ban reminded Vauxhall workers that transnational firms, like General Motors, organise their activities on a continental or global scale. They co-operate with one another and can set workers in one country in competition with those in another (Resource C). If workers' demands for better pay or working conditions are too great, the company may threaten to transfer production and jobs to countries where workers have less power. If workers take strike action, they are unlikely to bring the company to a standstill. Components and vehicles are made in several **locations** and the local market can temporarily be supplied from abroad.

In this situation car workers realised that they too would have to organise internationally. In 1987, the first international conference of autoworkers was held in São Paulo, Brazil. The 40 delegates from 15 countries agreed three priorities for action (Resource H).

Source: General Motors' *Workers' Voice*.

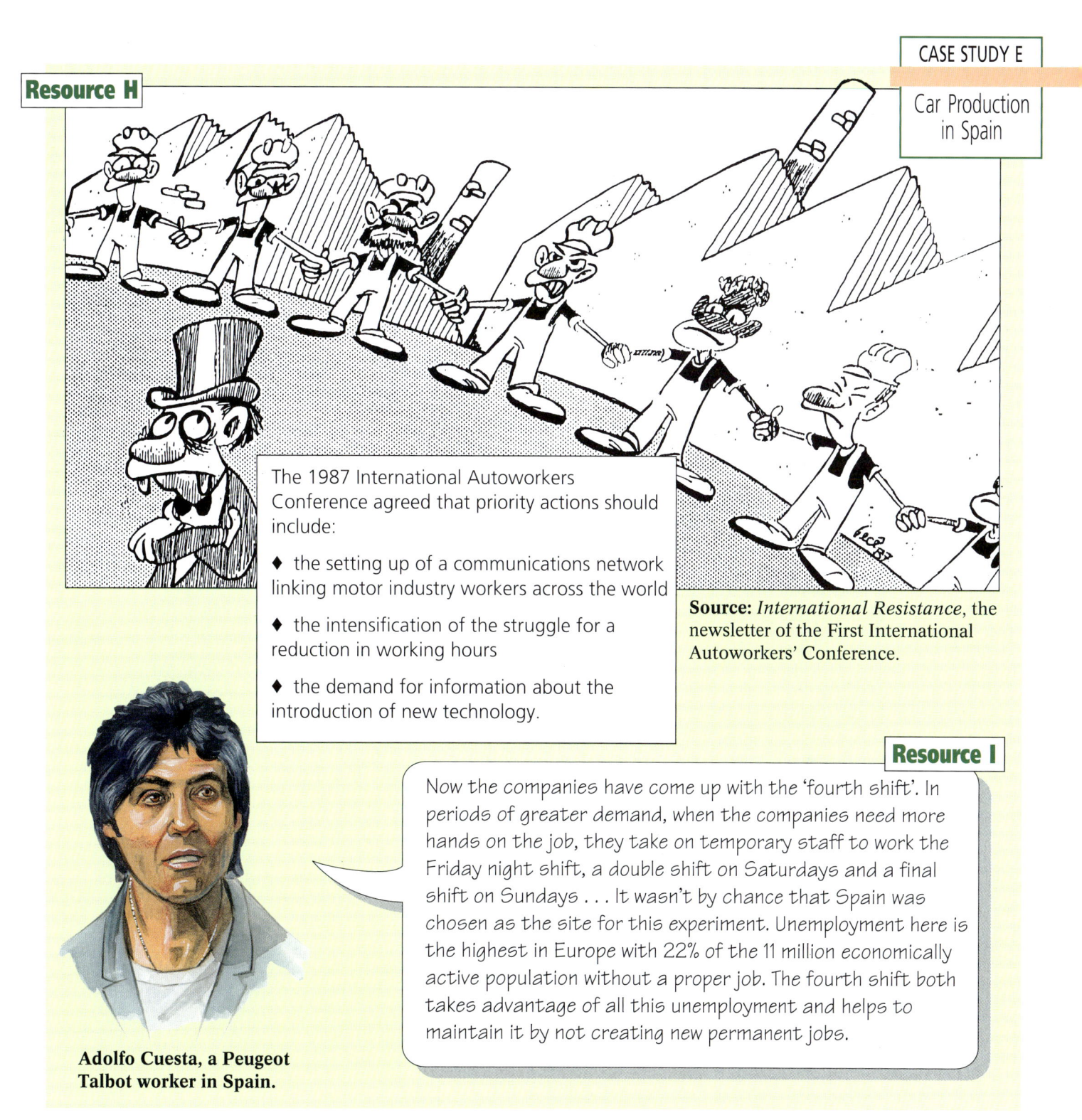

Resource H

CASE STUDY E

Car Production in Spain

The 1987 International Autoworkers Conference agreed that priority actions should include:

♦ the setting up of a communications network linking motor industry workers across the world

♦ the intensification of the struggle for a reduction in working hours

♦ the demand for information about the introduction of new technology.

Source: *International Resistance*, the newsletter of the First International Autoworkers' Conference.

Resource I

Now the companies have come up with the 'fourth shift'. In periods of greater demand, when the companies need more hands on the job, they take on temporary staff to work the Friday night shift, a double shift on Saturdays and a final shift on Sundays ... It wasn't by chance that Spain was chosen as the site for this experiment. Unemployment here is the highest in Europe with 22% of the 11 million economically active population without a proper job. The fourth shift both takes advantage of all this unemployment and helps to maintain it by not creating new permanent jobs.

Adolfo Cuesta, a Peugeot Talbot worker in Spain.

Activities

1 Imagine you are managing a factory for Peugeot Talbot in Spain. Write a letter to the company director in Paris requesting permission to introduce a 'fourth shift' (Resource I).

2 Design a poster encouraging dock workers to support the Nova ban (Resource F).

3 Draw another five frames in the cartoon story (Resource G). Suggest what the workers in the USA and Japan did next.

4 What would be the advantages of Ford or GM workers throughout Europe being members of a single transnational trade union?

CASE STUDY E
Car Production in Spain

Further activities

Short-answer tasks

1 Read the text in the box below. Should we try to do without cars in order to conserve resources and improve the environment?

> The motor industry uses 20% of all steel, 10% of aluminium, 35% of zinc, 50% of lead, 60% of natural rubber, and between 35 and 60% of all oil production (depending on the country).
>
> The car uses only 10–20% of the energy in that fuel. The rest is turned into noise, heat and pollution. In spite of lead-free petrol and catalytic converters, the car is still a major cause of air pollution and global warming.
>
> Other costs of private motor cars include road accidents, land lost to new roads and parking, traffic congestion and worsening public transport.

2 Work in a group. You have to decide where to build a new car factory in Europe. Try to agree on a ranking for the following factors, putting the most important at the top of your list.
- flat land
- cheap labour
- good transport
- skilled labour
- government finance
- low taxes on profits
- weak trade unions
- large market for cars
- attractive places for managers and directors to live
- component factories nearby
- low heating costs

Find out about . . .

1 Car design

After their Italian partners Fiat pulled out in 1980, the Spanish firm SEAT formed a new partnership with Volkswagen. SEAT's factories in Barcelona and Pamplona now make Volkswagen Polos, Passats and Santanas, many of which are exported. They also make a new range of SEAT cars: the Ibiza, Marbella and Malaga. Working with Volkswagen encouraged SEAT to make use of German engineers, and Italian designers in planning its new cars. They were designed by Giorgetto Giugiaro's Ital design team in Turin. It also designed the Volkswagen Golf and the Fiat Uno.

Collect a variety of brochures from car showrooms and study the designs. Carry out a survey to find out whether the design of small hatchback cars is a key factor in influencing the car buyer's choice.

Your CDT teacher may be able to show you how computers are used to aid the design of cars.

2 Balance of payments

In 1988/89 Britain's motor imports were valued at £3.42 billion more than motor exports. This gap between motor imports and exports was one of the major causes of Britain's growing balance of payments problem.

Find out about the link between Britain's growing balance of payments problems and the government's policy of encouraging Japanese car firms, such as Nissan and Toyota, to build factories in Britain. Can this policy be judged a success? What figures do you need to make this judgement?

Assessment activity

1 Look at the graphs (right).
a In which country were most cars made in 1987?
b Roughly how many cars did this country make that year?
c In which country were most cars bought in 1987?
d What percentage of those cars were imported?
e How many cars were made in Spain in 1987?
f How many cars were sold in Spain in 1987? (6 x 1 marks)

2a In 1986 Spain exported 672,792 cars to the European Community of which 91,313 were imported into the UK. In the same year the UK exported 136,886 cars to the Community of which 9,414 were imported into Spain. Also in the same year the UK imported 227,719 cars from Japan while Spain imported only 1,124 Japanese cars. The European Community imported a total of 1,104,634 Japanese cars that year. Draw a flow diagram to represent this information. (3)
b What could explain why the numbers of Spanish and Japanese cars entering the UK were so high? (2)
c Explain why the number of UK and Japanese cars entering Spain was so low. (3)

3 Write a short account of General Motors' operations in the UK and Spain. (3)

4 Spanish SEAT cars were first sold in the UK in 1985.
The graph (right) shows SEAT's sales statistics over the following four years. How might the following factors affect SEAT's future sales in the UK?
a Increased wages for car workers in Spain.
b The Spanish peseta falling in value relative to the UK pound.
c European Community regulations requiring a 'clean car'. (3 x 2)

5 Look at the cartoon (right) which is from a trade union newspaper. It shows one of the managers of a large transnational company and workers in two different countries. The manager wants the workers to be part of one big family and share the company's interests and values. The workers do not seem too keen on this idea.
 Explain why car workers may have different interests and values from the companies they work for. (2)

Total 25 marks

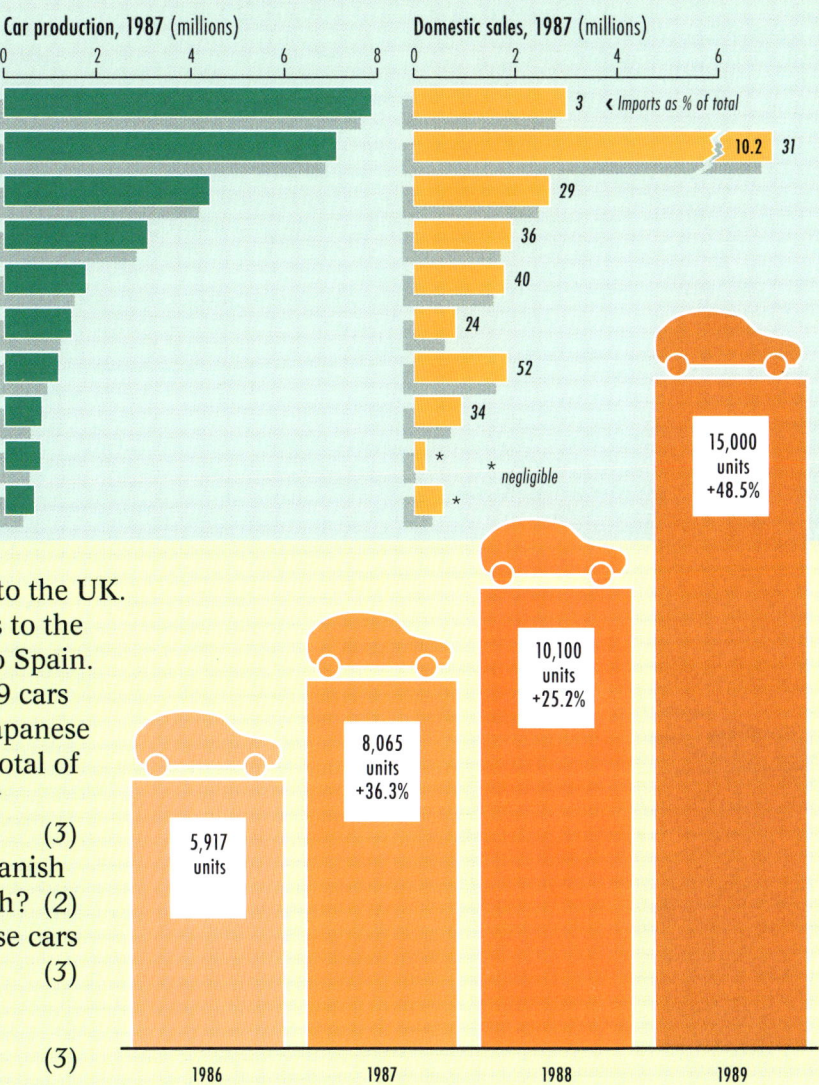

Car production, 1987 (millions)

Japan	~8
United States	~7
West Germany	~4.5
France	~3.5
Italy	~2
Spain	~1.5
Britain	~1.3
Canada	~0.8
South Korea	~0.8
Brazil	~0.5

Domestic sales, 1987 (millions) — Imports as % of total

Country	Sales	Imports %
Japan		3
United States	10.2	31
West Germany		29
France		36
Italy		40
Spain		24
Britain		52
Canada		34
South Korea		*
Brazil		*

*negligible

SEAT sales:
- 1986: 5,917 units
- 1987: 8,065 units +36.3%
- 1988: 10,100 units +25.2%
- 1989: 15,000 units +48.5%

Source: © *The Economist*, 15 October 1988.

"We must erode the boundaries imposed on us and further international solidarity!"

"WE ARE A BIG FAMILY!"

Source: *International Resistance*, the newsletter of the First International Autoworkers' Conference.

53

CASE STUDY E
Car Production in Spain

Library and research tasks

The European Charter of Social Rights

In 1992 the last remaining obstacles to free trade between the 12 countries of the European Community disappeared. The single market was first thought up by Europe's biggest transnational companies. If it is to benefit both these companies and the workers they employ, trade unionists believe that there will have to be some safeguards. In 1989 the European Trade Union Confederation supported the European Commission's proposed European Charter of Social Rights. This would guarantee workers minimum social and industrial rights and protect them from some of the likely effects of industrial re-organisation resulting from the single market. While Germany, France, Italy and Spain backed the social charter, Britain's government at that time opposed its introduction.

> Try to find out more about the European Charter of Social Rights. Was it actually introduced? When? What protection did it provide for workers? Did the attitude of the UK government change? Do you support such a charter?

Key Terms

consumer a user of energy, goods and services – all people play the role of consumer.

ethical consumer one who makes consumer choices according to a set of clear principles or priorities.

location position or situation in which a car factory is built. Locations are usually relative to each other; they have advantages and disadvantages.

trade unions organisations devoted to representing and protecting the interests of employees in industries. These interests are often in opposition to the interests of managers and shareholders.

Key Understandings

- Consumers can make choices. These choices are based partly on available information and partly upon the priorities of the individual concerned: are we to choose the cheapest, the best quality, the cleverest design, the most ethically produced or the most environmentally friendly?

- There is great pressure on motor vehicle producers to continue expanding. National markets are not large enough to support high-volume car industries and companies have had to become international. Many car firms are 'transnational companies'.

- The market for cars is not infinite. From time to time there is a crisis, because the car industry produces more cars than it can sell. So some factories may close. Occasionally whole companies go out of business. The intense competition to survive forces all companies to reduce costs; new technologies and materials can help save money, mostly by enabling the company to employ fewer people.

- An argument rages over the EC. There are those who see the EC only as a large international 'single market'. Others understand that for the new Europe to work fairly there must be international rules, laws and organisations designed to protect people from the uncontrolled power of the transnational companies.

Case Study F

The Farmers of Languedoc-Roussillon, and the EC Wine Lake

The newspapers sometimes carry stories about 'butter mountains', 'beef mountains' and '**wine lakes**'. All are a result of **surplus** production by farmers of particular products. The Languedoc region in southern France has been producing agricultural surpluses for decades – they even caused a minor war with Italy! Why do such surpluses occur, and what can be done about them?

> You have just joined the Directorate-General for Agriculture (DGVI) at the Headquarters of the European Community in Brussels as a trainee. The Directorate is concerned about agricultural surpluses, and your first assignment is to find out what causes these surpluses. You must also suggest what can be done to reduce overproduction. The area you are asked to look at is Languedoc-Roussillon in the South of France.

Languedoc-Roussillon region in southern France.

CASE STUDY F

Farmers and the EC Wine Lake

Key Question 1
What sort of farming takes place in Languedoc-Roussillon?

Resource A

Commission of the European Community

Farming in the Regions

Brief number 25 – Languedoc-Roussillon

The Languedoc-Roussillon region stretches along the Mediterranean coast of southern France between the River Rhône and the Spanish border. It comprises the five départements of Aude, Gard, Hérault, Lozère and Pyrénées Orientales, and has a population of just over 2 million.

Apart from the more northerly and mountainous département of Lozère, the region is warm and sunny and the local population is growing rapidly. The climate attracts tourists, and agriculture is also important. Farming accounts for 10% of the region's earnings, and employs 11% of the workforce. It is, however, declining in importance. In 1990 there were just 64,000 farms – less than half the number compared with 30 years ago.

The landscape of the area is varied. it is hillier towards the Massif Central in the north and the Pyrenees in the west, while the coastal plain is low and flat. The climate is too dry for many crops to grow without **irrigation**. Most soils are poor and rocky, though well-drained. Despite these difficulties, the warm summers and long growing season have led to many products being cultivated locally including peaches, melons, apricots and salad crops like lettuce and tomatoes.

Resource B

Over most of Languedoc-Roussillon, however, a special type of monoculture dominates the landscape and the economy – **viticulture**. Most of the grapes that are grown are used to make wine. This has been one of France's leading wine-producing regions since the last century. Unlike other parts of France where quality is high, the wines of this area are cheap *vins ordinaires* or *vins de table*, and are produced in large quantities.

About 70% of all the agricultural holdings in Languedoc-Roussillon are mainly concerned with vine-growing. Many of the farms are small, under 5 hectares in size. They are often run by elderly and part-time farmers, and function best as **co-operatives**. This means that small groups of farmers work together to market and distribute their wine. Over 40% of all French wine comes from such small co-operatives.

A vineyard in Languedoc-Roussillon.

CASE STUDY F

Farmers and the EC Wine Lake

Resource C

Climate

Employment structure
- Primary
- Secondary
- Tertiary

Conditions favouring grape cultivation
- Average summer temperatures of 20°C
- Well-drained soil is more important than fertile soil
- Sloping land increases exposure to sun and aids drainage
- South and south-east facing slopes are warmest
- Light early summer rainfall helps to swell the grapes
- June to August needs to be very sunny to ripen grapes and increase their sugar content

Agricultural land use
- Vineyards
- Pasture land
- Arable land
- Fruit orchards

Area of vines

339,000 hectares of vines in Languedoc-Roussillon

1.01 million hectares under vines in France

Value of agricultural output, 1991 (millions of francs)

Product	Aude	Gard	Hérault	Lozère	Pyrénées-Orientales
Quality wine	438	473	241	0	760
Table wine	1,369	979	2,028	0	335
Fruit and vegetables	221	1,849	363	14	1,853
Cereals	346	164	77	1	2
Animal products	329	268	192	466	77
Other	130	215	97	16	101
	2,833	3,948	2,998	497	3,128

Resource D

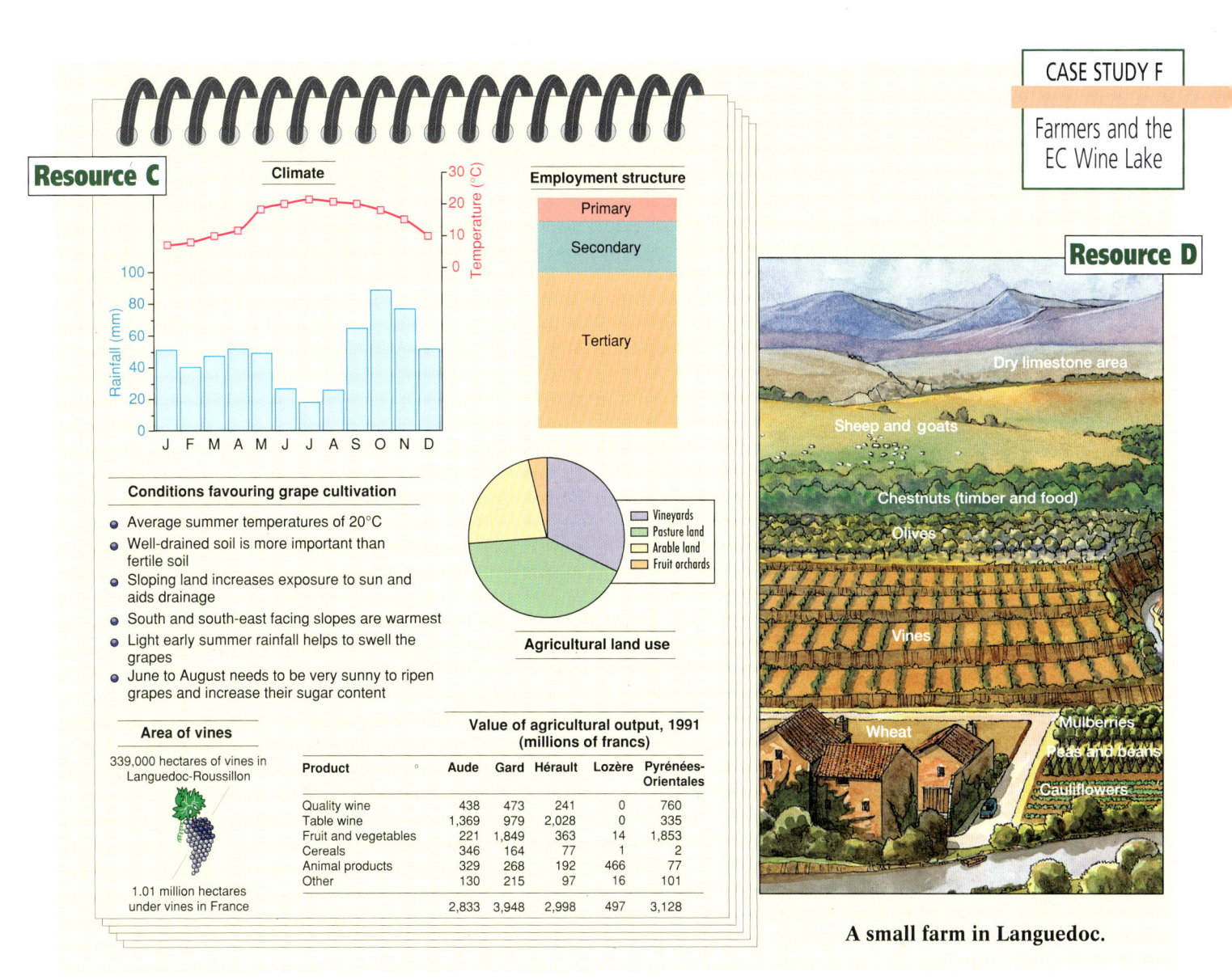

A small farm in Languedoc.

Labels: Dry limestone area; Sheep and goats; Chestnuts (timber and food); Olives; Vines; Wheat; Mulberries; Peas and beans; Cauliflowers

Activities

On examining the files you find the resources on these two pages. Study them carefully to familiarise yourself with the area. Now answer the questions below. Finally write a short report explaining why Languedoc-Roussillon has so much land (32% of the agricultural area) devoted to growing grapes for the wine-making industry.

1 In France about 7.5% of the population is involved in agriculture. How does this compare with the figure for Languedoc-Roussillon?

2 From Resource C find out:
a What is the *total rainfall* in the area?
b What is the *average summer temperature* (May–October)?
c What is the *temperature range*?

3a Describe the climate of this part of France.

b What aspect of climate might pose problems for farmers?

4 Look at the pictures of Languedoc farming in Resources B and D.
a What types of agricultural activity can you see?
b Which crop seems to cover the greatest area in Resource D?
c What sort of relief do vines prefer? Why?

5a Using the figures in Resource C, calculate the amount of money earned in 1987 by each product in Languedoc-Roussillon.
b What is the most important product of the region?
c What percentage of the total earned by agriculture came from this product?

Now write your report. You may wish to illustrate it.

CASE STUDY F
Farmers and the EC Wine Lake

Key Question 2
Why is there a surplus of wine in the European Community?

Resource E

Viticulture in Languedoc-Roussillon
Produced by: The Pennington Group – Agricultural Consultants

About half of France's wine-growers live in Languedoc-Roussillon. They produce two-thirds of all French wine from their 339,000 hectares of vines. As a result, this area is one of the largest wine-producing regions in the European Community, mainly producing low-quality 'table' wines.

In 1990 French wine production was just over 60 million hectolitres, while consumption was 40 million hectolitres. Much of this huge surplus of wine came from Languedoc-Roussillon. However, the over-production is not confined to France. In 1992, some 190 million hectolitres of table wine were produced in the European Community (EC), of which only 135 million hectolitres were actually drunk. Over several years large surpluses of table wine have accumulated forming the EC's so-called **wine lake**. At present the EC produces an average of some 20 million hectolitres of wine that is surplus to requirements each year.

To understand why the EC's wine lake has grown so big, five points need to be considered:

1 Although people in Britain today drink more wine than five years ago, in many other EC countries people now drink less wine than in the past. In France and Italy, wine consumption per person has dropped over the last 30 years.

2 Many vineyards have increased their productivity. Average annual production in the EC rose from 138 million hectolitres (1966–70) to over 180 million hectolitres (1986–90). Yields have also increased from 69 hectolitres per hectare in 1986 to 71.7 hl/ha in 1991.

3 Tastes have changed for various reasons. More people now drink the better-quality wines which are not often produced by the wine co-operatives of Languedoc-Roussillon.

4 Although wine consumption is rising in countries outside the EC, demand is not increasing as fast as it could do because of high taxes and duties.

5 Wine imports from non-EC countries like the United States, Australia, Chile, Bulgaria and Hungary have grown in recent years.

In the European Community wine consumption has slowly fallen in the last decade, while production has been gradually increasing. So unless action is taken, the wine lake will grow in size. Of course, wine is just one of the products in surplus in the EC. Grain, butter and beef have all been overproduced, partly because the European Community guarantees to pay farmers fixed prices for what they grow. Many problems are caused by these large surpluses, so the people responsible for organising and managing agriculture in the EC are trying to balance demand and production.

Countries with the highest wine consumption in the European Community (litres per head)

Country	1970s	1980s
France	104	80
Germany	20	26
Greece	–	32
Italy	95	71
Luxembourg	48	57
Portugal	–	70
Spain	–	49

Note: Where figures are not shown, this is because Greece, Portugal and Spain did not join the EC until the 1980s.

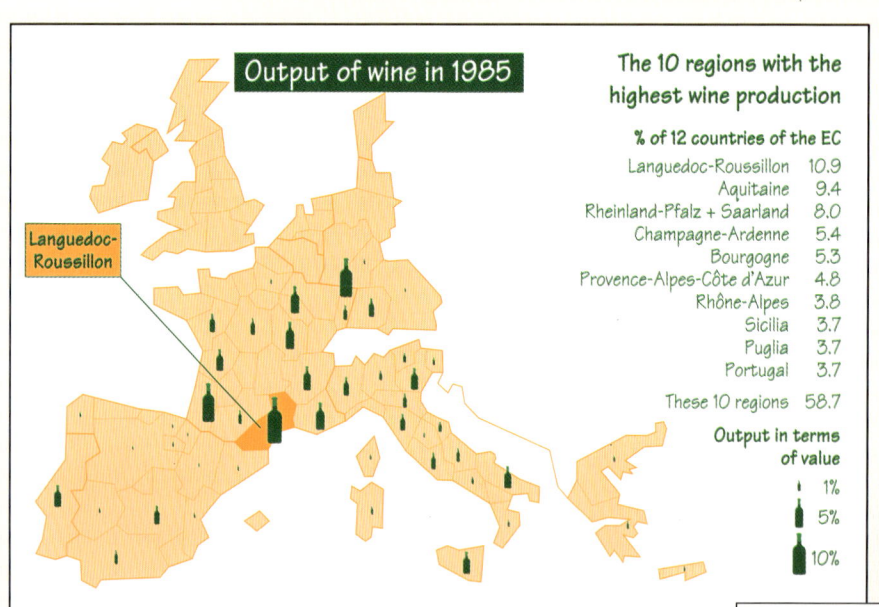

Output of wine in 1985

The 10 regions with the highest wine production

% of 12 countries of the EC

Region	%
Languedoc-Roussillon	10.9
Aquitaine	9.4
Rheinland-Pfalz + Saarland	8.0
Champagne-Ardenne	5.4
Bourgogne	5.3
Provence-Alpes-Côte d'Azur	4.8
Rhône-Alpes	3.8
Sicilia	3.7
Puglia	3.7
Portugal	3.7
These 10 regions	58.7

Output in terms of value: 1%, 5%, 10%

Resource F

Resource G

Changes in wine consumption, 1980–93.

1980
We drink wine quite a lot – it doesn't do you any harm, does it? Most weekends we have a bottle of wine with our Sunday lunch. We both have jobs, so can afford to drink wine when we like. We never spend more than £3 on a bottle. We eat out in the evening about once a week, and often drink wine then too.

1993
We are both very health-conscious, so we have cut down the amount of wine we drink – too much alcohol is bad for you, isn't it? We sometimes have wine on special occasions. We always buy the best wine we can afford. The wine shop has a good selection at about £5 a bottle. We both need our cars and so don't drink and drive.

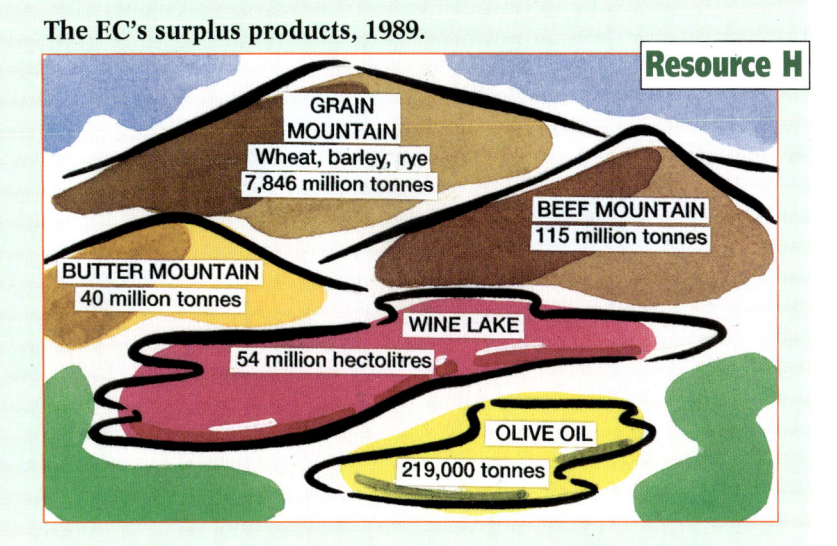

CASE STUDY F

Farmers and the EC Wine Lake

Resource H

The EC's surplus products, 1989.

- GRAIN MOUNTAIN — Wheat, barley, rye — 7,846 million tonnes
- BEEF MOUNTAIN — 115 million tonnes
- BUTTER MOUNTAIN — 40 million tonnes
- WINE LAKE — 54 million hectolitres
- OLIVE OIL — 219,000 tonnes

Activities

In a file labelled 'Wine-growing in the Community', you find a Consultants' Report. Study the report and the other resources on these two pages, then answer the questions below.

1 Using an atlas and Resource F, list five areas of Europe (apart from Languedoc-Roussillon) that are major wine-producers.

2 Examine the table in Resource E carefully.
a Name the EC's two leading wine-consuming countries.
b Describe what has happened to wine consumption in these two countries in recent years.

3a Write a paragraph to explain why there is a surplus of wine in the European Community.
b Can farmers be too successful for their own good? Talk about this question with a friend, then summarise your discussion.

4 Tom and Linda Bell (Resource G) were interviewed in 1980 and again in 1993. Read what they said, then explain why people are drinking less today than in the past.

5 What do you think can be done about the surpluses shown in Resource H? Should farmers be persuaded to grow less? How do you think this could be done?

Your answers to the questions above will form the basis of a presentation you will give to your Head of Department in Brussels. You must talk for 3–4 minutes, and attempt to answer the key question at the top of page 58. You should clearly identify the two most important causes of Europe's wine surplus.

You can work with up to two other people on your presentation, which must be delivered to your class/group. How successfully you answer the key question may determine the level of salary you receive in the next 12 months, so it is important to do a good job!

CASE STUDY F

Farmers and the EC Wine Lake

Key Question 3
What can be done to reduce wine production in Languedoc-Roussillon?

A reliance on growing vines has caused problems for Languedoc-Roussillon. These are being overcome as the French government and the European Community introduce changes. The resources here suggest what is happening, and may provide you with some ideas for helping to solve the problem of overproduction here and in other areas. Study the resources carefully.

Resource I

'In addition to creating a huge wine surplus in the European Community (EC), farmers in this region also caused a "wine war" with Italy in 1975. Unrest began when imports of cheap table Italian wine reached local shops. We were already having problems selling our own wine, so we tried to stop the imports.

The situation was very serious. Languedoc-Roussillon was clearly too **dependent** on wine production, so the EC set out to reduce the size of the area planted with vines. They banned us from planting new vines producing table wine, and gave grants to farmers who grubbed up their vines.

For many people here, wine production is a long family tradition. Elderly farmers were especially reluctant to dig up their vines and change their ways. Some, however, are planting better vines, which will result in higher-quality wines.'

Interview with Alain Gavanon, Secretary-General of the local 'Chambre de Commerce'

Resource J

NEW AVENUES FOR LANGUEDOC-ROUSSILLON

The French government has introduced several measures to **diversify** the economy of Languedoc-Roussillon and to reduce its dependence on wine production. These include:

1 Setting up the 'National Development Company for the Lower-Rhône & Languedoc' (BRL). Its aim was to provide sufficient irrigation water to increase the variety of fruit and vegetables grown. To date BRL has irrigated some 130,000 hectares through a network of pipelines and canals. Products now grown include melons, cherries, apricots, peaches and tomatoes.

2 Establishing agro-industries like fruit canning and frozen vegetable factories. These provide jobs in the processing of local produce.

3 Developing tourism on the coastal plain. In the last 20 years, 5 new resorts have been created along with marinas and golf courses. There are now over 1,000 hotels and 800 campsites. The number of tourists visiting the area has increased tenfold since 1965 to over 5 million per year.

4 Encouraging industrial development. Though it has little tradition of manufacturing, great efforts are being made to attract companies involved in electronics, computers and biotechnology. One major success was the move to Montpellier of the giant company IBM, bringing 3,500 jobs.

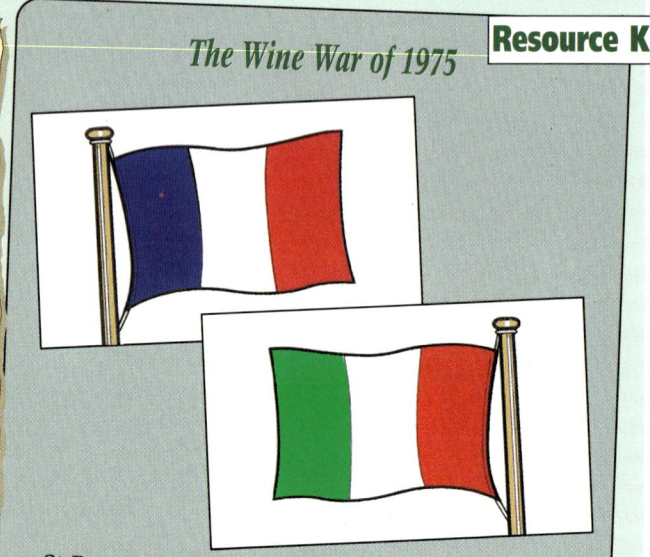

Resource K

The Wine War of 1975

- St Peter's Cathedral in Montpellier was occupied by protesting wine growers.
- Road signs were painted out to disrupt non-local traffic.
- The Béziers-Narbonne railway line was blown up.
- There were violent clashes between the wine growers and the CRS (French riot police).
- Finally the European Community intervened when the French government applied a 12% tax on imported wine – breaking EC rules.

CASE STUDY F

Farmers and the EC Wine Lake

Resource L

Irrigation works of CNABRL.

Tourist apartments at La Grande Motte.

IBM manufacturing plant, Montpellier.

Resource M

> I have farmed near Narbonne all my life. My grandfather planted these vines, and now they want me to dig them up. I have only 4 hectares here – not enough to grow anything else. If I grow fewer grapes our co-operative will go bust. At the moment I can just about make enough to live on – but at least I am happy.

> We got married last year, and are both training in hotel management. We want to work in a hotel at St Cyprien, near Perpignan, where we both grew up. Tourists are bringing a lot of money to our area and are helping to modernise facilities here.

Some local reactions to policies aimed at reducing the wine surplus.

Resource N

IT'S A MIRACLE – EC TO TURN WINE INTO PETROL
by Richard Caseby

The European Community has come up with a clever idea to empty its wine lake and help fight air pollution. It is converting 500 million bottles of wine into lead-free petrol.

The sale of wine converted into pure alcohol will rid the EC of an embarrassing hangover: what to do with a wine lake so large it can fill 5,290 Olympic-sized swimming pools.

The initiative will also be seen as environment-friendly because the alcohol, known as ethanol, can be used instead of lead to upgrade petrol.

However, the ludicrous economics of the move are bound to attract criticism.

Professor Andrew Porteous, an expert in fuel technology at the Open University, said: "Petrol from wine? It's such a waste. It's like a craftsman making a table and then chopping it up for firewood."

The new wine-fuel will be sold mainly in Germany, Belgium and Luxembourg, where petrol containing up to 5% alcohol is already on sale.

IT'S NOT ME OFFICER, IT'S THE CAR!

Source: *The Sunday Times*, 23 July 1989.
© Times Newspapers Ltd 1989

61

CASE STUDY F

Farmers and the EC Wine Lake

Activities

Write an account of how farmers in Languedoc-Roussillon can be encouraged to stop growing grapes. You should conclude your account by recommending one of the solutions you have read about (or think of one of your own). First, answer the questions below.

1 Some of the actions undertaken by the French wine-growers during the 'wine war' are shown in Resource K. Study this and read the interview with Alain Gavanon (Resource I).
a When was the 'wine war' and which two countries were involved?
b Why were the French wine growers so upset?
c What do you think of their actions? Do you agree with them, or not?

2a Why was it thought necessary to diversify the region's economy?
b In small groups, discuss how each of the photographs in Resource L shows that the region's economy no longer depends on wine production.

3 Was the European Community right to suggest that the wine producers should dig up their vines? If you think they were, then devise a poster to explain to the farmers why they must stop growing grapes. If you don't agree with EC policy, then write a letter explaining your views to the Director-General for Agriculture in Brussels.

4 Some people in Languedoc-Roussillon support the move away from agriculture, while others do not (Resource M). Do you support the move towards diversification or not? Explain your position.

5 Read the newspaper extract in Resource N, then describe what the European Community proposes to do with the wine surplus.

6 Study the document 'New avenues for Languedoc-Roussillon' (Resource J). Which one of the four suggested changes to the region's economy do you think:
a is the most likely to diversify the economy
b will probably be most resisted by local people?

Now write your account.

Further activities

Short-answer tasks

1 Try to sum up in a few sentences the type of farming found in Languedoc-Roussillon.

2 What is *irrigation*, and why is it necessary in the South of France?

3 Where is the 'wine lake' located? (Be careful!)

4 What are *agro-industries*?

Find out about . . .

1 Find a map in an atlas to show where grapes are grown. List six countries. What do you notice about the locations of grape-growing countries?

2 Write about one other area of **monoculture** somewhere in the world that you have studied. Name the crop and describe briefly how it is grown.

Library and research tasks

1 Write a paragraph about how grapes are grown. Try to include a description of what happens to the grapes when they are harvested.

2 In which parts of the UK are grapes grown and wine produced?

3 Visit your local supermarket to investigate where wine comes from.
a Look carefully at the labels on the wine bottles.
b List the countries that they come from.
c When you get home, colour all those countries on a map of the world.
d Compare your map with those of others in your class. Which supermarket stocks wine from the most countries?

Assessment activity

CASE STUDY F
Farmers and the EC Wine Lake

Wine production in Languedoc-Roussillon, 1991.

Département	Aude	Gard	Hérault	Lozère	Pyrénées Orientales	Total
Area under vines (hectares)	94,906	69,397	122,891	60	43,343	330,597
Production (million hectolitres)	6.4	4.1	8.0	0.1	1.8	_ _ _

1 Study the table above then answer these questions:
a Which département has the largest area under vines? *(1 mark)*
b Which département produced the most wine? *(1)*
c Calculate the total wine production. *(2)*
d Which département had the highest yield, Aude or Gard? *(2)*

2a Why do grapes grow successfully in Mediterranean areas like the Languedoc-Roussillon region of France? *(2)*
b Name two countries in the Mediterranean other than France where grapes are grown. *(2)*

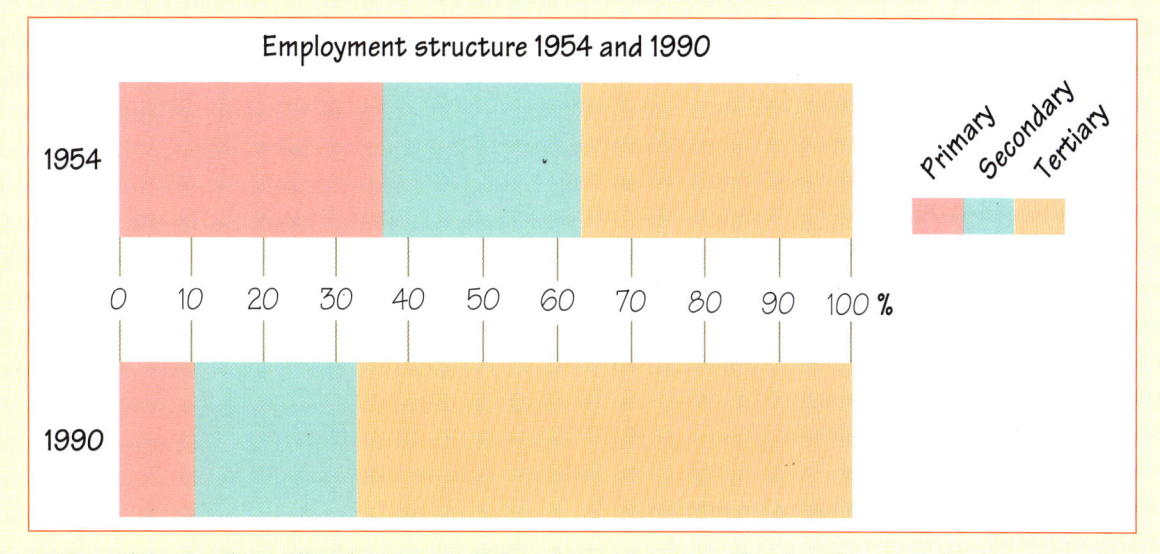

3 The diagram below shows Languedoc-Roussillon's employment structure.
a What percentage of the population worked in primary jobs in 1954 and 1990? *(2)*
b What happened to the region's employment between 1954 and 1990? *(3)*
c Explain the reasons for the change in primary sector employment. *(4)*

Employment structure 1954 and 1990

Primary, Secondary, Tertiary

4 Imagine you have lived on a small farm near Montpellier for 35 years. In that time you have grown grapes successfully and doubled your wine production. You are now getting old, and your daughter Annabelle, who is 25 years old, has left the area to work in a bank in Paris. One day, an EC official calls and suggests that you dig up your vines and plant citrus trees and salad crops in their place. The European Community will give you grants for this.

What is your reaction? Write a letter to Annabelle to let her know about the visitor and his suggestion. Tell her what you think about the offer made to you, and what (if anything) you intend to do. *(6)*

Total 25 marks

CASE STUDY F

Farmers and the EC Wine Lake

Key Terms

agro-industries industries associated with farming. They usually involve processing the products of agricultural activity, eg food canning, deep-freezing of vegetables, etc.

co-operatives formed when a few farmers group together to produce, market or distribute a product.

dependent when the economy of an area relies heavily on the production of one or a small number of products.

diversify to increase the number and variety of activities (and products) in an area, so that the area's dependence on one product is reduced.

irrigation the addition of water to the land by people using pipes, sprinklers and canals. Irrigation makes agriculture possible in areas where the shortage of rainfall would prevent farming, or cause yields to be too low.

monoculture the concentration of farming activity in an area on just one product.

surplus when more of a product is grown than can be sold at the normal market price, then the excess is called a surplus.

viticulture producing grapes from growing vines.

wine lake the surplus of wine resulting from more wine being produced than is consumed.

Key Understandings

- The climate and terrain of the Mediterranean coast of southern France have for many years suited the cultivation of grapes.

- For over a century the farmers in Languedoc-Roussillon have used grapes to produce huge quantities of table wine.

- A variety of factors, including increasing productivity, changing tastes and decreased wine consumption, has resulted in the production of much more table wine than people are drinking.

- Various attempts have been made by the European Community (EC) and by local officials to reduce wine production by encouraging farmers to grow other things, and developing alternative sources of income.

Case Study G

Cleaning-up the River Rhine

The Rhine is one of the longest rivers in Europe. It runs for over 1,300 kilometres from its source in Switzerland. At Basel the river is 200 metres wide. The Rhine flows on through France, Germany and the Netherlands. By the time it reaches the German/Dutch border at Lobith, the **discharge** is 2 million litres a second, and the river carries a lethal cocktail of pollutants. Since 1980 efforts have been made to clean-up the river, but there have been a number of accidental spills and other incidents which have worsened the situation.

You work as a trainee at the Institute of Environmental Pollution Studies in London. You are asked to attend a conference about managing pollution of the Rhine delta. The Institute has asked you to write an article about this subject for an environmental magazine. Begin your research by investigating why the River Rhine is so polluted, using the resources on the next two pages.

The Rhine's course through Europe.

CASE STUDY G
Cleaning-up the River Rhine

Key Question 1
Who is responsible for the pollution of the Rhine?

The Rhine: a cause for concern?

Resource A

The Rhine is Europe's most important river – more than 35,000 vessels regularly travel along it, or along a part of it, especially between the two main industrial centres, the Ruhr and Rijnmond. Apart from navigation, the river is used for fishing, tourism and recreation. Rhine water is used for domestic, industrial and agricultural purposes, and for generating energy. Last but not least, the Rhine is used as a drain or sewer.

As long as people have lived near the Rhine, they have thrown their refuse into the water. In the past the river was usually able to clean itself and break down pollutants. However, since the Industrial Revolution the volume of waste has risen greatly and the type of waste has changed. Today, industrial **effluents** mix with domestic waste, sewage, phosphates and heavy metals like lead and mercury. Not all of these pollutants are **biodegradable**, and some are highly **toxic**.

Since the 1970s the quality of Rhine water has improved: there is more public awareness of the pollution; politicians have taken action; and there is more legislation controlling the activities of industrialists. However, the River Rhine is not a healthy river yet.

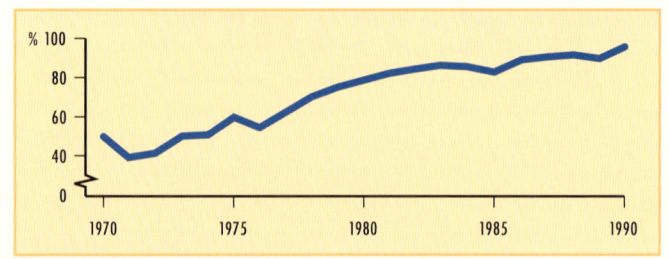

Source: International Rhine Commission.

Pollution of the River Rhine.

Who is responsible for all this pollution?

1. Many types of industry have established themselves along the banks of the river. The chemical industry disposes of waste containing heavy metals like cadmium, lead and mercury. The paper-making, brewing and the detergents industries also dump their waste into the river. Most of these emissions are properly authorised by the authorities. Some emissions, however, are not, and there is always the risk of accidental spills or leaks.

2. Households dispose of a variety of waste products: soap, detergents, leftovers and sewage. People also often throw things directly into the river, from pieces of paper to rusting bed frames and old bicycles.

3. Many agricultural practices lead to organic waste, chemical fertilisers and other waste products reaching the river. Fertilisers contain various chemicals from phosphates and nitrates to poisonous **hydrocarbons**.

Some indication of water quality can be gained by looking at the percentage of oxygen and the concentration of metals in the water.

Industry in the Rhine basin.

Resource B

- ✚ Paper industry
- ★ Chemical industry
- ■ Refinery
- ◆ Other industry
- ✕ Nuclear power station
- ▲ Conventional power station > 500MW

CASE STUDY G

Cleaning-up the River Rhine

Resource C

> Why did I choose to build my new aluminium plant near the Rhine? Well, first of all, the river provides a cheap form of transport. I also need a lot of water – 1,200 litres for every kilogram of aluminium produced. River water does nicely. And finally, I can easily get rid of all my waste materials. The discharge from the works is purified before we put it in the river. This is entirely legal – I have all the permits required.

Mr Joseph Schwartz, industrial manager.

Resource D

A source of pollution of the River Rhine.

Resource E

Some measures of changing water quality, 1970–90.

Measurements taken at:
- Lobith (dotted)
- Mannheim (solid)

*Readings for chlorine and nitrogen at Mannheim are not available.

Source: Central Bureau of Statistics, Algemene Milieustatistiek [General Earth Studies].

Activities

Check your understanding of the resources on these two pages by answering the following questions, then prepare a simple diagram with notes to explain who are the main polluters of the Rhine.

1a Why has the River Rhine proved to be such an attractive industrial location?
b Describe the main industrial areas along the Rhine in Germany. For each one, list its main towns and the industries there.

2a Which parts of the River Rhine do you think will be most polluted and which parts will be least polluted? Explain your answers.
b How might the industrial areas in Switzerland affect the quality of river water in other countries?
c Examine the levels of chrome pollution found in samples taken at Mannheim in central Germany, and downstream at Lobith. Explain the differences between them.

Chrome µg/litre*	1970	1975	1980	1985	1990
Lobith	109.0	35.0	20.0	7.6	6.5
Mannheim	16.0	21.0	10.0	5.5	4.9

* One-millionth of a gram per litre

3 Since the Industrial Revolution the amount and type of waste have changed. Give two reasons why the amount has changed. What kinds of materials are thrown away today that weren't thrown away a hundred years ago?

4a Samples of water from the River Rhine show that its quality is improving (Resource E). Calculate the percentage change in each sample from 1970 to 1990.
b What measures may have helped to reduce pollution by:
- industry
- farmers
- individuals and households?

5 Make a list of the River Rhine's main pollutants (see Resource A). Name the group most responsible for releasing each one. Underline the main producer of each pollutant. For example:

Copper	individuals, farmers, <u>industry</u>
Paper	
Nitrates	

CASE STUDY G

Cleaning-up the River Rhine

Key Question 2
What are the consequences of Rhine pollution for the Netherlands?

At the Conference, a special workshop is devoted to the Dutch situation. Being at the mouth of the river, the Netherlands has had to deal with pollution problems that were caused hundreds of kilometres upstream. Two specific problems are dealt with by guest speakers.

Resource F

Hank de Boer, Port Admiral of Rotterdam Harbour

As you know, the port at Rotterdam is vital for the Dutch economy. We are constantly dredging the harbour so that large ships can berth here. Why do we have to do this? Well, like every large river, the Rhine transports a lot of **silt**. This settles near the river banks, and here in the harbour. Each year we dig out 23 million cubic metres of silt.

The problem now is that the river is polluted by metals like lead and cadmium. These attach themselves to silt particles, so we cannot dump the polluted silt in the North Sea. We have built a special depot to accommodate it. This, however, is not a real solution. We have found out, through water sampling, which factories are causing the pollution – 95% of it is caused by Swiss, French and German heavy industrial plants. These plants have been asked to stop releasing metals. If they don't, we will send them a bill to share the costs of building these special polluted-silt depots.

Rita de Hoop, Director of the Drinking Water Purification Plant, Neiuwegein

The pollution of the Rhine causes many problems. If we didn't purify the water, for example, heavy metal contamination could seriously affect public health. Phosphates, which are in high concentration, pose a different problem. They stimulate the growth of **algae**, and algae clog our pipelines and filters. We have a similar problem with silt.

There is also a lot of salt in the water. This not only gives the water a nasty taste, but it also helps to corrode the pipelines. Saline discharges from mines in Germany make water in the Rhine unsuitable for market gardening in the Netherlands.

Almost every year we have to close down for a few days, and stop taking in water supplies from the river. This is usually because of some kind of serious pollution incident upstream. In 1987, for instance, after the Sandoz incident, we had to close for four days. Luckily we have large reserves of purified water, so our customers are not inconvenienced too much.

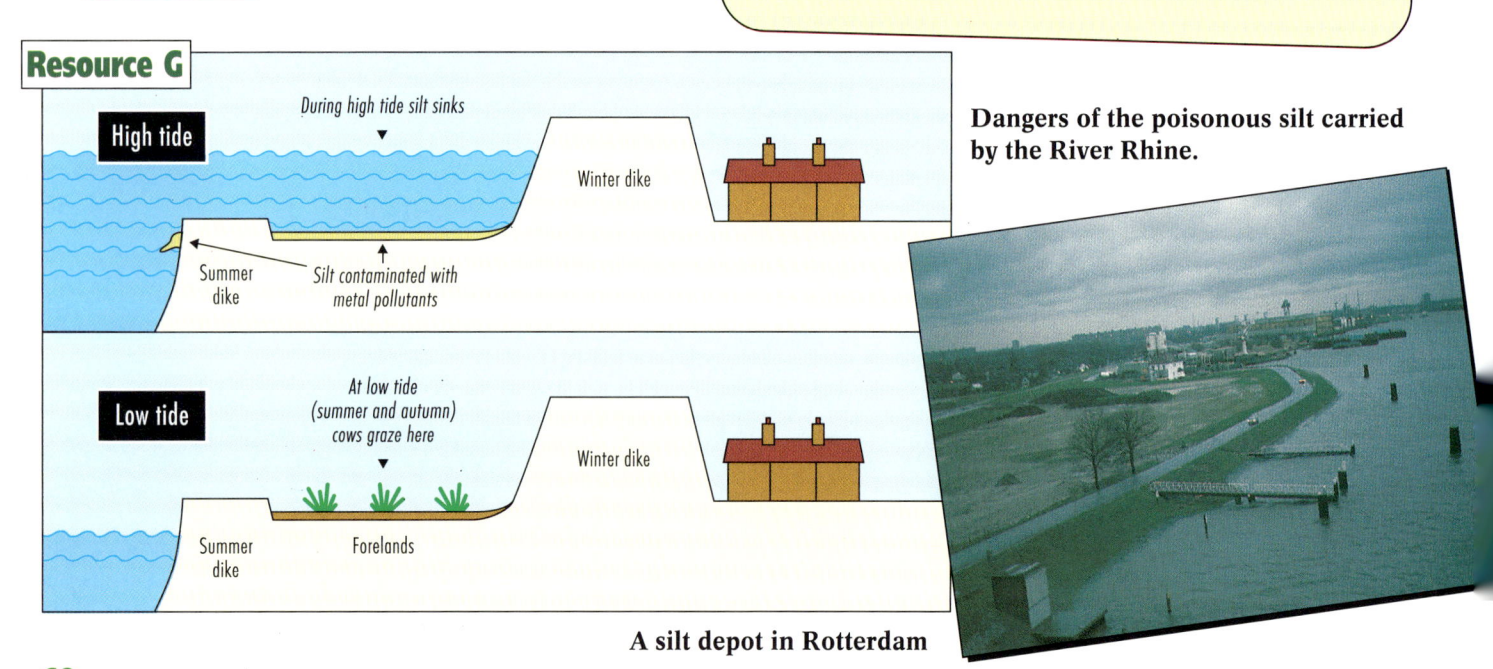

Resource G

Dangers of the poisonous silt carried by the River Rhine.

High tide — During high tide silt sinks — Winter dike — Summer dike — Silt contaminated with metal pollutants

Low tide — At low tide (summer and autumn) cows graze here — Winter dike — Summer dike — Forelands

A silt depot in Rotterdam

Resource H

The drainage basin of the River Rhine.

POLLUTANTS ENTERING THE NETHERLANDS, 1985	
Chloride	1,117,600 tonnes
Phosphate	3,560 tonnes
Copper	460 tonnes
Cadmium	10 tonnes

RHINE BASIN
Population: over 50 million
Area: 225,000 km²

Map shows: Rotterdam, Duisburg, Cologne, Bonn, Frankfurt, Mannheim, Ludwigshafen, Karlsruhe, Strasbourg, Basel, Lake Constance. Legend: River Rhine drainage basin; Urbanised industrial areas.

Resource I

The graphs on this map show the concentration of HCB (hexachlorobenzene) and PCBs (polychlorinated biphenyls) in eels caught in the Netherlands. These graphs can be compared with the allowed limit in Germany (500μg/kg). In almost every case the maximum is exceeded.

μg/kg lipid weight — scale 0 to 1500. Maximum allowed shown.

Resource J

◀ A drinking water purification plant on the Rhine near Rotterdam.

Year	Demand
1960	505
1970	870
1980	1,011
1988	1,161

The growth in demand for drinking water in the Netherlands (million m³).

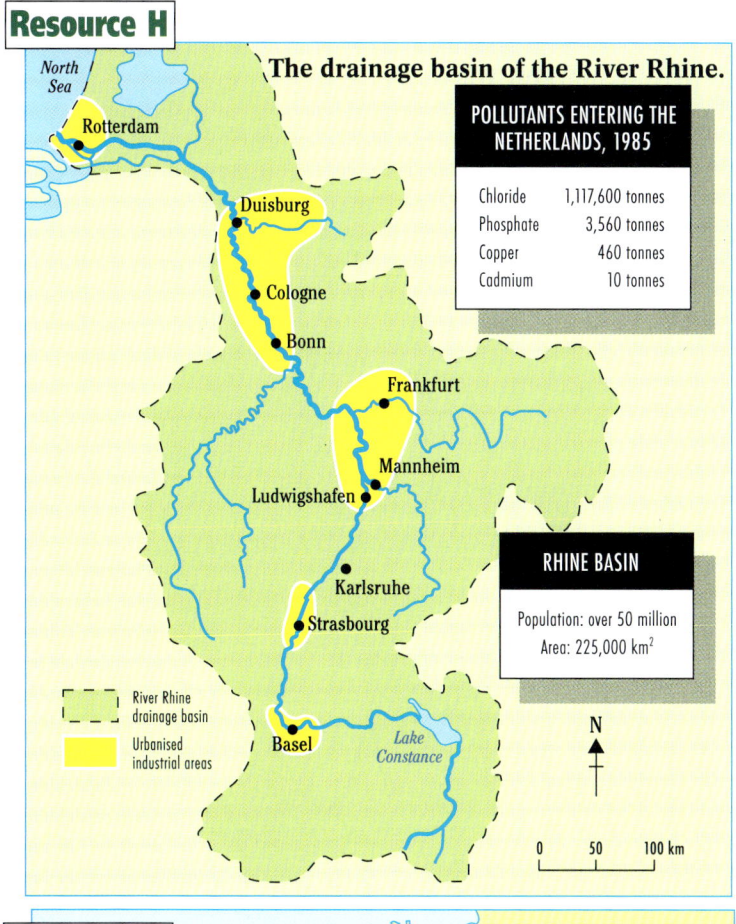

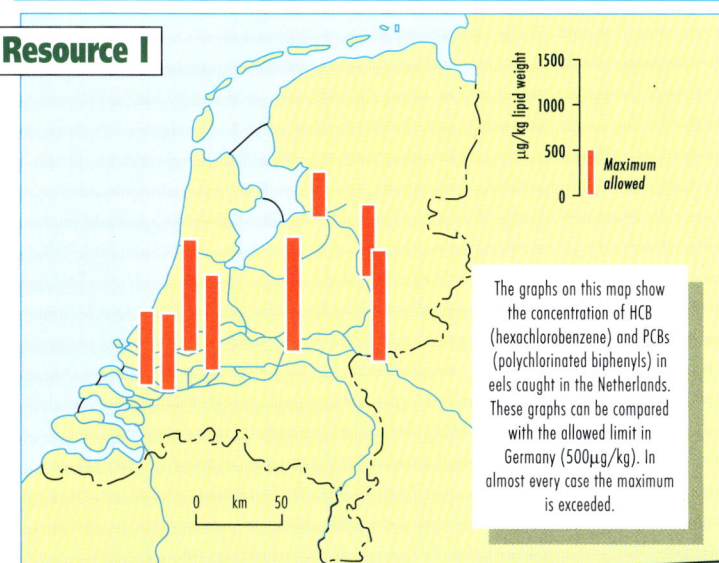

CASE STUDY G
Cleaning-up the River Rhine

Activities

After attending the Conference you decide to write a letter to the *Nederlands Observer*, a Dutch national newspaper, summarising what you have learned about the situation faced by the Dutch people, and offering them the support of your own employers, the Institute of Environmental Pollution Studies. Before you do this, answer the questions below.

1 List five functions of the River Rhine. What is likely to be the consequence of pollution for each of these functions?

2 Silt sinks near the banks of the Rhine and in Rotterdam harbour. In the Netherlands, the river banks are used to grow grass. During the summer, cows graze here (Resource G). What will be the consequences of the poisonous silt for agriculture?

3 A Dutch environmental group hands you some evidence which shows pollution levels in eels caught along the Rhine (Resource I). What do you learn from this map? Is the group right to be concerned?

4a At the Conference you meet the Mayor of Rotterdam. In a few lines, try to summarise the problem he faces.
b List some questions you could ask him so that you are better informed about the situation faced by city residents and other people living along the Rhine.

5 Study Resource J.
a Copy and complete the following.
In 1960 _____ million m³ of drinking water was used in the Netherlands. By 1988, this had grown to _____ million m³. This represents a growth of _____ %. Activities for which we use a lot of drinking water are _____ and _____.
b What kind of pollution do you think is the worst for the purification plant?

Now write your letter to the *Nederlands Observer*.

CASE STUDY G
Cleaning-up the River Rhine

Key Question 3
What can be done to stop or reduce pollution?

Everyone at the Conference recognises the River Rhine's pollution problem, and the environmental groups are sure of the solutions to that problem. However, politicians have to take different interests into account.

Resource K

ACTION ON SALT

Facts
- Every year almost 40 million tonnes of salt drain into the Rhine.
- 40% comes from French potassium mines, and 40% from the Alsace sodaworks.
- The high concentration of salt poses problems for the water purification stations, for some industries also using water, and for horticulture. Dutch market gardeners have to desalinate water before using it to water their crops. This is expensive.

Action
Two main actions have been taken to reduce the high salt concentrations in the Rhine:

1. International
In the 1960s, negotiations were started between the countries through which the Rhine passes. This resulted in a Convention in 1976 which stated that French potassium mines should halve their salt output by 1990. All signatories would contribute to the costs.

2. Local
Three Dutch farmers started a legal action against the French potassium mines. They wanted compensation for the damage caused to their produce by salty water. The farmers' case was backed by 'Stichting Reinwater' (The Rhinewater Foundation).

Solution
In trying to find ways of storing salt produced by the potassium mines, the French faced opposition from local environmental groups and trade unions, as well as technical and financial problems. They finally decided to store salt near the mines and to reduce the potassium output of the mines. While this was going on, the Dutch farmers won their court case. Between 1986 and 1987 salt output was reduced by 6% – a small beginning!

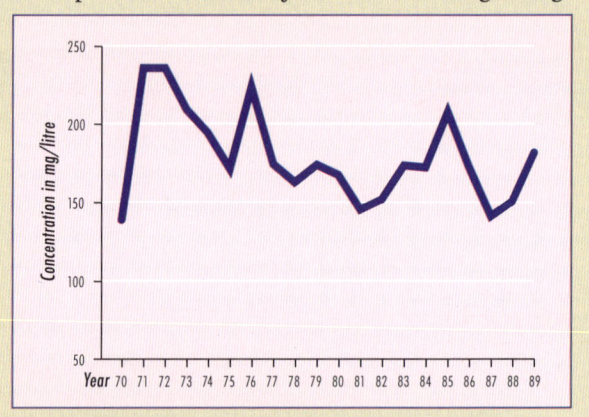

Salt (chloride) concentrations in the River Rhine in the Netherlands.

Resource L

RHINE ACTION PROGRAMME

International co-operation over the River Rhine goes back to 1887 with a treaty prohibiting the discharge of wastes dangerous to fish. By 1946, the situation had deteriorated further and the International Commission for the Protection of the Rhine Against Pollution (ICPR) was formed.

More recently still, following a serious incident in 1986, the *Rhine Action Programme* (RAP) was developed, and adopted by all the countries bordering the Rhine. By the year 2000, the programme aims to achieve a return to the river of species like the salmon which once thrived there. They also want to safeguard the use of the river for extracting drinking water.

The specific aims of the *Rhine Action Programme*, approved by a Conference of Ministers on the Protection of the Rhine against Pollution, in Strasbourg in 1987, are:
- to accelerate the reduction of permanent pollution from all sources
- to reduce the risk of accidents and spillages
- to improve hydrological and other conditions in the river.

CASE STUDY G

Cleaning-up the River Rhine

Resource M

ACTION AGAINST RIVER POLLUTION

What is done at a national level . . .
- National laws are made stating how much waste material can be discharged.
- Industrial plants are obliged to have a permit for their emissions.
- Pollution taxes are imposed on individuals and industrial plants.
- Purification and measuring stations are built.

. . . and at an international level?
- There is more co-operation between the countries that share the Rhine.
- There is an alarm system for every time the concentration of a certain material exceeds its permitted value.
- Plans are made for the conservation and restoration of natural landscapes.

INTERNATIONAL COMMISSION FOR THE PROTECTION OF THE RHINE AGAINST POLLUTION

Ecological Master Plan for the Rhine

"Salmon 2000"

Activities

1a Why was it considered necessary to reduce salt concentrations in the River Rhine?
b Representatives of several countries were involved in the agreement to reduce salt emissions. Which countries do you think were involved, and why?
c Did the agreement on salt reduction reached in 1986 have any lasting effect?

2 Action on river pollution can be taken at national and international levels (Resource M).
a If pollution taxes are introduced, how best could these taxes be spent?
b How can a system that allows factories to release specified quantities of pollutants into rivers be policed?
c Why is it necessary, when considering action on cleaning-up rivers such as the Rhine, to involve representatives from several countries?

3 The *Rhine Action Programme* aims to restore the Rhine to a condition suitable for habitation by salmon and other species, by the year 2000. Outline some of the measures which may be adopted as part of the river cleansing strategy.

4 Many factors play a role in the struggle against the pollution of the Rhine delta. There are lots of interest groups – politicians, industrial managers, farmers, environmental groups, ecologists, etc. List these groups, and for each one, try to decide:
a why they are concerned about river pollution
b to what degree they are committed to doing something to resolve the pollution problem
c what other interests they have which might influence their views.

You have now attended the Conference, and have to write a short article entitled 'Improving Water Quality in the River Rhine' for an environmental magazine. Use what you have learned from this case study for your articles. You should include illustrations, tables and statistics where appropriate. You have a maximum word limit of 400 words.

CASE STUDY G

Cleaning-up the River Rhine

Further activities

Short-answer tasks

1 Who is responsible for polluting the River Rhine?

2 The Netherlands is very active in searching for international solutions for the pollution problem. Why is this?

3 What can you as an individual do about pollution?

4 Why do industrial managers choose to locate near to the Rhine? What is their main aim? What role is 'protecting the environment' likely to play in their overall policy?

Find out about . . .

The chemical industry appears to be one of the Rhine's biggest polluters. However, we cannot do without this industry. Make a list of chemical products we use at school and at home. Add to your list some of the chemical products used in medical care and in the production of foodstuffs.

Library and research tasks

1 The Rhine is not only known for its pollution. It also is the focus of a thriving tourist industry. Look in a few travel brochures to see what the river and the area around it have to offer.

a How might tourists travel in the area, and what is there for them to see?

b If a large number of tourists visited the area, what consequences might there be for the river and its immediate environment? Make two lists: (i) positive (ii) negative.

2 This case study has only looked at the River Rhine. Try to make some comparisons with another large river. Be sure to choose a large and important river, like the Thames, the Tyne or the Clyde. Find out about its length, importance, different functions, industry, pollution levels and controls, etc. Write a short report on these matters. Include a sketch map to show the river's course, and any important factors affecting it.

Key Terms

algae very small water plants containing chlorophyll.

biodegradable description for material which readily decomposes, usually into organic components.

discharge the amount of water flowing in a river in a given time.

effluents materials that are released into rivers directly or indirectly by farmers or factories.

hydrocarbons chemical compounds derived from oil or coal.

silt the fine muds carried downstream by rivers.

toxic poisonous.

Key Understandings

- A variety of agents may be responsible for polluting rivers, including individuals, farmers, industries, energy generators, etc.

- Pollution may be due to deliberate actions or be the result of an accident.

- The effects of river pollution are often felt along the entire course of the river, but may be concentrated downstream.

- Pollutants are quite likely to change the water's chemical composition, and so may affect aquatic life. If fish are affected and are eaten by humans, then the impact of pollution can pass up the food chain.

- In order to control river pollution, particularly in a large catchment, international action is needed along with measures taken on a national scale.

Case Study H

The French Energy Dilemma

France is a major industrial nation. It needs energy on a large scale for its factories, farms and homes. Like other Western countries, France faces important choices in how to meet its energy needs.

You are an adviser to the French government on energy issues over the period between 1974 and 1989, a time when France urgently needed to develop a clear energy policy. You must keep the President and government ministers informed about all the issues involved in developing such a policy.

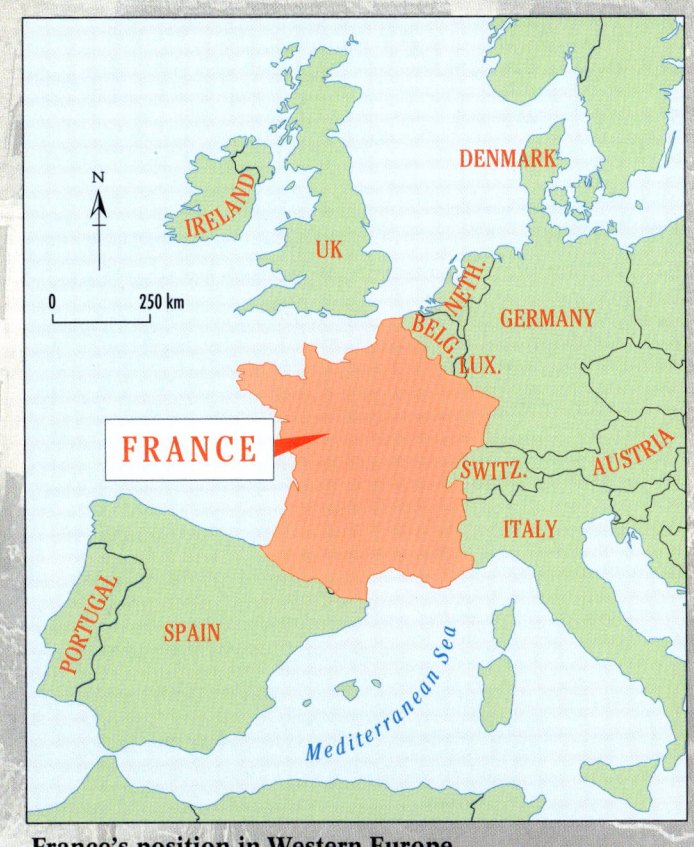

France's position in Western Europe.

CASE STUDY H

The French Energy Dilemma

Key Question 1
Why did France opt for large-scale nuclear energy?

Dateline ..... 1974 .....

France is facing an energy crisis. Major problems have arisen because conflict in the Middle East has cut off the oil supplies on which the country heavily depends. Some urgent decisions now need to be made about how France's future energy requirements will be met.

The country has elected a new President, the conservative Giscard d'Estaing. He appoints you as his adviser with special responsibility for energy issues. You are immediately asked to advise on the best course of action to prevent future energy crises. You must quickly find out about the current situation so that you can give advice to the President. Luckily you discover a report and some other documents in the file of your predecessor, which sum up France's energy situation.

Resource A

12th November 1974

Energy in France

France needs power for industry, fuel for transport, and heat, light and power for the home. This energy can come from five sources: coal, oil, natural gas, hydro-electric power and nuclear reactors. All of them can be used to make electricity, but only oil can be used to fuel road and air transport. Unlike Britain, France has no oil of its own. It depends on oil supplies from North Africa and the Middle East, which are threatened by political instability. Oil, therefore, is scarce and expensive. Future supplies cannot be guaranteed.

The French coal industry is in decline. Mines are closing and output is falling. Like oil, coal is a **non-renewable** resource. It is possible to import it cheaply from overseas but this is bad for the **balance of payments** and still leaves France vulnerable to future shortages.

France has no share in the large natural gas fields of the North Sea. It has one small inland field at Lacq in the south-west, but this will be exhausted by 1985. In future gas may be imported from Algeria.

Hydro-electric power is a **renewable** resource. Water is used to drive turbines and generate electricity. It is an important source of energy in France, but virtually all suitable sites have now been exploited.

France has large domestic resources of uranium which is used to generate nuclear electricity. Considerable expertise and experience has already been built up in nuclear power generation. Though the industry is small at the moment, plans to expand it have already been approved.

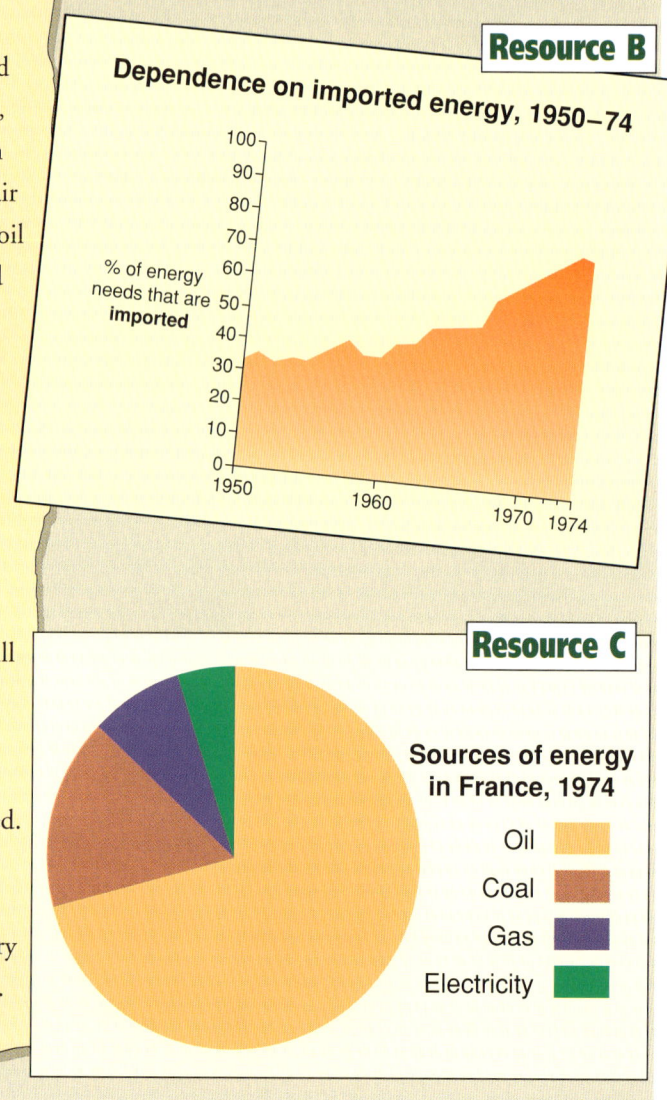

Resource B

Dependence on imported energy, 1950–74

% of energy needs that are imported

Resource C

Sources of energy in France, 1974

- Oil
- Coal
- Gas
- Electricity

> Because of the oil crisis we've decided to switch to electric central heating. We're also going to double-glaze the windows and insulate the walls and loft. Maybe our energy bills won't be so high. We might even buy a smaller car.

CASE STUDY H

The French Energy Dilemma

Resource D

(a) The French coal industry in decline.

(b) HEP site in the Gorges de la Dordogne, Corrèze.

(c) Natural gas plant at Lacq.

(d) Pressurised water reactor at St Laurent-des-Eaux on the River Loire.

Resource E

Activities

The new President also has a copy of the report that you have found. After reading it, he sends you a list of questions. These are set out below. Using the resources on these two pages to help you, write a short report, making sure that it answers each of the questions below, and that it responds to Key Question 1 on page 74.

1a What are our major energy sources at the moment (1974)?
b What proportion of France's energy needs must we import now (1974)?

2a Which energy sources are imported now, or could be imported in the future?
b Suggest one *advantage* and one *disadvantage* of importing energy from overseas.

c As the President's Energy Adviser, on balance do you think it is wise for France to continue relying on such a high proportion of imported energy?

3 Which sources are *renewable* and which are *non-renewable*?

4a How can France reduce its dependence on imported energy sources?
b How can France become more independent in the production of electricity?

5 In what ways is it possible to cut down on our use of energy:
a as individuals and
b as a nation?

75

CASE STUDY H

The French Energy Dilemma

Key Question 2
How did the French achieve their nuclear ambitions?

Dateline ..... 1981 .....

France again has a new President, the socialist Francois Mitterand. The President asks you for a brief history of the nuclear programme up to 1981, and a forecast of developments up to 1990. He wants to know how far France has progressed to independence in electricity generation. Your draft report is on these pages. Before presenting it to the President you must re-read and check it.

Resource F

REPORT ON THE HISTORY OF NUCLEAR ENERGY IN FRANCE, AND ITS PROSPECTS FOR THE FUTURE

1 History to 1981

The commercial nuclear programme began on a small scale in the late 1960s with French-designed gas-cooled reactors. Plans for expansion were laid in 1970 when a series of **pressurised water reactors** (PWRs) were ordered from the USA. At present (1981) 21 of these have been built and 11 more are planned or are under construction. They provide 39% of all French electricity. In addition, France has extended its control over other areas of the nuclear fuel cycle. This begins with the mining of uranium ore. About 25% of this comes from the former colonies of Niger and Gabon in West Africa. This proportion will increase to 60% by 1990 to allow domestic supplies to be conserved. The concentrated ore is **enriched** at a large plant at Tricastin: this produces the high-quality fuel needed by PWRs. The enriched uranium is made into fuel rods at four different **fabrication** sites, before it is placed inside the reactors. From time to time the burned-out fuel rods are removed from the reactors and reprocessed at Cap de la Hague to retrieve unburned fuel and to separate and store radioactive waste.

2 Prospects to 1990

During the 1980s France intends to switch from American reactors to PWRs that are designed and built in France. Twenty of these 1300 megawatt reactors are planned. A **fast-breeder reactor** will be built at Creys-Malville and this new technology should prove more efficient than any existing PWR. **Reprocessing** facilities at Cap de la Hague will be extended and these developments should give France virtual independence in electricity supply. We anticipate that 70% of all electricity will come from nuclear reactors by 1990.

J Laval
Adviser to the President
2nd December 1981

Resource G

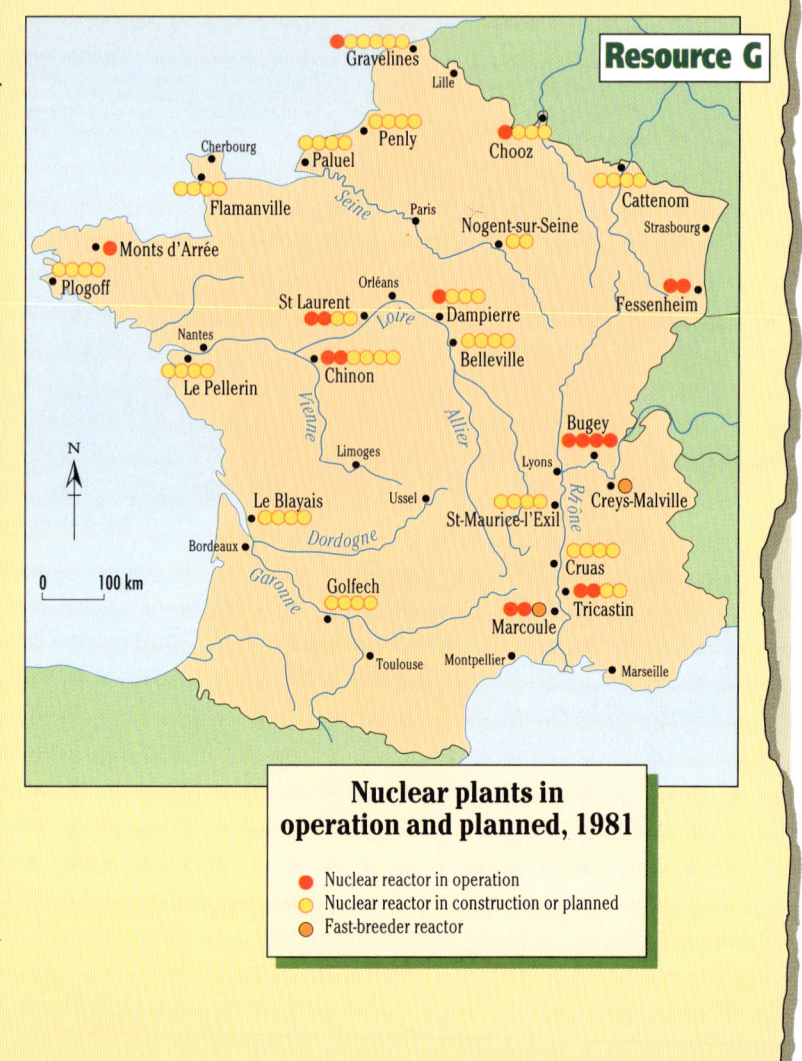

Nuclear plants in operation and planned, 1981

- ● Nuclear reactor in operation
- ● Nuclear reactor in construction or planned
- ● Fast-breeder reactor

Resource H

Location of fuel cycle operations
- ⊙ Uranium mining and milling
- ⊗ Uranium refining
- ○ Uranium enrichment
- ■ Fuel fabrication
- ⛴ Power station fabrication
- ⊙ Reprocessing and vitrification

CASE STUDY H
The French Energy Dilemma

Resource I

(a) Uranium mine.

(b) Uranium enrichment plant at Tricastin.

(c) Uranium oxide fuel pellet.

(d) Gravelines on the Channel coast – six 900 mW reactors.

(e) Reprocessing plant at Cap de la Hague in Normandy.

CASE STUDY H
The French Energy Dilemma

Resource J

910 MW Series

Site	Opening date	Capacity (MW)
Fessenheim 1	1977	880
Fessenheim 2	1977	880
Bugey 2	1978	920
Bugey 3	1978	920
Bugey 4	1979	900
Bugey 5	1979	900
Tricastin 1	1980	915
Tricastin 2	1980	915
Tricastin 3	1981	915
Tricastin 4	1981	915
Gravelines 1	1980	910
Gravelines 2	1980	910
Gravelines 3	1980	910
Gravelines 4	1981	910
Gravelines 5	1984	910
Gravelines 6	1985	910
Dampierre 1	1980	890
Dampierre 2	1980	890
Dampierre 3	1981	890
Dampierre 4	1981	890
Le Blayais 1	1981	910
Le Blayais 2	1982	910
Le Blayais 3	1983	910
Le Blayais 4	1983	910
St Laurent 1	1981	880
St Laurent 2	1981	880
Chinon 1	1982	870
Chinon 2	1983	870
Chinon 3	1986	870
Chinon 4	1987	870
Cruas 1	1983	880
Cruas 2	1984	880
Cruas 3	1984	880
Cruas 4	1984	880

1300 MW Series

Site	Opening date	Capacity (MW)
Fessenheim 1	1977	880
Fessenheim 2	1977	880
Paluel 1	1984	1,290
Paluel 2	1984	1,290
Paluel 3	1985	1,290
Paluel 4	1986	1,290
St Alban 1	1985	1,300
St Alban 2	1986	1,300
Flamanville 1	1985	1,290
Flamanville 2	1986	1,290
Cattenom 1	1986	1,265
Cattenom 2	1987	1,265
Cattenom 3	1989	1,265
Cattenom 4	1991	1,265
Belleville 1	1987	1,275
Belleville 2	1988	1,275
Nogent 1	1987	1,275
Nogent 2	1988	1,275
Golfech 1	1990	1,275
Golfech 2	1993	1,275
Penly 1	1989	1,290
Penly 2	1991	1,290

PWRs built or planned, 1970–93.

Source: Adapted from *The French Nuclear Electricity Programme*, EDF, 1988.

Activities

The President asks for some simple statistics to back up your written report. He also asks you to illustrate the **nuclear fuel cycle**, and he wants your opinion on the nation's progress towards electricity independence. His questions are below. Prepare an illustrated report to answer these questions, and to respond to Key Question 2 on page 76.

1a What was the increase in nuclear capacity (in megawatts) between 1970 and 1981? Use the data in Resource J to help you.
b Look again at Resource G and describe briefly the locations of nuclear plants in France. How good a national coverage has been achieved?

2 By how much will France's nuclear capacity increase between 1981 and 1990?

3 Draw a flow diagram to represent the nuclear fuel cycle. Before you try this, re-read your report and examine the photographs in Resource I.

4a What percentage of total nuclear capacity will be provided by French-designed reactors in 1990?
b Which countries does France mainly rely on to provide uranium?

5 What is your opinion of the progress France has made towards establishing independence in electricity production?

Key Question 3
Has the nuclear programme created any problems?

CASE STUDY H
The French Energy Dilemma

Dateline ..... 1989 .....

President Mitterand has just learned that the British are to abandon plans to expand their nuclear industry. This seems to be because of the high costs involved. The President needs more information before a meeting of French cabinet ministers at which the energy situation will be discussed. You find a recent report on the subject, and pass it to him.

Resource K

Problems ahead for the French nuclear industry?

In many ways the expansion of the nuclear industry in France has been a great success. Building and output targets have been met and a surplus of electricity can be produced which can be exported. In relative terms, coal and oil imports have fallen, and 70% of electricity now comes from nuclear reactors. However, there are a number of problems.

1 Nuclear electricity is costly. Official figures suggest that it costs 19 centimes per kilowatt hour, compared with 34 centimes to produce the same amount of electricity from coal. Unofficial figures, though, estimate the real cost of nuclear electricity as high as 46 centimes per kilowatt hour.

2 The British have abandoned further expansion partly because of the costs of dismantling reactors when they reach the end of their productive life. Sooner or later these costs will fall on the much larger French industry as well. At present, nobody really knows how great they will be.

3 Electricity demand has not grown as rapidly as predicted. The industry now suffers from **overcapacity**. Even allowing for exports, some reactors do not work at full power or efficiency. This increases costs further.

4 With the exception of a planned nuclear complex at Plogoff in Brittany, public opposition has failed to force the cancellation of any part of the nuclear programme. As the number of reactors increases, however, the risk of accidents grows. A major accident could seriously damage public confidence in the industry.

5 Although the fast-breeder reactor was completed at Creys-Malville in 1986, it has never worked well, and there are no plans to further develop the fast-breeder technology.

6 Most reactors are sited along rivers, and use river water for cooling. In drought years, like 1989, falling river levels mean that electricity output must be cut back in order to prevent over-heating in the rivers and the consequent death of aquatic plants, fish and other organisms.

Resource L

RADIATION FEAR IN NUCLEAR BLAZE

France urged to show care over Channel nuclear waste

Fault found in French nuclear plants

Nuclear plant stays open despite leak

Problems in the nuclear industry.

CASE STUDY H

The French Energy Dilemma

Resource M

Drought threatens import of French nuclear power

Paul Brown
Environment Correspondent

Supplies of nuclear generated electricity imported from France via the Channel cable may be cut off because of a serious drought and technical problems, according to internal papers of Electricité de France.

Half the 53 French nuclear stations are out of action or running well below capacity because reduced river levels and warmer water have made cooling the stations less effective.

Emergency supplies of coal and oil are being imported to re-open mothballed fossil fuel generating stations to try to make up for the shortfall.

Mr R. Jacob, head of the French national grid, says that if November is a cold month, supplies to Britain will have to be cut off to prevent power cuts in France. If the temperature drops well below normal, France will have to appeal to Britain to sell them electricity.

The difficulties are an embarrassment to the nuclear lobby on both sides of the Channel. Lobbyists hold up the French industry as a shining example for Britain to follow. Under privatisation proposals, Britain had considered doubling the 2,000 megawatt capacity of the cable but the latest difficulties make this seem less attractive.

In theory, France has a large overcapacity for generating electricity, with less than 60 per cent of power plant in use at one time. More than half the power stations are nuclear, providing more than 70 per cent of the country's electricity.

The French papers show that the drought has seriously reduced the flow of some French rivers and warmed the water. This means a number of French nuclear stations cannot run at full power. If the drought continues, at least six will have to shut by January, a time of peak demand.

Hydro-electric schemes are also in difficulty with the water level only 30 to 40 per cent of normal.

A strike last year held up maintenance of some stations which are still closed. In some older stations, safety problems have meant closure. Technical difficulties in a third group of stations mean they are out of action.

In the summer, oil and coal stations – normally used only at peak periods – were started up to make up for the shortfall but they have run through large stocks of fuel normally kept for emergencies.

The report says supplies of coal and oil are well below that required. Supplies are being imported but in the worst case scenario, France will suffer power cuts unless power can be imported.

A spokesman for the National Grid said they were aware of the French difficulties. France was continuing to supply the 1,500 megawatts and there has been no suggestion that it was going to be cut off, although there was provision for this in the contract.

Source: © *The Guardian*, 30 November 1989.

Resource N

Plogoff says no to nuclear power

For five years, citizens of Plogoff in Brittany have waged a bitter fight against the proposed installation of a nuclear power station, now cancelled by the new socialist government.

Activities

After reading the item (Resource K), the President sends you the following list of questions. He needs the answers for his high-level meeting with French cabinet ministers the next day. Answer these questions, then respond to Key Question 3.

1 In your opinion, has the high cost of the nuclear programme been justified by the degree of independence it provides for France?

2a Do you think that the policy of locating nuclear electricity production close to markets has been successful?
b Draw a map to show which areas of France are more than 75 kilometres from a nuclear reactor.

3a Are the French public aware of any problems caused by using nuclear means to generate electricity? The newspaper headlines (Resource L) may provide some clues.
b Are there any other problems associated with the French nuclear programme?

4 What percentage of nuclear capacity is likely to be affected by drought (Resource M)?

5 Leaving aside your neutral position as the President's adviser on energy, if you were an anti-nuclear campaigner, what arguments would you present against government policy?

Further activities

Short-answer tasks

1 What do you understand by the terms *overcapacity* and *nuclear fuel cycle*?

2 Use the pie-chart (right) to rank the major sources of energy used in France.

3 Make a list of renewable sources of energy, and another list of non-renewable sources.

4 Using the figures in the table (right), plot a series of line graphs (on the same axes) to show the changes in relative importance of the different forms of energy in electricity generation. Label the lines carefully and provide a key.

Percentage contribution of different fuels to the production of electricity in France, 1975–90.

France's total energy consumption, 1990
- Nuclear
- Coal and gas
- Oil
- Other (including HEP)

CASE STUDY H

The French Energy Dilemma

Fuel	1975	1980	1985	1990	1992
Oil and gas	39	23	4	4	4
Coal	17	25	11	8	7
HEP	34	28	20	14	16
Nuclear	10	24	65	74	73

Source: Electricité de France.

Find out about . . .

1 Make a list of the countries, apart from France, which might be affected if there was a major accident at a French nuclear power station. Use an atlas to help you, and explain your answer.

2 Find a map which shows the physical geography of France. Use it to consider which areas are most suitable for HEP production. Present your conclusions as a labelled map.

3 Design a newspaper advertisement to promote the French nuclear industry. Consider carefully the information it should contain.

4 Compare energy use in the following countries with that in France:
- United Kingdom
- Italy
- USA
- Japan.

Which country makes the greatest use of renewable sources?

5 Design a poster to advertise an anti-nuclear energy protest meeting.

Library and research tasks

1 Use library books and the resources in this case study to list some advantages and disadvantages of nuclear power in general.

2 Try to discover which countries in Europe, apart from France, have nuclear power stations, and which do not. Suggest possible reasons to explain your findings.

3 Find out what you can about the current situation in the British nuclear industry, and write a short report about it. If you wish, give your own opinions about nuclear power at the end of your report.

Role play

The French President asks you to participate in a discussion on energy problems. Also present will be a representative of the oil industry, an expert on energy conservation, and an anti-nuclear campaigner. The subject of the discussion is 'The Future of French Energy Supplies'.

Ask your teacher to set up this discussion, chaired by the President. Appoint one person to play each role. Write a short summary of the outcome of the talks.

CASE STUDY H

The French Energy Dilemma

Postscript

Electricité de France (EDF) is now the largest producer of nuclear power in Europe. In 1991, it provided 72% of France's electricity from 55 operational nuclear stations. EDF is also an exporter of electricity, to Switzerland, Germany and Italy, and to the UK through the cross-Channel cable.

Key Terms

balance of payments the difference between the money earned by selling goods and services abroad and the money spent buying goods and services from other countries.

enrichment the process which increases the content of usable fuel in refined uranium.

fabrication the production of uranium fuel elements for installation inside reactors.

fast-breeder reactor a sodium-cooled type of reactor which is capable of creating more fuel (plutonium) than it consumes.

non-renewable energy energy sources such as coal, oil, gas and uranium whose supplies are finite.

nuclear fuel cycle the entire nuclear process from the mining of uranium, through electricity generation, to fuel reprocessing and the final disposal of radioactive waste.

overcapacity the ability to produce more of something than is required.

pressurised water reactor (PWR) a water-cooled reactor which burns enriched uranium.

renewable energy energy sources including the sun (solar power), wind, tides, running water and geothermal heat, which are not depleted in use.

reprocessing the separation of unburned uranium and other useful fuel isotopes like plutonium from the useless by-products of the nuclear reaction.

Key Understandings

- Unless a country meets all its energy needs from domestic sources, a variety of factors can influence the supply of energy.

- Strategically it is useful for a country to have a mix of fuels from more than one source.

- Each type of energy has a different cost structure, as well as advantages and disadvantages in the short or long term. Nuclear energy, for example, is often regarded as a cheap option, but the costs of storing or reprocessing waste and decommissioning old stations add to this cost. There are also environmental costs.

- In the 1980s France developed the largest nuclear industry in Europe. It now supplies over 70% of the electricity needed by France.

- Despite such apparent success, however, the industry faces persistent problems with its economics, safety, technology and environmental impacts.

Case Study 1

All Change for Farmers of the Former Soviet Union

The last few years have seen major changes in the former Soviet Union. Many of these were initiated in 1985, when Mikhail Gorbachev became the country's leader. In 1991, the Soviet Union broke up and the former **communist state** was replaced by the Commonwealth of Independent States (CIS). This included Russia and 10 new nations. Throughout this period, there were major changes in agriculture. However, improving farming in these countries is not an easy task, with farmers facing so many difficulties. What are the new reforms and will they make any difference?

A group of British farmers will visit several farms in Russia next year. They have been invited for an exchange of views with their counterparts. The Moscow government is keen to encourage Russian farmers to adopt Western practices. British farmers will examine farming methods and look at the problems facing their Russian colleagues. In addition the group will be interested to see how farming in Russia today is different from that in 1985, when the country was still governed by state communism.

As a junior civil servant working for the Ministry of Agriculture, Fisheries and Food (MAFF) in London, you have been asked to brief the delegation before they leave the UK. The documents in this case study should help you.

Russia and the former Soviet Union.

CASE STUDY 1

Farming in the Soviet Union

Key Question 1
How was Soviet agriculture organised up to 1985?

Resource A

Memo from:

**British Embassy Moscow
Economic Affairs Division**
December 1985

Since 1950, the output from Soviet farms has grown more quickly than the country's population. This suggests that Soviet farmers should be able to grow enough food to feed everyone, and that agriculture is well organised and efficient. The reality is rather different: there are severe food shortages, long queues outside shops and even rationing of some items.

As the USSR is so large, and covers a range of latitudes, many different types of agriculture are found. About half the farming land is used for growing grain, including wheat. Huge areas of grassland support cattle, sheep and pigs.

As well as fruit and vegetables, other items, including cotton, rice, sugar beet and even grapes, are cultivated.

A variety of factors influence how people farm.

Physical conditions: although the nation has a massive land area, not all is suitable for agriculture. Adverse climate rules out about 30% of the area, and there are also large mountainous areas. **Tundra** and **permafrost** are widespread in the north, whereas further south, desert conditions are common.

Economic and political organisation the USSR has a communist government, so agriculture is organised in a different way from most of Western Europe:

- Almost all land is owned by the state, and not by the farmers who work it.
- Individual farmers do not make decisions about what to grow.
- All farming activity is planned by the government. It decides how much of each type of crop must be grown, and what price will be paid.
- Farmers either work on a **kolkhoz** (collective farm) or a **sovkhoz** (state farm). Both types of farm are large and employ many workers. The average sovkhoz in this year has an area of 16,100 hectares and a labour force numbering 530 workers.
- There is a lot of interference from the state. Individual farmers have no incentive to show initiative or enterprise.

In general, industry attracts more government money and attention than farming. As a result, food-processing facilities are poor, storage and distribution facilities are inadequate, and salted, dried and pickled foods are found more often than frozen produce. The **infrastructure** is poorly developed – country roads are so bad that a lorry loses at least 10% of its load between field and farm, and a further 10% between farm and railhead. Ordinary people as well as the country's leaders have become concerned by the situation.

Resource B

Queues for food outside a shop in Moscow in the late 1980s.

CASE STUDY I
Farming in the Soviet Union

Resource C

We live in a small town called Shahan in Kagaranda region. We have three children – the youngest is just one year old. My husband works at the Shakhtinskaya Mine. I work at another mine, though I'm on maternity leave now.

It was Sunday yesterday and I went out to buy some butter. I took my youngest child. You should have seen the crowd outside the shop. How was I to get anything when I had a small child with me? I just turned round and went home.

Life is supposed to be getting better, but we are always short of something in our town. Biscuits are in short supply, as well as sausages, cheese, sugar, margarine and a lot more. Yet judging by the papers, food production is increasing every year. So where is this food if the shops are empty? True, we've got canned fish, and meat is sometimes available, but it's expensive.

Think about the problems of feeding a family in such conditions – the children are growing, and my husband works hard.

Letter from a young woman called Dudareva, printed in *Pravda*, 23 November 1987

The reality is that we just do not produce enough agricultural output. The state is forced to make large purchases abroad of grain, meat, fruit, vegetables, sugar and other products.

We continue to trail behind developed countries – large and small – in labour productivity, in crop yields from fields, in livestock productivity and in the variety and quality of foodstuffs.

A speech made by former President Mikhail Gorbachev on 15 March 1989

Resource D

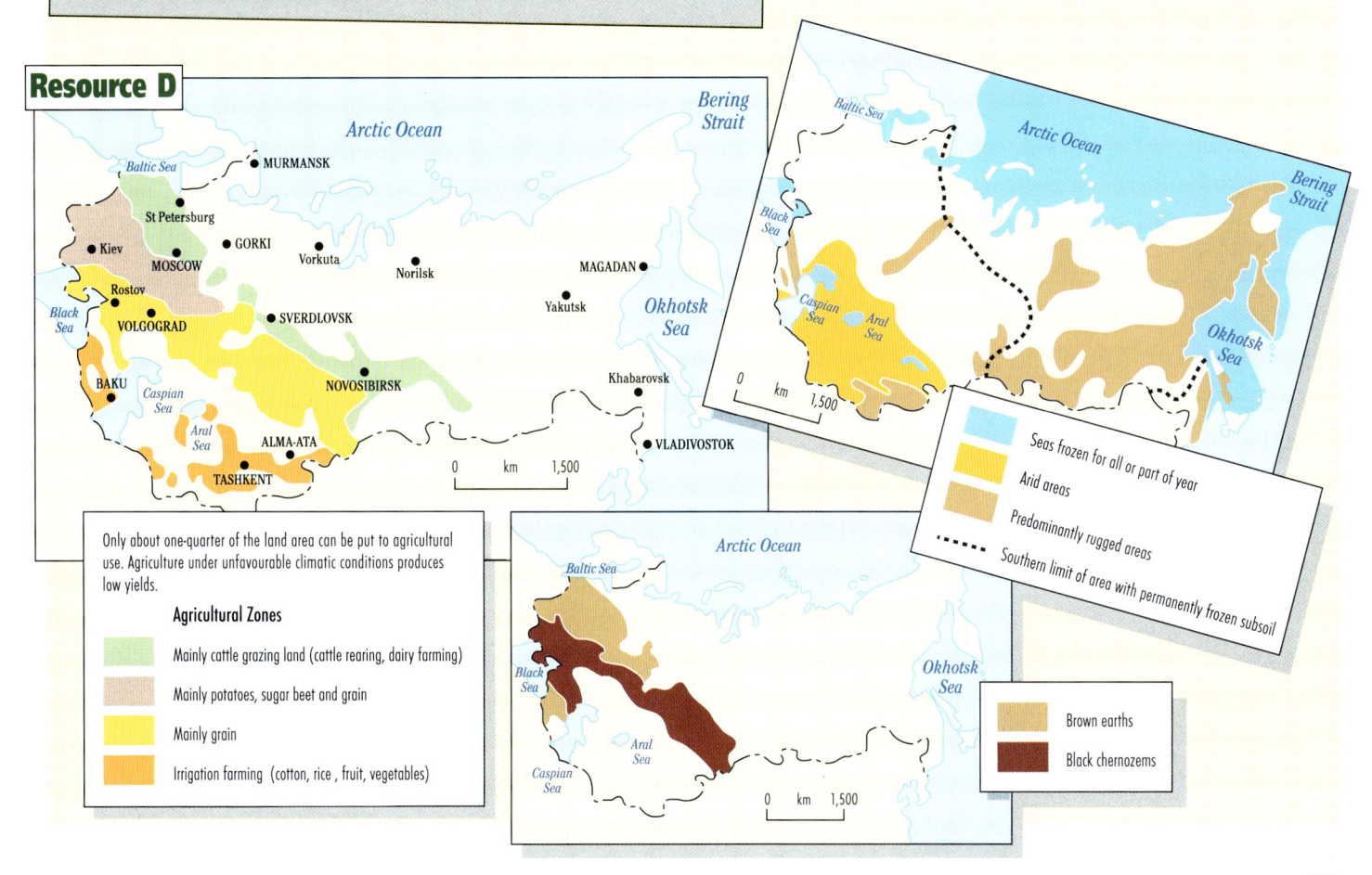

Only about one-quarter of the land area can be put to agricultural use. Agriculture under unfavourable climatic conditions produces low yields.

Agricultural Zones
- Mainly cattle grazing land (cattle rearing, dairy farming)
- Mainly potatoes, sugar beet and grain
- Mainly grain
- Irrigation farming (cotton, rice, fruit, vegetables)

- Seas frozen for all or part of year
- Arid areas
- Predominantly rugged areas
- Southern limit of area with permanently frozen subsoil

- Brown earths
- Black chernozems

CASE STUDY 1

Farming in the Soviet Union

Resource E

Million tonnes (unless stated)	1968	1981–85 (average)	% change
Grain	172.2	183.1	–
Sugar beet	95.8	77.6	–19.0
Potatoes	103.8	79.6	–
Vegetables	19.3	29.6	–
Milk	83.6	96.1	+14.9
Meat	11.8	16.4	–
Raw cotton	6.0	8.4	+40.0
Wool ('000 tonnes)	421.0	457.0	–
Eggs (billion)	35.7	74.4	–

Some indicators of agricultural output in the former Soviet Union, 1968–85.

Resource F

'And this is the storehouse for the paperwork to do with the preparation of the vegetables.' (In the background is the storehouse for the vegetables themselves.)

Activities

Before they visit Russia, the British farmers need to know something about the country and its farming. Initially you decide to provide them with a briefing paper which details the state of Soviet agriculture up to 1985, when Mikhail Gorbachev came to power, and reforms began. Use the resources on pages 84–86 to answer the questions below, then try to produce a briefing paper which summarises the organisation of Soviet agriculture and lists its main problems.

1a Read what Dudareva has to say (Resource C). How are Dudareva and her family affected by problems in Soviet farming?
b What problems does Mikhail Gorbachev note in his speech?

2 The maps (Resource D) show some of the physical factors affecting Soviet farming.
a List the towns and cities where farming is difficult. Next to each town's name give one reason to explain why you think farming there is difficult.
b The south-west of the Soviet Union is **arid**. What does this mean? How can farmers overcome this difficulty?

3 Changes in the output of some agricultural products between 1968 and 1985 are shown in Resource E.
a List all the products in the table, then calculate the percentage change for each item. Sugar beet, milk and raw cotton have been done for you.
b Now make another list, putting the products in rank order. Those with the largest increases should be at the top of the list.
c Look carefully at the type of product whose output has increased most. On the basis of these figures, do you think that Soviet agriculture has failed over the last 20 years? Explain your answer.

4 The cartoon above appeared in a Soviet magazine. Discuss with a partner what problems it is trying to highlight.

5 'There are many advantages for a country whose government owns all the land, and decides what crops farmers will grow, where they will grow them, and in what quantities.'
a List the advantages referred to in this statement. Then list some disadvantages.
b Do you agree with the statement? Explain your answer.

Key Question 2
How has agriculture in Russia changed since 1985?

CASE STUDY I
Farming in the Soviet Union

Resource G

BRIEFING PAPER PRODUCED BY
THE CONFEDERATION OF NEW RUSSIAN FARMERS
Agricultural Change: 1985–1990

The organisation of our agriculture is starting to change, and it certainly needs to! In 1985, our country's manufacturing industry produced 22 times more than it did in 1940, while agricultural output was just 2.5 times greater. We are producing more fruit, vegetables and meat than ever before, but an average Russian farmer today can only feed 8 people, whereas a Dutch farmer can feed up to 112 people. Over 1 million people leave our countryside for the cities each year.

Once Mikhail Gorbachev became the Soviet leader in March 1985, the situation began to change. He was well qualified to improve agriculture, as he was a trained **agronomist**, and a former Minister for Agriculture. Immediately Gorbachev began to restructure the economy. This **perestroika** aimed to reduce government control and interference, and to encourage more individual initiative and enterprise.

Gorbachev's Reforms
By the end of 1985 a total re-organisation of agriculture was proposed. 'Collective' farms effectively became 'state' farms, and one State Agro-Industrial Committee was formed from the 13 different Ministries responsible for agriculture. The following year, state and collective farms were allowed to sell one-third of their produce to local shops and markets. Here the prices could be fixed locally instead of by the government. Farmers were given incentives to work harder.

In 1989, families and small groups were allowed to rent land and machinery. Produce belonged to the leaseholder who could decide whether to use it and keep any profit made. By December 1990, a new Land Law allowed private land ownership. Farmers were permitted to own, not just lease, their share of the collective farms, use the land for life and pass it on to their heirs.

The government has allowed farms to be organised in various ways: there are more co-operatives, family contracts and leasing arrangements. The aim is to reduce state control and encourage private enterprise.

Resource H

Our family plot is quite small, only about half a hectare. There are 34 million private plots like it in the country, mostly on collective or state farms.

We use this land to grow vegetables and fruit. We also have a few chickens and a goat.

Private plots cover only 2% of the total farmed area in the country, but produce over one-quarter of the gross agricultural output.

Private plots produce about 30% of our country's milk, meat, eggs and vegetables, and 60% of the potatoes, honey, fruit and berries.

One of Russia's many new private plots

CASE STUDY I
Farming in the Soviet Union

Resource I

A food market in Russia.

DATELINE.....1992.....USSR BREAKS UP.....CIS FORMED

PROGRESS ON PRIVATISATION
Some state farms are now setting up as shareholding companies. Shares in the farm are distributed to all workers.

PEASANT POWER
Peasant farmers and sharecroppers in the former Soviet Union now occupy 6% of the cultivated area, but account for only 3% of agricultural production.

WORLD BANK SURVEY BLOW
December 1992

A report published in Washington by the World Bank yesterday indicates just how little progress is being made in the Russian farm sector, and how much is still to be done. The World Bank estimates up to 'one-third of food produced is lost through poor storage, waste, theft and inadequate transport facilities'.

NO CHANGE ON FARMS
Russian agriculture is still dominated by state farms and large co-operatives. However, many important changes are increasingly being guided by free-market forces.

Resource J

What progress had been made by 1992?

Resource K

The collective farm where I work is near Novosibirsk. We grow mainly wheat and maize, but there are some pigs and sheep too. I earn 178 roubles each month (£185). I'm concerned about the new reforms. How would I manage the land if suddenly it belonged to me? What would I grow? My family could starve if we had bad weather, or if I fell ill. It is safer to work collectively. The better the farm does, the more comfortably everyone in the village will live.

A Soviet farmer on an arable collective farm.

CASE STUDY I

Farming in the Soviet Union

Activities

Just before the British farmers leave for Russia, they are summoned to London, where Anatoly Chapinsky of the Confederation of New Russian Farmers will tell them about recent changes. The resources on pages 87–88 form part of this updating meeting. Answer the questions below, then summarise the two changes you think will make most difference to Russian farmers in the future.

1a Which has made more progress since 1940, Soviet agriculture or industry?
b What were the main problems of Soviet agriculture in 1985?

2a How important are the private plots that state and collective farm workers are allowed to have (Resource H)?
b Should produce continue to be bought by the government at a guaranteed price, or should farmers be allowed to sell their goods at local markets (Resource I)?
c What disadvantage might there be for a farmer moving from a system where the government guarantees a market price for his produce to a free market situation?

3 Accounts of the present situation in Russia often appear in our newspapers. Study the brief extracts in Resource J.
a What reasons does the World Bank give for the poor performance of Russia's farms?
b List some of the changes which have been introduced into Russian farming since 1985.
c Does any real progress seem to have been made between 1985 and 1992?

4 If you had worked on a large collective farm for 20 years, and were told that you could now lease some land, how would you feel about it? Would you be worried like the farmer in Resource K? Discuss your feelings with a partner.

5 Do you think the changes initiated by Mikhail Gorbachev will improve Russian farming? What else needs to be done?

Further activities

Short-answer tasks

1 Why was Mikhail Gorbachev the ideal man to start reforming agriculture in the former Soviet Union?

2 What does 'perestroika' mean? What changes has perestroika brought to former Soviet farms?

3 Draw up a list of five questions that the British farmers could ask during their visit.

4 Using the data (right), plot a line graph to show grain production in the former Soviet Union between 1976 and 1990. Is it possible to predict from the graph what grain output will be next year? Explain your answer.

5a Give two reasons why Russia and the other former Soviet republics need to keep increasing their agricultural output.
b Suggest two ways in which increased output can be achieved.

6a A combination of physical and human factors has influenced farming in the former Soviet Union. Copy the list of factors below and write the letter P (physical) or H (human) next to each one to show which group of factors they belong to:
- land ownership
- inadequate storage
- dense vegetation
- state subsidies
- permafrost
- drought
- government pricing policy
- poor transport.

b Which group of factors do you think is most important? Why?

Grain production in the Soviet Union, 1976–90.

Year	
1976	224
1977	196
1978	237
1979	179
1980	189
1981	158
1982	187
1983	192
1984	173
1985	192
1986	210
1987	211
1988	195
1989	211
1990	300

CASE STUDY I

Farming in the Soviet Union

Find out about . . .

1a What sort of physical conditions (climate, soil, etc.) does wheat need, to grow well?

b Draw a map to show the main areas of the world where it is grown.

2 Using an atlas, compare the location, size and extent of Japan, the USA and the former Soviet Union. In which country do you think the conditions most favour agriculture? Do these countries share any common problems related to agriculture?

3 Are there any similarities between the organisation of farming in China and the former Soviet Union?

4 If you were a British farmer, which part of the former Soviet Union would you like to visit most, and why? In which part of that country does farming differ most from your own home area?

Library and research tasks

1 Soviet farming was 'collectivised' in the 1920s. What did this actually mean to ordinary farmers? Do you think it was a good idea?

2 What was the 'Virgin Lands Scheme' and why was it needed?

3 Find out how the average consumption by Soviet people of the important food items shown in the table below compares with that in Britain.

Cereals	131
Meat	63
Milk (including butter)	243
Potatoes	105
Vegetables	100
Eggs	270

Food consumption in the Soviet Union, 1987 (kg per head).

Key Terms

agronomist person who has studied agriculture.

arid lacking in water, dry.

communist state the old system of government in the Soviet Union in which private ownership of property (such as farms) was not allowed, and the making of profits was illegal.

infrastructure network of services needed to allow economic activities like farming to take place, eg electricity, water, gas, roads, etc.

kolkhoz a collective farm where output is varied and workers share the profits according to the work done.

perestroika the restructuring or re-organisation of the former Soviet Union's economy.

permafrost permanently frozen soil and rock below the surface, found in areas where the temperature rarely rises above zero for long periods.

sovkhoz a state farm run like a factory. Workers receive weekly wages. State farms are larger, more mechanised and more specialised than collective (kolkhoz) farms.

tundra type of vegetation found in northern latitudes consisting of mosses and sedges with patches of lichens. It is too dry, and the winters are too long, for any trees to grow.

Key Understandings

• The huge extent of the former Soviet Union means that a large variety of agricultural products can be grown. However, physical factors limit the area that can be easily farmed, and economic and political factors determine what is grown, and where it is grown.

• Low investment in food production in the Soviet Union for many years has resulted in food shortages, with shops lacking even basic foods like bread. Many farmers had no interest in their work because they did not own the land they farmed.

• Political changes and the restructuring of the economy are slowly altering farming in Russia and the other republics.

• New laws mean that farmers can own or lease land for the first time and make profits. Other aspects of free-market forces are also being encouraged.

• Rural infrastructure is being improved to help improve the efficiency of farmers.

Case Study J

Western USA's Water Crisis: The Case of Mono Lake

The western part of the USA covers 60% of the nation's land area, yet receives just 25% of the annual precipitation. Despite very low rainfall totals, the region supports a growing population and a large agricultural sector. To allow such growth to occur, aquifers have been pumped dry, huge reservoirs constructed and extensive canal systems built to transfer water to where it is most needed. Water shortages still occur, however, and some aspects of the region's environment show signs of stress. Water provision has become a highly controversial political issue.

> Mono Lake in northern California is an important bird sanctuary and tourist attraction. However, its level has been considerably reduced since the streams which feed it were diverted to supply water to cities in southern California. Senator Beverley Wallach is a local politician who is keen to protect the lake for the future. As a student of geography, and someone with a keen interest in the environment, the Senator asks you to investigate what is happening to Mono Lake.

Mono Lake in the western USA.

CASE STUDY J
Western USA's Water Crisis

Key Question 1
Why do the water resources of the western USA need to be managed?

Dry East and Wet West – A Divided Nation?

Resource A

The USA may be divided into two parts by the 100th meridian (the 100° W line of longitude), as the map below shows.

To the east of this line America is wet, rainfall is generally plentiful and the rivers are large and reliable. To the west of this line, America is dry. Until the 1860s the Great Plains which sit astride the 100th meridian were better known as the Great American Desert. This area was regarded as a national boundary, 'up to which population and agriculture could advance … and no further'.

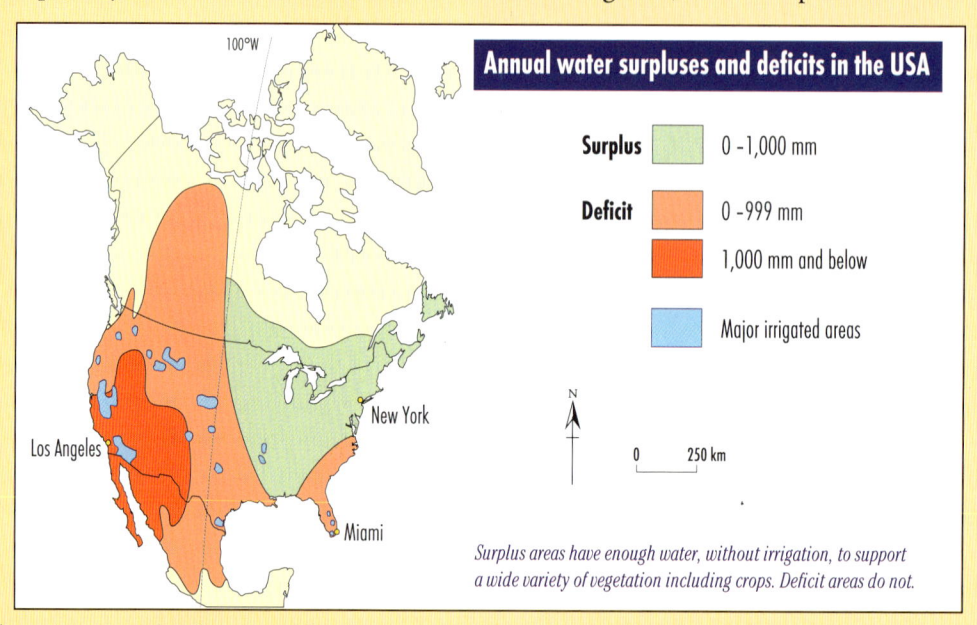

Annual water surpluses and deficits in the USA

- Surplus: 0 –1,000 mm
- Deficit: 0 –999 mm
- Deficit: 1,000 mm and below
- Major irrigated areas

Surplus areas have enough water, without irrigation, to support a wide variety of vegetation including crops. Deficit areas do not.

The development of the American West was only possible owing to a relentless quest for the most precious of resources: water. Water management and transfer schemes have transformed the west – great circles of centre-pivot **irrigation** now dominate the farmland of the plains and the valleys of the west. Huge dams and reservoirs control the flow of the region's major rivers.

Centre-pivot irrigation in the Midwest.

Glen Canyon dam and Lake Powell, Arizona.

Exotic palm trees, lush golf courses and even a 170-metre fountain in Phoenix proclaim people's victory over the desert. However, the cost of this victory has been huge, not just in financial terms, but also – and more seriously – in terms of the environment.

Resource B

CASE STUDY J

Western USA's Water Crisis

A PARCHED LAND

In the western half of the USA, a combination of low rainfall and high rates of evaporation produce dry ground. This is difficult to settle, useless for cultivation, and may also be liable to erosion. Irrigation has been developed, and the western states now use 12 times more water for farming than those in the east.

Cities also make huge demands on water surpluses. The original site of Los Angeles, for example, was chosen because it had a reliable source of water – the River Los Angeles. This supply quickly ran out, however, and today the local supply of water has to be pumped from below ground. This is called **groundwater**.

Water transfer schemes have also had to be built to meet the needs of farms and cities in southern California. Three major schemes have come to the rescue as Los Angeles' groundwater supplies have proved inadequate:

1 The State Water Project (SWP) which transfers water from northern California.
2 The Los Angeles Aqueduct, which first brought water from the Owens Valley, but was extended in 1941 to include the catchment area of Mono Lake.
3 The Colorado River Aqueduct – a supply of water which Los Angeles may lose as the Central Arizona Project nears completion.

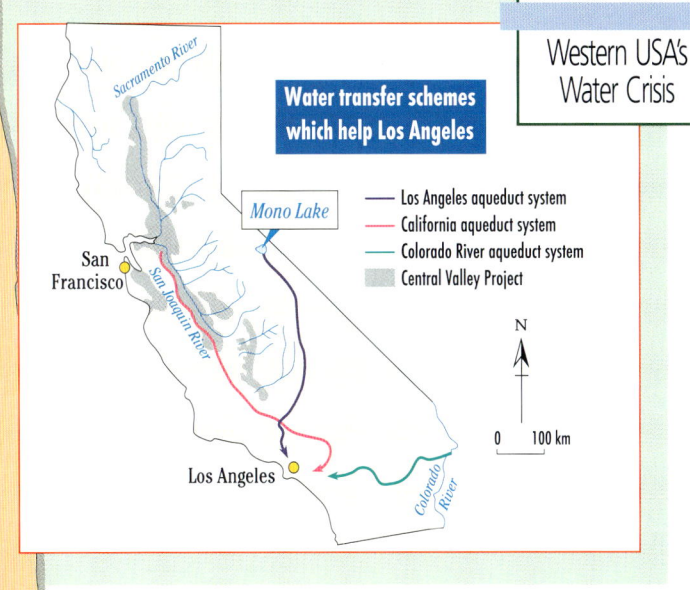

Water transfer schemes which help Los Angeles

- Los Angeles aqueduct system
- California aqueduct system
- Colorado River aqueduct system
- Central Valley Project

Resource C

Climate graph for Los Angeles

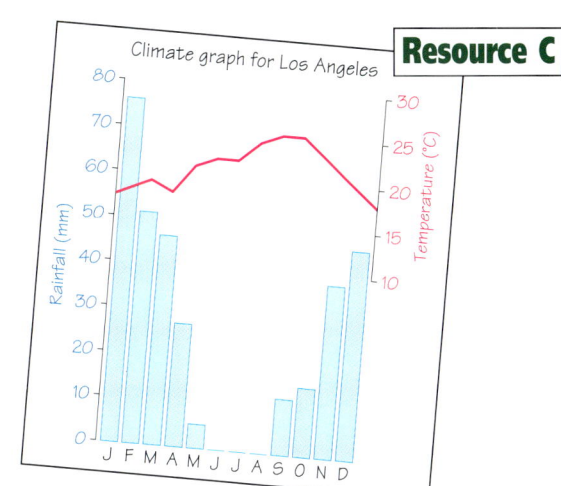

Activities

To refresh your memory about water availability in the USA, you look back in your school geography file, and find the material on these two pages. Answer the questions below, then make sure you can answer Key Question 1 at the top of page 92.

1a Read the article 'Dry east and wet west'. Explain why it describes the USA as 'a divided nation'.
b List as many economic activities as you can that depend on the use of water.

2 The data in the table (right) contrasts water use in the eastern and western USA.
a Draw two divided bars, one for each region, to show how its total water use is made up. To do this you will need to calculate the percentage of the water used for each of the activities shown.
b What differences do you notice about water use across the USA?

West	Used for	East
661,900	irrigated agriculture	49,800
34,700	domestic demand	93,300
20,700	manufacturing	210,400
10,500	energy	393,600
10,200	minerals	21,600
12,700	other uses	4,400
750,700	*total* used per day	**773,100**

3 Describe the climate of Los Angeles using the climate graph (Resource C), and state the particular problems posed by such a climate for farmers and city dwellers.

4 Read the magazine extract 'A Parched Land'. Use a ruler and the scale of the map to estimate the distances involved in the schemes developed to supply Los Angeles with water.

CASE STUDY J

Western USA's Water Crisis

Key Question 2
What is the ecological impact on Mono Lake of continued water diversions to Los Angeles?

Beautiful lake threatened

Resource D

Mono Lake is one of the oldest continually existing lakes in North America – it is one million years old. The lake lies in a basin in northern California, just to the east of Yosemite National Park. The unique ecology of this **terminal lake** has been put at risk by the water needs of the City of Los Angeles. Four of the five main streams that feed the lake have been diverted, causing the water level to fall 13 metres. Since the diversion started in 1941, the lake's volume has halved and its salinity has doubled.

Mono Lake supplies 17% of Los Angeles' water and 2% of the city's electricity

— Los Angeles aqueduct system
— Hydro-electric power plants

The location of Mono Lake.

Environmentalists regard Mono Lake as a scenic and ecological treasure. The lake is well known for its limestone formations called **tufa** towers, which were originally formed under water. Ironically these towers have only become visible and become a tourist attraction since the lake's water level began to fall.

The lake is also one of California's most important bird sanctuaries. Mono Lake's abundant brine shrimp attract over 280 species of bird. There are huge colonies of California gulls and important numbers of phalaropes, grebes and snowy plovers. As the water level drops and the salinity of the lake increases, the tiny brine shrimp on which the birds depend die. Birds are also abandoning their nesting islands all over the lake, because land bridges form when the water level drops, allowing coyotes and other predators to raid the nesting areas.

Fragile tufa towers.

An oasis for birds.

The drop in the level of Mono Lake is the basis of a major dispute between conservationists and the Los Angeles Department of Water & Power (LADWP). The conservationists are worried that the lake's ecosystem will soon completely collapse. No one knows exactly how low the level of the lake can fall before a catastrophe occurs. The impact of Los Angeles' growth on Mono Lake is obvious, but so far is not irreversible.

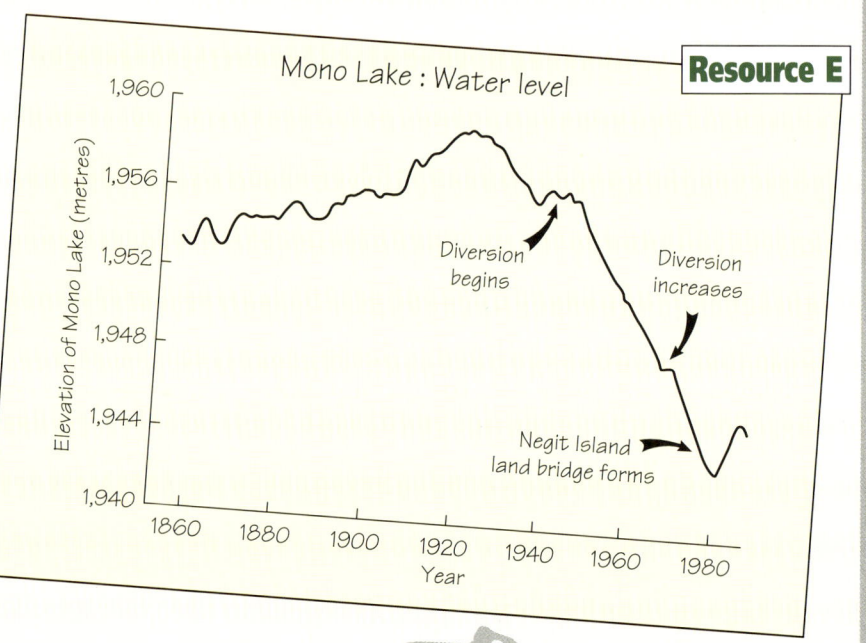

Resource E

Mono Lake : Water level

(Diversion begins; Diversion increases; Negit Island land bridge forms)

Resource F

Mono Lake's ecosystem.

Resource G

The changing shape of Mono Lake

Natural shoreline 1941
1,960 metres above sea level

Water level 1990
1,945 metres above sea level

Final estimated shoreline
1,930 metres above sea level

CASE STUDY J

Western USA's Water Crisis

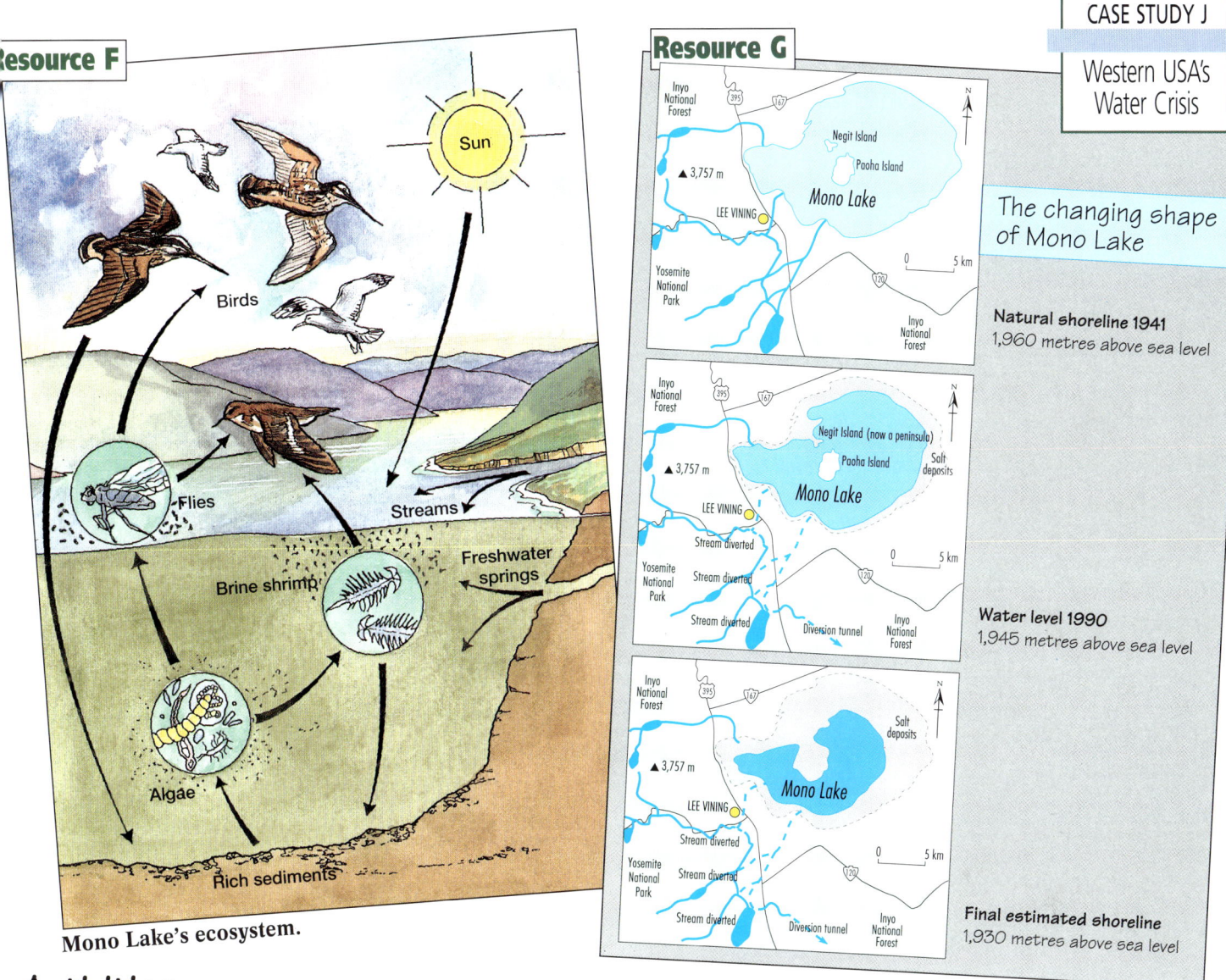

Activities

One of the groups trying to stop Mono Lake from being drained further has written to Senator Wallach enclosing the article, photographs and other resources shown here (Resources D–G). Examine the materials carefully, then write a report for the Senator, setting out the case for **conservation**. Explain the reasons for preserving the lake, and stopping further water diversions.

1a From the photographs and magazine article here, what attractions do you think that the Mono Lake area has for visitors?
b Why do you think local people are keen to protect the lake?

2a What effect has diverting rivers had on the water level in Mono Lake (Resources E and G)?
b Explain two other effects on the lake since water diversions began in 1941.

3 If water diversions continue, what do you think the landscape of this area will look like in 100 years' time? Draw 'present' and 'future' field sketches of the Mono Lake area, using the resources here to help you.

4a How far will the shoreline of Mono Lake fall before it stabilises (Resource G)?
b What changes will this fall in water level bring to
- the length of shoreline
- the two islands that existed in 1941
- the lake's ecology?

Now write your report. Make sure you set out the case for protecting the lake clearly, by explaining the many effects that water diversions are currently having.

95

CASE STUDY J — Western USA's Water Crisis

Key Question 3
Can the ecology of Mono Lake be preserved?

California's water problems are due to imbalances of supply and demand. Some 75% of the state's rainfall occurs in the northern third of the state, while 80% of water consumption takes place in the southern third. Two opposing groups are at the heart of the conflict – the Mono Lake Committee, determined to protect the lake, and the Los Angeles Department of Water & Power. Both groups provide position statements for Senator Wallach and submit some of their literature for inspection.

Resource H

The Mono Lake Committee

1. The assault on our earth, air and water has reached epic proportions. There must be one place to hold the line on the destruction of our natural heritage … one place where concerned people can successfully concentrate their energies … one battle that we can win. *Here* is the place … it is Mono Lake.

2. Since diversions began in 1941, Mono Lake has fallen about 13 metres and doubled in salinity. Trout fisheries in the streams have been devastated. Unless diversions are cut, increasing salinity will poison Mono Lake's unique ecosystem.

3. It is not only the lake that is at risk. Caustic dust, swept up by the wind from the thousands of hectares of recently exposed lake shores, is polluting the clean air of the eastern Sierra.

4. This tragedy is unnecessary. Experience from recent droughts has proved that conservation could easily save more than enough water to protect Mono Lake. We have enough water to avoid further damage if only we manage our resources wisely.

Resource I

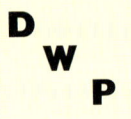

DWP Los Angeles Department of Water & Power

1. Water diversions by the Department of Water & Power (DWP) from the Mono Lake basin are an important source of high-quality water for Los Angeles. Mono Lake basin water also produces a substantial amount of clean hydro-electric power for the city.

2. The Department believes that the Mono Lake ecosystem is currently in a healthy and productive state, particularly with regard to the lake's ability to provide food and a habitat for large numbers of migratory birds.

3. The Department must view the water needs of the residents of the city as its first priority. The DWP, however, acknowledges its responsibility to do what it reasonably can to maintain the lake in an environmentally healthy condition. The Department also recognises that to do so will at some point in time require a reduction in the city's authorised diversions, which will have to be replaced from a different source.

4. The Department of Water & Power will continue to pursue vigorously the practical implementation of water conservation and reclaimed water projects.

Resource J

War of words over Mono Lake.

CASE STUDY J

Western USA's Water Crisis

Activities

Having examined all the available evidence, you recommend to Senator Wallach that she should support the campaign to protect Mono Lake, and that this is likely to increase her appeal with many voters, with the possible exception of those living in southern California. Answer the questions below, then devise a poster to help convince even residents of Los Angeles that they should support the aims of the Mono Lake Committee.

1 The materials sent to Senator Wallach to examine get mixed up. You must sort them out. Which of the booklets and pamphlets shown in Resource J do you think were produced by the DWP and which by the Mono Lake Committee?

2 Study the statement provided by the Mono Lake Committee (Resource H).
a Apart from the fall in water level, what other risks does the statement from the Mono Lake Committee draw attention to?
b How does the Committee suggest that Californians should deal with water shortages?

3 Study the statement from the Los Angeles Department of Water & Power (Resource I).
a Is there any indication that the DWP does not intend to use Mono Lake water for ever?
b How might the DWP provide water for Los Angeles residents in future years?
c You are asked to recommend five ways that the citizens of Los Angeles could save or conserve water. Prepare a list.

4 Devise an attractive campaign poster for the Senator, which sets out the three most important reasons for protecting Mono Lake for the future.

CASE STUDY J

Western USA's Water Crisis

Further activities

Short-answer tasks

1a What is *irrigation*?
b Why is irrigation so necessary in the western USA?

2 What is a *terminal lake*? Why are terminal lakes so salty?

3 The water from Mono Lake's streams also provides power for Los Angeles. What type of power is this likely to be, and how is it generated?

4 Study the cartoon (right). Explain the confusion being experienced by the water droplet shown.

5 The limestone tufa towers in Mono Lake were formed under water. Are they similar to any other limestone features you have come across?

"....AND HERE I AM ON MY WAY TO L.A. INSTEAD OF MONO LAKE!"

Find out about . . .

1 Find out about one of the other water transfer schemes in the western USA, eg the Central Valley Scheme, the State Water Project, the All-American Canal, the Colorado Aqueduct or the Central Arizona Project. For any one of these schemes:

a Draw a sketch map to show the main dams, lakes, canals, pipes, etc.
b Find out where the water is going, and what it is used for.

2 One way of making the most of the water available is to use *dry farming techniques*. Find out about such methods and describe the main dry farming techniques in use in the American Midwest.

3 Find out about the water supply to your own area. You may have to contact your local water company for help here. Compare the distance your water travels from its source with the length of the Los Angeles Aqueduct.

4a Calculate how much water is used by your household each day.
b What measures could you suggest which would reduce your household's water consumption?

5 Many hotels in the American West are urging visitors to use water carefully. Plastic tags like the one shown here are left hanging on bathroom doors, suggesting that you 'shorten your shower'. Design two other plastic tags for different rooms of the house. Each should be attractive, and carry a slogan urging people to conserve water.

WATER CRISIS
PLEASE CONSERVE
SHORTEN YOUR SHOWER
WE'RE ALL IN THIS TOGETHER

This water conservation effort is sponsored by the San Luis Obispo Chamber of Commerce, the City of San Luis Obispo, and this establishment.

CASE STUDY J

Western USA's Water Crisis

Library and research tasks

1 Using an atlas and holiday brochures, plan a two-week fly-drive holiday to California for two people. Devise an itinerary (a route with stopping places) and include a visit to Mono Lake. Choose other interesting places to visit. You can use Los Angeles or San Francisco airport (or both).

2 Use library books to find out about the problems of water supply in Latin America. In particular try to find out about the Sertão in north-eastern Brazil. Why have large reservoirs and water management schemes been so unsuccessful in this area?

Key Terms

conservation the act of protecting a landscape or habitat, usually to prevent people from damaging the environment.

ecosystem the plants and animals that rely on each other within a certain area.

groundwater water found below the surface in a permeable rock.

irrigation to water farmland artificially using canals, ditches, pipes and sprinklers.

terminal lake a lake with no outlet or overflow.

tufa a form of limestone precipitate.

water transfer scheme moving water from an area of surplus to one of shortage.

Key Understandings

- Areas of high water demand are not always the same as those of high natural water supply. This inequality creates areas of water shortage.

- Water-short areas can have their natural water supply supplemented by water imported via pipelines, aqueducts and canals.

- Water transfer schemes, like the one that diverts water from Mono Lake to Los Angeles in the south of the state, may have consequences for the environment and wildlife of the area from which water is being transferred.

- Mono Lake (and areas like it) is regarded by some people as an environment that needs special protection. This creates a conflict over its future use.

CASE STUDY J
Western USA's Water Crisis

Postscript

The war of words between the Los Angeles Department of Water & Power and the environmentalists, as represented by the Mono Lake Committee, has spilled over into the courts. The environmentalists have tried to stop or limit the Mono Lake diversions – with some success – as the newspaper extract below shows.

Newspaper extract from the *Fresno Bee*.

The Fresno Bee   Friday, April 19, 1991

Court extends order barring LA from diverting Mono water

Associated Press

SOUTH LAKE TAHOE – In a victory for environmentalists, a judge has issued another order preventing Los Angeles from diverting water from Mono Lake streams until the lake level reaches 6,377 feet above sea level.

"If the injunction is denied and the lake is allowed to recede further, there is an obvious threat to its value as an economic, recreational and scenic source," Superior Court Judge Terrence Finney said in an opinion released Thursday.

He issued a preliminary injunction requiring Los Angeles to maintain the lake level at 6,377 feet until the state Water Resources Control Board decides how much water Los Angeles can take from the lake basin.

The new order is, in effect, an extension of a preliminary injunction Finney handed down in August 1989.

Because of the drought, the city has been unable to release enough water to bring the lake to that level or to resume diversions. Currently the lake is at 6,375 feet, according to Martha Davis, executive director of the Mono Lake Committee, an environmental group.

Los Angeles has been diverting water from Mono Lake streams since 1941, using a dam-and-aqueduct system to ship the water from the eastern side of the Sierra Nevada to Southern California.

The diversions have dropped the lake level about 40 feet and, environmentalists say, damaged the lake environment. Mono is a huge salt lake described by its admirers as starkly beautiful.

The Los Angeles Department of Water and Power said Finney's decision would cost the city about 100,000 acre feet of water over the next two years.

James Wickser, the department's assistant general manager for water, said the department was disappointed with the ruling because evidence showed "that no significant impact to the lake's ecosystem would occur if planned diversions were resumed."

But Finney disagreed, saying that diversions had already caused "irreparable harm."

He described 6,377 feet as "simply a minimum level necessary to protect the resources at Mono Lake."

"It may well be that after the public trust values have been weighed by the Water Resources Board, it may conclude that 6,377 feet is not adequate to protect those values," Finney said.

Wickser said the city would be required to increase its purchases from the Metropolitan Water District at more than twice the cost of water from the Mono Basin.

Davis said the city could tap a $60 million fund created by the state to protect the lake and find water to replace the diversions.

Case Study K

Irrigating India

You are a Project Officer for Oxfam. Your job is to help farmers in India to improve their quality of life. You have to examine different kinds of evidence – government reports, newspaper articles, scientific journals – to see whether it is worth spending more money on irrigation. Using the resources provided, you will have to decide whether or not to put Oxfam money into extending irrigation, and write a report explaining your decisions.

India is a huge country with a rapidly growing population. Tamil Nadu, one of its 22 states, is home for nearly 50 million people, almost the same number as live in the United Kingdom, and food must be provided for these people. All farmers need to ensure an adequate water supply for their crops. This is even more necessary in a country like India where resources are scarce, and where the provision of basic food is essential. In Tamil Nadu and other parts of India, new crop varieties require larger amounts of water, and a more regular supply. The question of whether more water should be provided through irrigation is therefore a very important one.

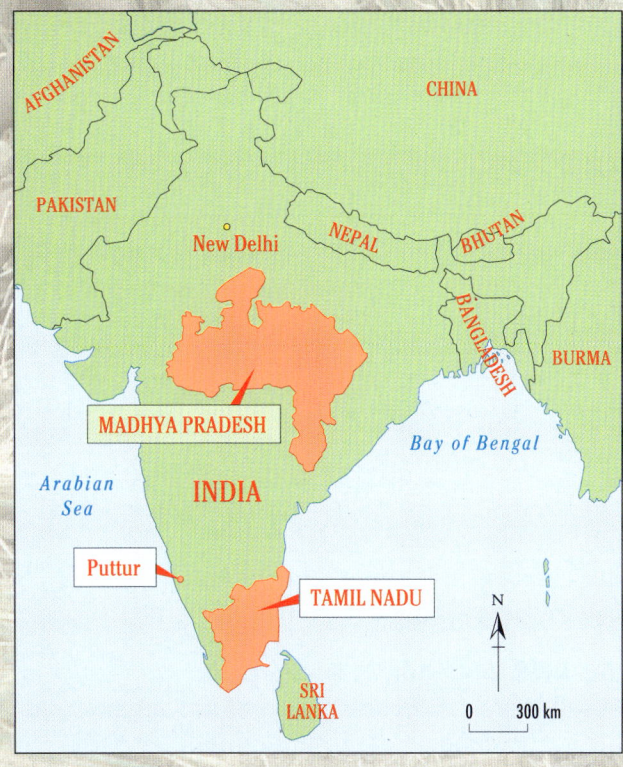

The states of India.

CASE STUDY K

Irrigating India

Key Question 1
How important is irrigation for India?

Resource A

Report to: The Minister of Agriculture
The Government of India

From: The Director of Irrigation, Tamil Nadu

Government report No. 1507

URGENT AND CONFIDENTIAL

PRESENT NEEDS FOR IRRIGATION IN INDIA

Most parts of India have suffered below normal rainfall in several recent years. In Tamil Nadu we had disastrous failure of the **monsoon** rains in 1987, as well as for several years before that. In north-western India wheat production fell from 47.1 million tonnes in 1986 to 45.6 million tonnes in 1987 as a result of the failure of rains. Rice production has also fallen.

Actual rainfall received as a percentage of normal rainfall

	1979	1982	1986	1987	1991
All India	77	89	85	89	99
West	85	84	78	76	94
North	52	95	89	63	90
East	84	88	84	104	100
South	95	89	90	76	115
Centre	69	93	87	77	92

In 1990 there were 114 million people working in agriculture out of a total population of 800 million. As the population grows by nearly 15 million every year, agricultural production must continue to rise by more than 3% a year if living standards are to rise. Is there enough water to go round? Just over half the total water resources are now developed. We estimate that 110 million hectares (66%) of India's agricultural land can be irrigated, divided roughly equally between medium- and large-scale irrigation projects and small-scale projects like wells and **tanks**.

Modern wells, using electric or diesel pumps, give farmers more control over the timing and the amount of water that goes onto the fields than do canals. In the north and north-west, unlike the rest of India, there are massive groundwater resources in the deep **alluvium**, so modern well irrigation has become very important there.

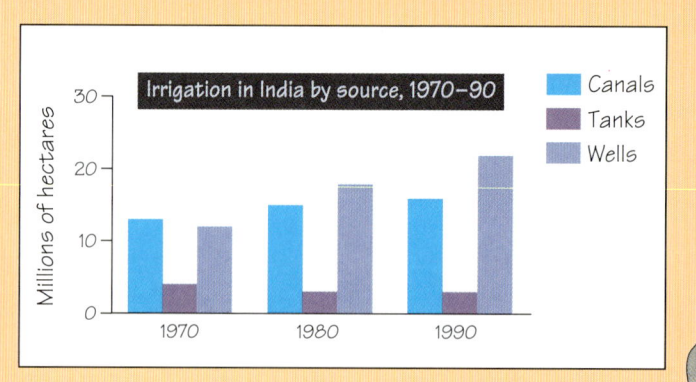

Irrigation in India by source, 1970–90 (bar chart showing Canals, Tanks, Wells in millions of hectares for 1970, 1980, 1990)

In view of the obvious benefits of irrigation, I propose that the government urgently develops irrigation schemes in the area.

Activities

Review the resource on this page by answering the following questions. Then write a report for Oxfam, explaining the importance of irrigation.

1a What are the effects on agricultural production of a failure to receive normal rainfall?
b What changes in farming practices may a farmer have to introduce to benefit from irrigation?

2 Using the information in Resource A:
a Find the average for each region of the actual rainfall as a percentage of normal rainfall.
b Rank the regions of India in order of their average actual rainfall as a percentage of normal rainfall for the five years given.
c Which region most needs irrigation?

3 Convert the information given in the graph in Resource A into three pie-charts showing the proportion of India's land irrigated from different sources in 1970, 1980 and 1990.

4 Outline the factors which influence the availability of groundwater for farming.

5 Draw a poster encouraging farmers to buy *either* fertiliser *or* pumpsets.

Key Question 2
How is irrigation important for individual farmers?

CASE STUDY K

Irrigating India

The Ramnad Times

Resource B

Irrigation comes to Puttur
By J.V. Krishnamurthy

I have come to the village of Puttur in southern Tamil Nadu, some 80 kilometres from the nearest large town, to see how farmers are making use of irrigation water.

Puttur lies on a dry, flat plain, but although the soil all looks very similar I've seen a wide variety of crops – rice, chillies, oilseeds and millets. Temperatures here allow crops to grow all the year round – if they have enough water. However, the rainfall of less than 750 mm is concentrated between October and December, and irrigation is essential to allow crops to grow outside that period.

Groundwater here is **saline**, and the nearest canal is over 50 kilometres away, so the village depends on its tank. I have come to the farm of Thangaswamy Pillai. He farms two hectares – above average, by Indian standards – divided into five fields, scattered across the village. His three best fields are irrigated from the main tank, which in most years has water for four months. The other two fields are on dry land.

On two of his irrigated fields Mr Pillai has recently introduced hyv rice, and chillies. He has also started using chemical fertilisers. As a result, his rice yields have gone up from under 1 tonne per hectare to nearly 3 tonnes. How has that been possible?

'I have used seed provided by the government, and I've bought fertiliser. But I've had to use **pesticide** because the hyvs are attacked more than local varieties. It's only worth it where I can guarantee enough water. That's why I've stuck to local varieties on my unirrigated land,' he says. 'They take less water because they only need 90 days to mature compared with 120 days for the hyvs that are available. Even then,

An Indian farmer, Mr Pillai.

I only have enough water in the rainy season,' he goes on. 'But on the dry land, I've started growing oilseeds to sell instead of rice to eat at home. Buses come right past the village, and it's now cheap and easy to get them to market.'

Irrigation has obviously made a difference to Mr Pillai's farming, but as he says, it's also vital to get his produce to market and to sell it at a good price. Where all those things have come together, millions of India's farmers have shown that they can change traditional farming practices very quickly.

Resource C

Irrigation in India has encouraged other changes in farming. Where farmers have irrigation water they are also using new varieties of seed – high-yielding varieties (**hyv**). By the early 1990s over 80% of wheat and nearly 60% of rice sown was hyv, nearly all of it on irrigated land.

Nitra Sharma is a Block Development Officer, responsible for encouraging farmers in her district to adopt new techniques in farming.

CASE STUDY K
Irrigating India

New practices and technology are helping to raise productivity.

Resource D

Resource E

The different stages of cultivating rice.

(a) (b) (c) (d)

CASE STUDY K
Irrigating India

Resource F

Wet and dry land in Puttur

- Dry land
- Wet land
- Settlement
- Water

0 metres 500

INDIA — Puttur

Resource G

Water demands of rice and millet

Crop	Rice	Millet
Duration (days)	120	110
Total water requirement (mm)	965	508

Resource H

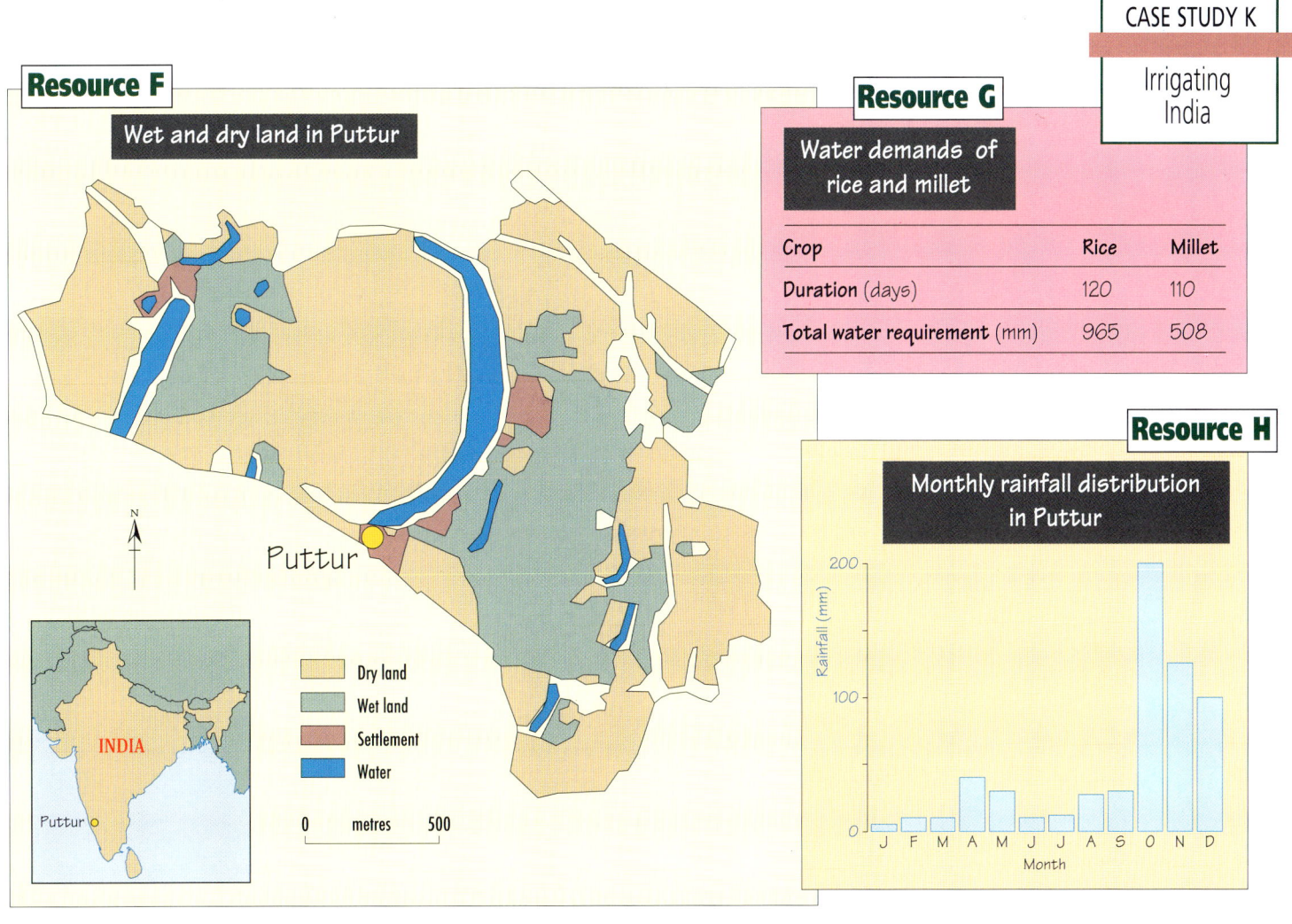

Monthly rainfall distribution in Puttur

Activities

You are asked to advise the government on designing a campaign to encourage farmers to adopt new farming practices. Answer the questions below, then write a brief report suggesting what the government should do to encourage change.

1 Complete the following paragraph:
Puttur is a village in _____ State, India, where crops such as rice, _____ and _____ are grown. The village depends on a _____ for its irrigation. The total rainfall is usually less than _____ mm a year. On irrigated land the farmers grow _____ and _____, and on unirrigated land they grow _____.

2 Look at the photos in Resource E. Match the labels below with the appropriate photo. Put them in order of the agricultural stages.
   Transplanting
   Threshing
   Growing
   Harvesting

3 Using Resources F and G, copy the map showing categories of land and mark the areas where you would plant rice and millet.

4 In what ways has irrigation made it possible for Mr Pillai to change his farming?

5 Using the resources on pages 103–105, describe the main differences in cropping patterns between wet and dry land. Why do these differences exist?

6 How may improved transport affect Mr Pillai's farming?

7 Study the text and Resource H.
a In which months are the crops grown in Puttur likely to be (i) sown and (ii) harvested?
b If the growing season for hyv rice is 120 days, use the figures in Resource G and the rainfall figures in Resource H to calculate how much *extra* water would be needed from irrigation for the rice crop to mature.

CASE STUDY K
Irrigating India

Key Question 3
Does irrigation always bring benefits?

The Indian Scientist – Update

Resource 1

Editorial

New evidence is coming to light that if India's irrigation potential is to be developed to the full there may be high costs as well as rich potential benefits.

Irrigation in India has been practised for centuries. Traditional means of raising water onto agricultural land, such as **Persian wheels** and **kavalais**, helped to increase yields. Over the last hundred years the building of huge dams has made it possible for over 16 million hectares to be irrigated by canals.

As the government develops plans for more canal irrigation, some scientists are suggesting that the costs may outweigh the benefits. The biggest scheme under discussion today is the *Narmada River Project*. The Narmada River is the largest westward flowing river in India. It is 1,300 kilometres long, and flows through central India to the sea north of Bombay. The government plans to build over 3,000 dams, large and small, along the Narmada River. The largest will be over 250 metres high, and large lakes will be created.

The benefits for those downstream may be dramatic. Nearly 2 million hectares of land will be irrigated, and 400 megawatts of **hydro-electric power** generation capacity will be created. Much higher productivity from the land may result.

But what of the costs? Research published in *The Ecologist* magazine suggests that more than 100,000 hectares of forest and good agricultural land will be drowned.

The sheer weight of the water trapped in the reservoirs could trigger earthquakes. As many as 1 million people will have to leave their homes and be re-housed outside the flooded area. Furthermore, if irrigation is not accompanied by good drainage to take surplus water off the fields, they may become **waterlogged** and saline, and consequently unusable for crops.

The Narmada River Project.

These costs are leading many people to press for a re-think on the project. They argue that small-scale schemes could produce just as great benefits without the damage either to people or to the environment that such a huge scheme will cause. In 1993, political opposition forced the World Bank to withdraw its support for the scheme, although the Indian government says that it is determined to go ahead.

One thing seems clear: while millions of farmers in India are crying out for extra water for their fields, it can't be provided free, and there are major costs as well as benefits that come with the development of irrigation.

Resource J — Large- and small-scale methods of irrigation.

(a) Persian wheel.

(b) Kavalai.

(c) A large dam.

CASE STUDY K

Irrigating India

Resource K — Not everybody is happy with large-scale irrigation schemes.

We spend too much money on large dams.

No one actually realises what environmental damage large dams cause.

Thousands of people like me will lose their homes when our land is flooded.

Unless the project is planned, some areas downstream may become waterlogged, and salinisation is a further problem.

Ordinary people are never consulted about these schemes.

Protest against the dams.

Activities

As part of your report to Oxfam you have to explain why there is opposition to some irrigation schemes in India. Using the information on these two pages, summarise the disadvantages of some large-scale irrigation schemes.

1 If you were a member of a family who lived just above the dam site and had to move and be re-housed because of the dam, how would you feel? Write a diary entry for the day you and your family were forced to move out of your home.

2 If you lived downstream of the dam site, how would you feel if you discovered that the government had decided *not* to build the dam and that as a result your land would not be irrigated? Describe what changes you had been planning to make on your farm when the irrigation water arrived.

3 Divide into groups. One half of each group prepare to argue the case *for* building a large dam for irrigation and electric power. The other half of the group prepare the case *against*. Discuss.

CASE STUDY K
Irrigating India

Further activities

Short-answer tasks

1 The importance of water cannot be underestimated. Study the diagram below, then list at least four reasons why water is important to the people shown.

Some uses of water in India.

2 Name three types of irrigation practised in India.

3 Outline the main advantages of large-scale irrigation schemes.

4 The figures below show how food grain production (measured in million tonnes) in India has changed over the last 40 years. What is the main trend here? How might it have been achieved?

	1950–51	1960–61	1970–71	1980–81	1990–91
Million tonnes grain	50	82	108	130	176

Find out about . . .

1 Several large-scale irrigation projects have been developed in Africa – the Aswan Dam in Egypt, the Kariba Dam in Zambia and the Volta Dam in Ghana. Find out about *one* of these schemes. List the main advantages and disadvantages of the project you choose.

2 Many of the new crops being planted in India are hyvs.
a What does this term mean, and what advantages do these crops have for a country like India?
b What was the 'Green Revolution'?

CASE STUDY K

Irrigating India

Library and research tasks

1 Find out how much aid has been sent to India since 1985, and how much of that aid has been spent on agriculture by:
a the UK government's Overseas Development Administration (ODA)
b by all other countries together.
(The ODA publishes brief summaries of overseas aid.)

2 Contact two charities that support work in India. Find out how much each one spends on agricultural and irrigation projects in India. Do their projects focus on large-scale or small-scale irrigation projects?

Group activity

You have already learned a little about the controversy over the building of dams along India's Narmada River. The diagram below summarises the main locations of the project and outlines some of the scheme's main benefits and consequences. Study it carefully.

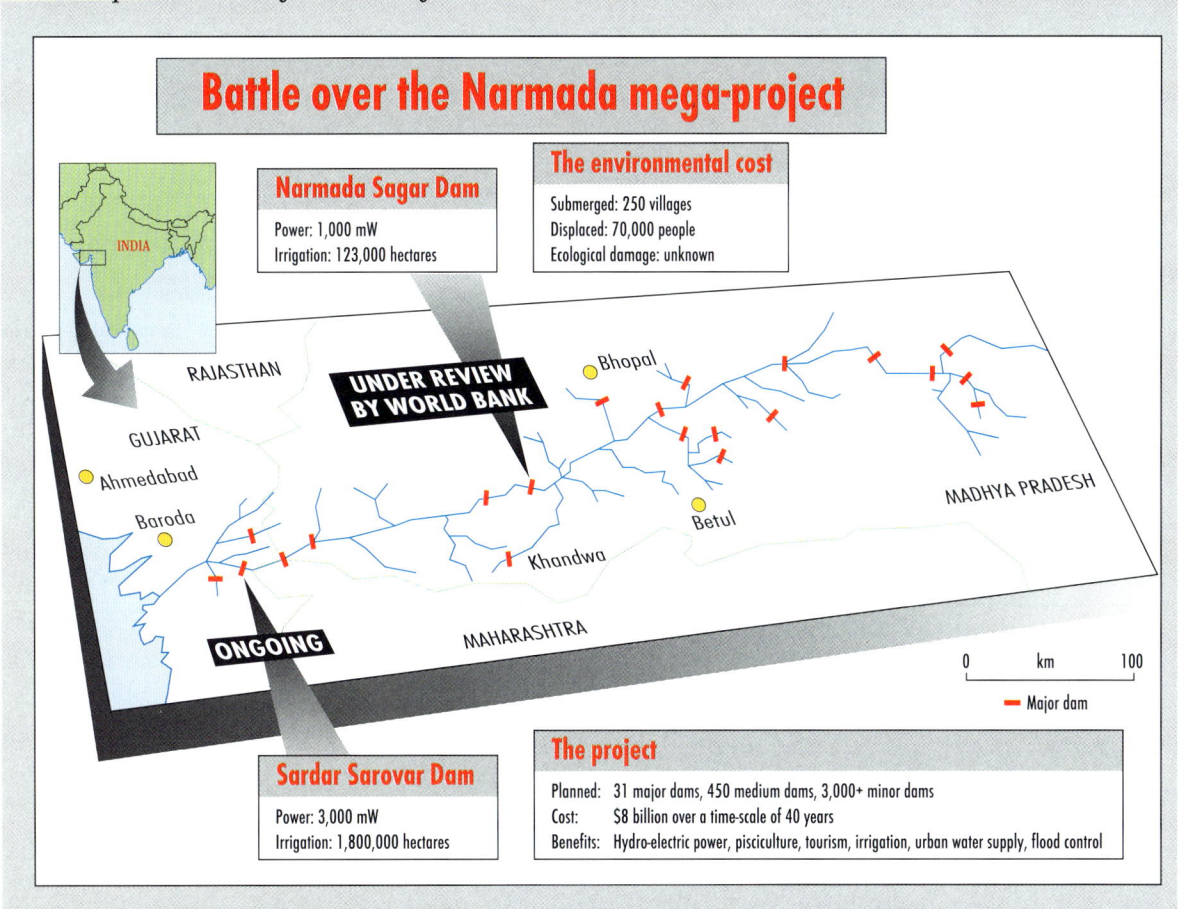

Battle over the Narmada mega-project

Narmada Sagar Dam
Power: 1,000 mW
Irrigation: 123,000 hectares

The environmental cost
Submerged: 250 villages
Displaced: 70,000 people
Ecological damage: unknown

UNDER REVIEW BY WORLD BANK

ONGOING

Sardar Sarovar Dam
Power: 3,000 mW
Irrigation: 1,800,000 hectares

The project
Planned: 31 major dams, 450 medium dams, 3,000+ minor dams
Cost: $8 billion over a time-scale of 40 years
Benefits: Hydro-electric power, pisciculture, tourism, irrigation, urban water supply, flood control

Community leaders from near the site of the proposed Narmada Sagar Dam write to your school asking you to join their protest against the project. In small groups, discuss whether you would support local people in their fight against the further development of dams on the Narmada River.

If your group votes to support the protest, what help could you actually give? If your group decides not to support the protest, write a letter explaining to the protesters why you decided not to support them.

CASE STUDY K
Irrigating India

Key Terms

alluvium sands and gravels deposited by rivers. In the Ganges valley these can be over 3,000 metres thick. They are porous and so store enormous quantities of groundwater.

hydro-electric power electricity generated by using the energy of falling water.

hyv high-yielding variety, bred to increase yield of grain.

kavalai well irrigation system. Bullocks walk down a ramp, raising the water by pulling up a bucket attached by a rope over a pulley.

monsoon an Arabic word meaning 'season'. It refers to the main rainy season, which over most of India is between June and November.

Persian wheel another traditional system of well irrigation. Bullocks operate a wheel by constantly turning a heavy wooden axle. Buckets attached to the wheel are lowered into and raised from the well, emptying automatically into the irrigation channel.

pesticide chemical designed to kill pests in the soil and on plants.

saline water salty water. High concentrations of salts may develop in the soil as a result of poor drainage associated with irrigation. Crops will not grow if there is too much salt in the soil.

tank small artificial storage reservoir, common in south and east India.

waterlogged soil soil that is badly drained, permanently marshy.

Key Understandings

- Rainfall in most parts of India is often not enough to guarantee full agricultural production, so irrigation is important. Already 33% of the total area is irrigated, and this could be doubled.

- Irrigation has encouraged the use of new seed varieties, chemical fertilisers and pesticides. Crop production has more than doubled since 1960 as a result.

- Other factors have also encouraged farmers to change: the growth of towns means bigger markets; improved roads have made it easier and cheaper to get goods in and out of the villages.

- Despite the benefits of irrigation, it may also have high costs. Many people may have to be moved to make way for big schemes. Good land and forest may be spoiled or flooded.

- Despite the costs, irrigation remains one of the most important demands of farmers in India today, as it offers the best guarantee of improving crop yields and living standards.

Postscript

Agricultural production has grown considerably over the last four decades, but the cost of achieving the increase in output has been high. About one-third of government spending on agriculture each year at the end of the 1980s was on irrigation – but much of this was for maintaining existing projects rather than developing new ones.

Today, about 40% of India's potential for irrigation remains undeveloped, and many existing projects are falling into disrepair.

Case Study L

Sokoto River Project, Nigeria

Nigeria is a large country in West Africa. It stretches from the edge of the arid Sahel south to a humid rainforest environment on the coast. It has a population of nearly 90 million people. Its economy used to be based on agriculture and cash crop exports, particularly of cocoa, palm oil, cotton and groundnuts. However, oil became the mainstay of the economy in the 1960s and '70s. Unfortunately, agriculture was neglected, and with low oil prices in the 1980s, Nigeria suffered, finding it difficult to pay for the food it now had to import. There is still a great deal of poverty.

> In your school holidays you are asked by Rural Action, a charity running projects in the developing world, to report on the success of water resource development in Nigeria. You decide to focus on the dry north-west of the country. Your job is to find out about the existing development projects and assess how successful they have been, so that you can advise Rural Action on how to design their own new projects.

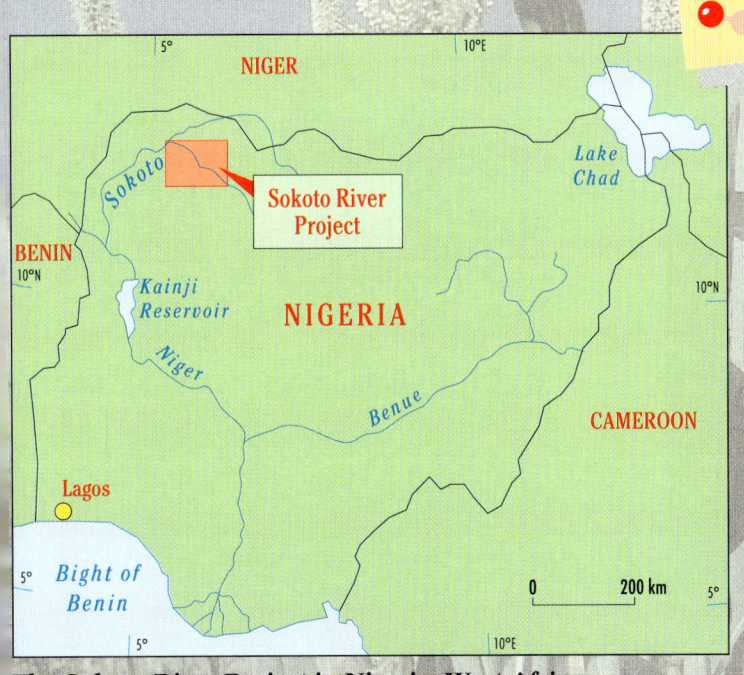

The Sokoto River Project in Nigeria, West Africa.

CASE STUDY L
Sokoto River Project, Nigeria

Key Question 1
How have local farmers adapted to the environment of northern Nigeria?

Resource A

Tsamiya, Nigeria, 27th September

Dear John and Cathy

I'm writing this at the end of September, sitting in Tsamiya village where I've been working in the flat land above the Sokoto River. The village, with its thatched mud houses, is quiet. It hasn't rained now for almost two weeks, and I think the **dry season** has begun. It will not rain again until next May or June. The grass is still green, but already the crops in the fields are turning yellow as harvest-time approaches.

The fields are an amazing sight, because the Hausa people plant several crops together in the same field, and the millet and sorghum are over 3 metres high. The farmers will soon bring in the millet, followed in November by the sorghum. Both are important **subsistence** crops, and much will be stored in thatched (mud) granaries and eaten through the year. Later on, other crops like cotton and groundnuts (peanuts), will be harvested. After that, the fields on the higher land will stand bare until the rains next year. However, they're still important, because the village animals and cattle herds of nomadic Fulani will graze on the thick stubble.

Meanwhile the farmers will be busy on the low-lying land by the river. Much of this has been flooded during the wet season. They grow rice in the wettest parts, and flood-resistant sorghum elsewhere. Once they are harvested, the vital dry-season vegetable cultivation begins. The range of crops is vast, for example onions, tomatoes, potatoes, green and red peppers, tobacco, different kinds of melon and calabash. They also grow cassava, which is important when the rains fail.

It's amazing how farming is adapted to the cycle of the seasons. The main crops don't have very high yields, but all are resistant to drought. Also, all farmers have fields on both high and low land. Crops on high land away from the river depend on rainfall entirely. If there's a drought, these crops can fail. Land near the river, which is irrigated naturally by floodwater, is very important in dry years, although if there's a lot of rain there can be damaging floods. Either way, the dry-season vegetables are an important source of food and cash. Some farmers even irrigate them using wells dug into the **water table**.

Love, *Sally*

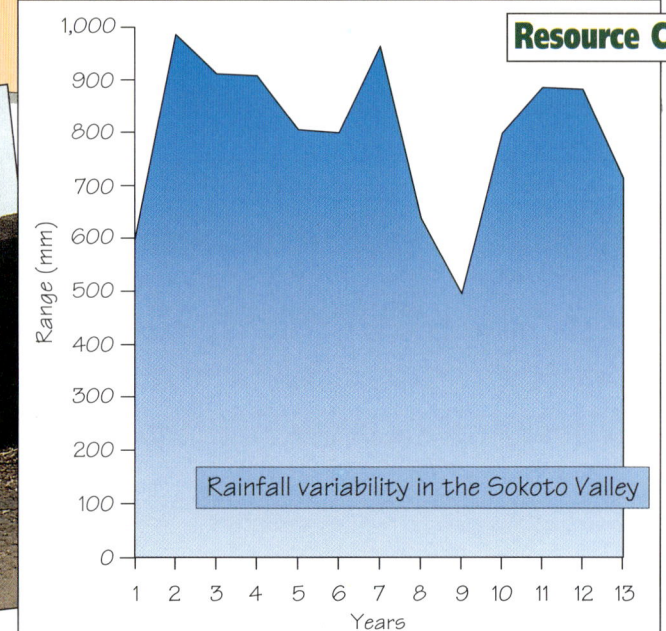

Resource B

A Hausa village in northern Nigeria.

Resource C

Rainfall variability in the Sokoto Valley

CASE STUDY L
Sokoto River Project, Nigeria

Resource D

AGRICULTURAL CALENDAR

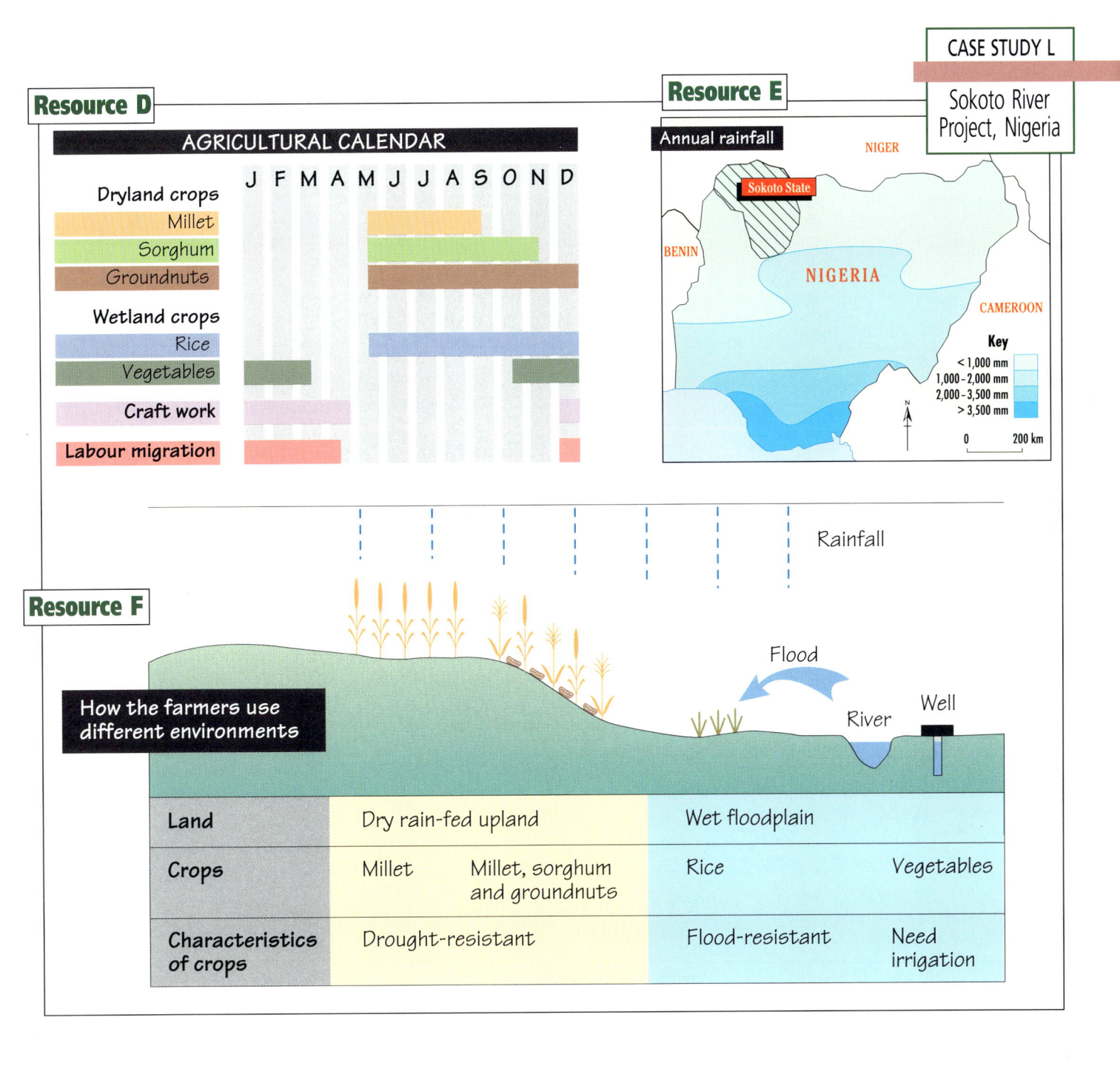

J F M A M J J A S O N D

Dryland crops
- Millet
- Sorghum
- Groundnuts

Wetland crops
- Rice
- Vegetables

Craft work

Labour migration

Resource E

Annual rainfall

Key
- < 1,000 mm
- 1,000 – 2,000 mm
- 2,000 – 3,500 mm
- > 3,500 mm

0   200 km

Resource F

How the farmers use different environments

Rainfall · Flood · River · Well

Land	Dry rain-fed upland		Wet floodplain	
Crops	Millet	Millet, sorghum and groundnuts	Rice	Vegetables
Characteristics of crops	Drought-resistant		Flood-resistant	Need irrigation

Activities

Rural Action shows you the letter and the other resources on these two pages, and asks you to write a short report about farming in the Sokoto Valley for their Africa Director. Answer the questions below to check that you understand the situation, then write your report.

1 When is the rainy season in northern Nigeria?

2 Which season do you think is shown in the picture of the village (Resource B)?

3 What could farmers do in the dry season if they could not make dry-season gardens?

4 Make a list of the ways in which farmers deal with **a** drought and **b** flood.

5 Make a list of the main crops grown on the high land and the low riverside land.

Now write your report.

CASE STUDY L

Sokoto River Project, Nigeria

Key Question 2
How could development projects improve on existing local agriculture?

Resource G

IRRIGATION IN SOKOTO VALLEY
THE OPTIONS

The biggest problem in the Sokoto Valley is the short **rainy season**. Crop **yields** are low, and drought is a constant problem. As a result, although local farmers work hard, agriculture is unproductive. At the same time, the river is full of water which runs to waste. There are several different ways in which the area could be developed.

1) Improved rain-fed cultivation: Crop yields could be improved in spite of the short rainy season and dry years, if existing cultivation methods are improved. Drought-resistant varieties of sorghum or millet could be introduced, and plant-breeding at agricultural stations could improve local varieties of crops. Higher yields could also be obtained using chemical fertiliser and pesticides. These chemicals are costly, but if they help give higher yields, farmers will be able to pay for them. Almost all farmers could benefit, but even if they adopted the new technology they would still be exposed to serious droughts.

2) Large-scale irrigation: If a dam were built across the river, surplus water could be stored in the wet season. This could then be used to irrigate a large area in the dry season. A canal would carry water from the dam site to the area of best soils. A further network of smaller canals would be needed to distribute the water onto the crops. The dam and **irrigation** scheme would be expensive, but it would improve yields. It would also allow crops to be grown continuously, with high-yielding maize in the wet season followed by wheat in the dry season. High yields will also demand 'green revolution' chemicals like the improved dryland cropping strategy described above. Farmers will pay for them by selling their crops. They can also be made to use some of their extra profits to pay the government back for its investment. The result will be a modern agricultural project which could contribute to national food needs. The danger is that the cost of developing the project would be so great that the extra crops could never pay for it. There is also a risk that farmers would themselves not make enough money to pay for their water and chemicals.

3) Small-scale irrigation: The main problem with large-scale irrigation projects is that they are expensive both to build and to run. They also demand that farmers work together in large groups. Farmers may be reluctant to tie themselves down in this way. Another strategy is to encourage small-scale irrigation, using small petrol pumps and shallow wells. These are cheaper, and could be subsidised for a few years until their use becomes widespread. Farmers could borrow money to buy a pump and to pay for a well to be dug, and then pay the money back over three years by selling their crops. This could only be done where water is close to the ground surface, near a river. Only a few farmers could gain from this form of irrigation, but it would not cost the government much to establish the programme and farmers could each choose whether to get involved.

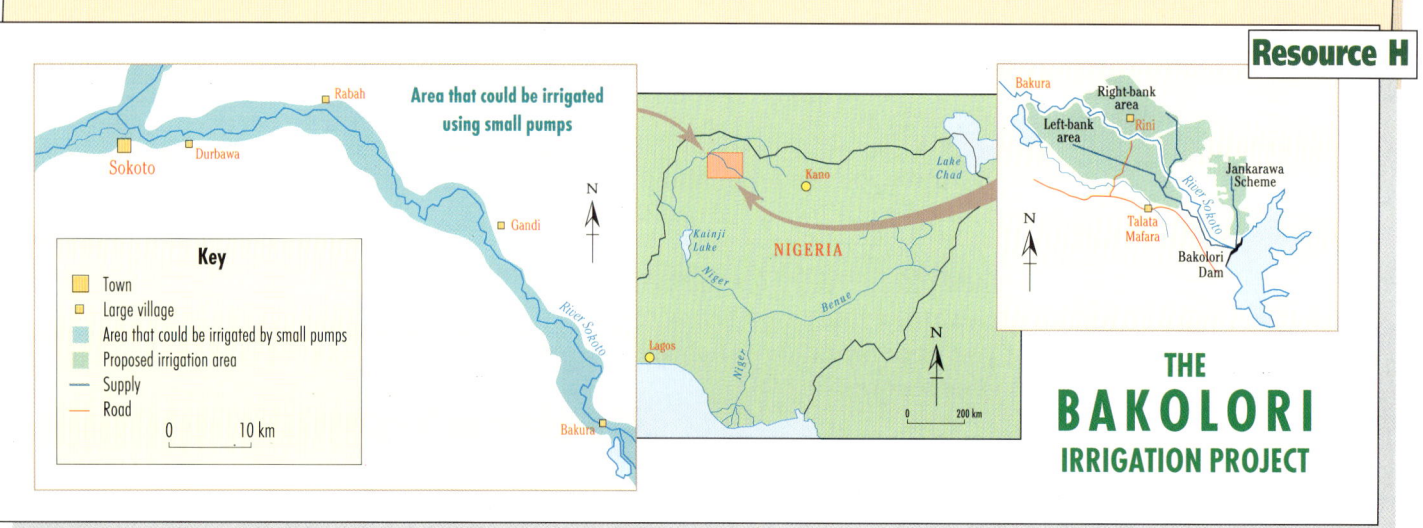

Resource H

THE BAKOLORI IRRIGATION PROJECT

Resource I

Rainfed crops in the Sokoto Valley.

CASE STUDY L

Sokoto River Project, Nigeria

Resource J

A petrol pump used for small-scale irrigation in northern Nigeria.

Activities

The development charity Rural Action has a small technical committee. After you have read the consultant's report (Resource G), they ask you to recommend which of the three development options you think would be best for the local farmers. Give reasons for your answer.

Now use the resources on pages 114–115 to answer the following questions. They could be used in a class debate about small-scale versus large-scale irrigation.

1 What is the biggest problem facing agriculture in Sokoto?

2 Why does irrigation increase crop growth?

3 How can crop yields be increased without irrigation?

4 How are the costs of irrigation, fertiliser or pesticide to be paid for?

5 Give two reasons why small-scale irrigation might be better than large-scale irrigation projects.

CASE STUDY L

Sokoto River Project, Nigeria

Key Question 3
How successful is the irrigation project on the Sokoto River?

The development option actually selected in the Sokoto Valley in the 1970s was the large-scale irrigation scheme supplied by a dam. The project is called the Bakolori Agricultural Project. The dam covers 12,000 ha, and the irrigation scheme 30,000 ha. It was finally finished (after some delays) in 1982.

New Dam – a Mixed Blessing

Resource K

Our reporter Sunday Ugbe writes from Sokoto

It is harvest time on the massive irrigation scheme on the Sokoto River. The huge fields dwarf the few farmers standing on the irrigation canals watching the imported combine harvesters plough into the sea of ripened wheat. All around the project is **unproductive land**. The bush is dry and desolate, as the dry season comes to its end. Almost 9,000 hectares of wheat is being grown under irrigation using water stored in the dam, at a time of year when there is normally no cultivation. This is an impressive achievement, but there is a cost. Large areas are not cultivated, either because of water shortages due to broken pumps and canals, or because farmers cannot afford to pay for water. Yields are poor, because the area is too hot for wheat. Also, supplies of fertiliser are limited, and the tractors keep breaking down.

The reservoir is filling up with silt caused by soil erosion upstream. Many farmers further down the river claim that the dam has reduced the floods which once irrigated their own rice fields and allowed them to grow vegetables in the dry season. They say the dam has simply moved the irrigated area, not extended it. The fishermen downstream also complain that the dam has reduced their catch. As a result, many fishermen have had to move away. Some have come to the dam to fish, but their hopes of finding lots of fish in the reservoir have been disappointed, so only a few can fish there.

The project cost far more than expected, and it is not paying for itself. Farmers cannot afford the full cost of supplying water because their yields are too small, and the government is having to buy crops at high prices to help farmers keep going. This helps the larger farmers, but many small farmers have given up and gone away. Others have left because there are new problems with diseases. Mosquitoes and other parasites breed in the water in the canals, and many children have fallen sick. The new road to the project makes the farmers realise that other areas may offer a better chance, and many have left to start again elsewhere. Only the large farmers and those with wages from jobs with the project itself are doing well.

The Bakolori Dam.

Resource L

I think the irrigation project is a good idea, because I have had all my land developed. My son works in the agricultural office and I get my fertiliser and pesticide from him. Now, my yields are much higher, and I have managed to buy more land. I grow maize and wheat and sell them to the project.

Umaru Dan Galadima, a large-scale farmer

I have lost because of the project. I only have three fields, and one of those was buried under a canal. I'm still waiting for compensation and new land. I can't afford fertiliser and pesticide, and the tractor driver doesn't come when I need him. I try to grow millet and sorghum as I used to before the project, but they are still growing when the tractors arrive to plant wheat, and sometimes my crops are destroyed. They say it is illegal to grow traditional crops, but I can't pay for water, so I have to grow them. Last year I had to sell a field to buy grain for my family.

Ali Maradun, a small-scale farmer

CASE STUDY L

Sokoto River Project, Nigeria

Resource M

Potential and actual crop yields on the Bakolori Irrigation Project

Crop	Potential yield (kg/ha)	Actual yield (kg/ha)	Actual as percentage of potential
Groundnuts	2,250	1,555	69
Rice	3,500	1,952	56
Wheat	3,000	1,250	
Beans	6,225	1,770	
Tomatoes	18,500	6,225	
Maize	4,000	900	
Cotton	2,100	351	

Resource N

A comparison of the planned area of irrigation on the Bakolori Project, and the area actually irrigated

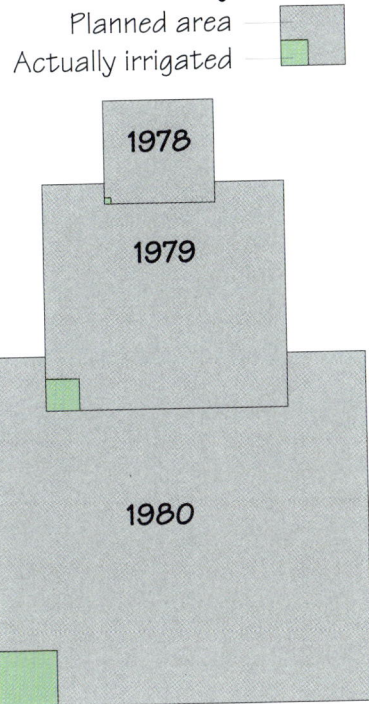

Key
- Planned area
- Actually irrigated

1978
1979
1980

Resource O

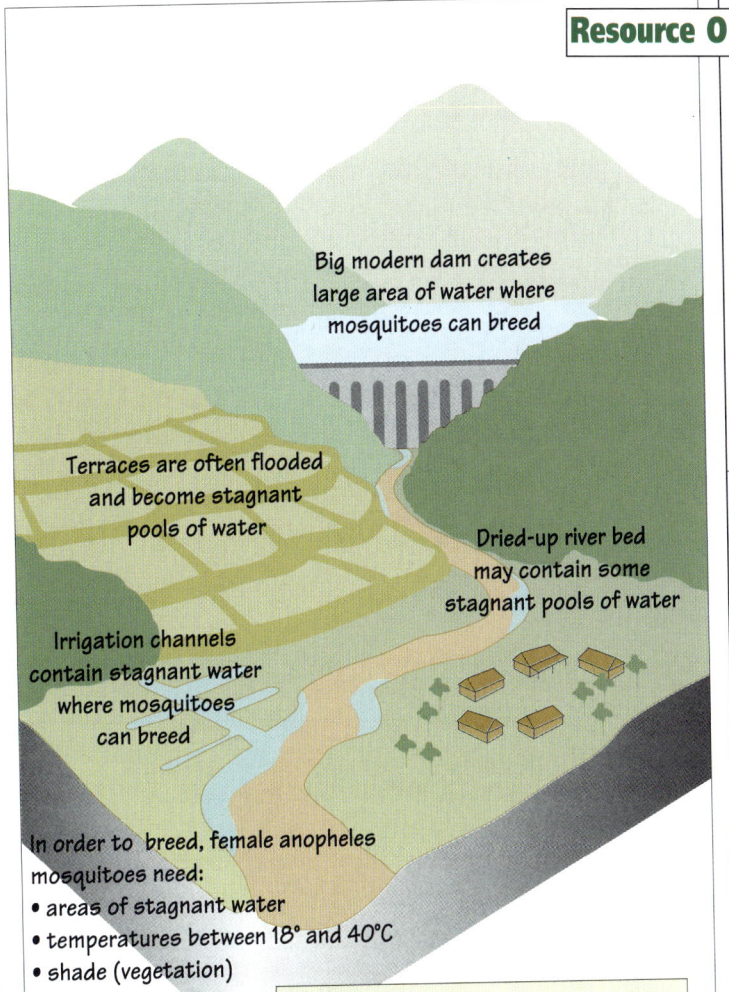

Big modern dam creates large area of water where mosquitoes can breed

Terraces are often flooded and become stagnant pools of water

Dried-up river bed may contain some stagnant pools of water

Irrigation channels contain stagnant water where mosquitoes can breed

In order to breed, female anopheles mosquitoes need:
- areas of stagnant water
- temperatures between 18° and 40°C
- shade (vegetation)
- plentiful rainfall
- a nearby source of human blood

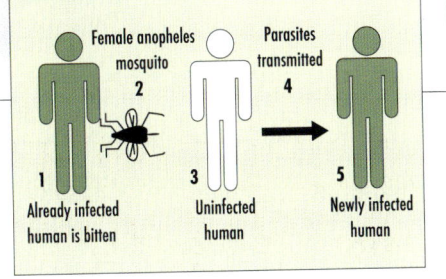

1. Already infected human is bitten
2. Female anopheles mosquito
3. Uninfected human
4. Parasites transmitted
5. Newly infected human

Resource P

Number of farmers growing rice and dry-season vegetables before and after the dam was built

	% of farms	
	Before dam	After dam
Growing rice	68	25
Growing dry-season vegetables	91	18

CASE STUDY L

Sokoto River Project, Nigeria

Activities

Rural Action has heard that the irrigation scheme developed on the Sokoto River as a result of the consultant's report has not been successful. The charity asks you to investigate this claim, and presents you with the resources on pages 116–117 as evidence.

When you have read the newspaper article and other resources, you must decide whether, on balance, the chosen scheme was a success or not. Answer the questions below individually.

1 Examine Resource M. How do the actual yields achieved compare with those which should have been possible? Copy the table, and complete the final column.

2 What problems seem to have been caused by the dam? Which local groups of people are suffering as a result?

3a From Resource N, estimate the area that is actually being irrigated compared with the area that was planned. Does this suggest the scheme was a success?
b Why are some areas in the irrigation scheme not receiving any water?

4 Why does the introduction of irrigation and the building of the dam cause an increase in malaria?

5a If you were a small farmer, what do you think you could do to keep your family alive and well fed?
b Get together with a small group of friends to discuss your answers. On balance, do you think that building the dam was a success or a failure?

Now write your final report to Rural Action. What kind of agricultural development projects should have priority in the future?

Further activities

Short-answer tasks

1 What problems face farmers in areas like Sokoto in the dry zone of West Africa? Give three examples.

2 Using the map below, in which other countries would you expect farmers to have similar problems to those in Sokoto?

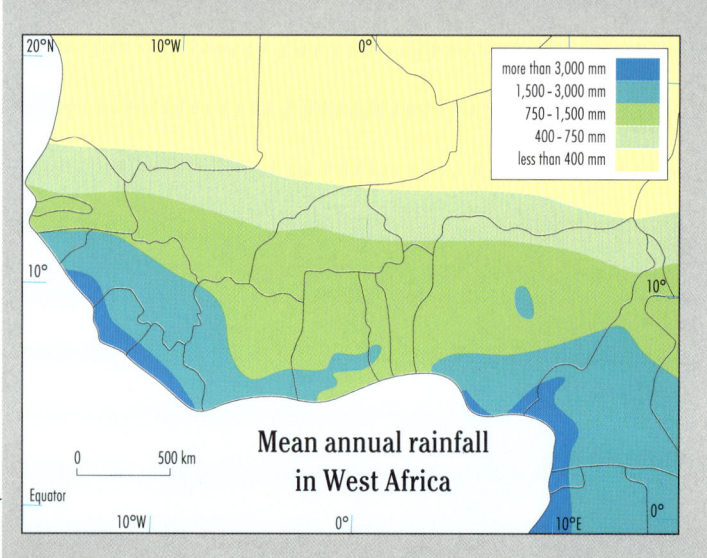

Mean annual rainfall in West Africa

3 What do you think those people involved in 'agricultural development' are trying to achieve?

4a Using the table (right), which shows monthly rainfall in northern Nigeria, calculate the total annual rainfall.
b Draw a bar graph to represent this data.
c Identify and list the three months with the highest rainfall and the months with the lowest rainfall in the year.
d Which months would be most suitable for growing crops?

Month	Mm
January	0
February	0
March	0
April	2
May	23
June	172
July	162
August	200
September	242
October	37
November	0
December	0

Monthly annual rainfall at Sokoto Airport in northern Nigeria.

5 Suggest three good aspects and three bad aspects of irrigation as a way of achieving agricultural development.

CASE STUDY L

Sokoto River Project, Nigeria

Find out about . . .

1 Find out about industry in Nigeria. Make a map of the location of the largest cities. Try to find Lagos, Abuja (the federal capital), Warri, Ibadan and Kano. Mark on the map the area where oil is found, and the routes of railways and major roads.

2 Write a short report outlining reasons why the Nigerian government might want to develop agriculture as well as industry. You might like to consider the following ideas:

- Without successful agriculture, people will flood to the towns where there are too few jobs for them.
- Unless agriculture is successful, there will be no food for workers in industries to eat.
- Unless agriculture is successful, rural people will not have the money to buy the goods produced in the factories.
- Successful agriculture is needed to produce cash crops which can be exported.

3 A number of projects are suggested for development in the Sokoto area of Nigeria. These are listed below with their costs. There is a total of £150 million to spend. You are asked by Rural Action to suggest which projects it should recommend to the Nigerian government. List those schemes you would fund, and say why.

Project	Cost (£ million)
Building better roads to the south	50
Building a hospital	85
New agricultural research on high-yielding crops	25
Research on drought-resistant crops	20
Agricultural experts to train farmers	35
Programme for farmers to train each other	20
New large irrigation scheme	100
Repair of existing irrigation schemes	50
Subsidised fertiliser for farmers	65
Subsidised irrigation pumps for farmers	35

Library and research tasks

1 Find out how the annual rainfall in other African countries compares with that in Nigeria, and consider what agricultural problems they may have. You might look in particular at Ethiopia, Kenya, Sierra Leone and Zimbabwe.

2 Find out about the problem of drought in the Sahel and Ethiopia. Write a short report on the ways in which farmers have traditionally responded to the problems of rainfall in Africa, and the problems they currently face. (Case Study O develops this theme further.)

3 Using an atlas, plan a three-week trip in West Africa which would enable you to learn more about the problems of agriculture in different environments.

CASE STUDY L
Sokoto River Project, Nigeria

Key Terms

dry season for much of the year, Nigeria experiences high atmospheric pressure, which means there is little chance of rain.

irrigation the application of water to crops, particularly in areas where rainfall would otherwise be inadequate for those crops to grow. It is important to apply the right amount of water at the right time.

rainy season when the sun is at its most intense (around June in the northern hemisphere), the tropics experience low pressure which sucks in moist air, giving a high probability of heavy rain.

subsistence many small farmers only grow crops for their own and their household's use. These are *subsistence crops*.

unproductive land land that is infertile and grows poor crops is unproductive.

water table the level underground at which rocks are saturated with water. This water can be reached by sinking wells.

yield the amount of useful material obtained from a food crop in a single growing season, usually described in kilograms per hectare.

Key Understandings

- Farming activity is usually adapted to the physical conditions of the environment in which it is located.

- Technology can be used to alter patterns of farming activity with beneficial as well as sometimes unforeseen consequences.

- Different methods of irrigation are appropriate for different circumstances.

Case Study M

The Mexican Oil Industry

To understand any country's attempts to make its way in the world, we need to know about its geography and its history. Mexico is no exception. It is part of the Spanish-speaking world: why? It is an economically developing country, but next door is the USA, which is the most powerful nation on earth: does this cause any problems and what opportunities does it provide? What resources does Mexico have, and how successfully are they being developed?

Mexico has had an oil industry for nearly a century. Since the early days of the industry the Mexicans have been suspicious of large transnational companies developing the **oil** (and taking the profits). At one stage all the foreign companies were nationalised – without compensation, which made Mexico very unpopular with its rich neighbour, the USA.

> You work for an international oil company. At a conference last week in Dallas you heard that Mexico was looking for partners to expand its oil production. You think your firm should move in. However, before you can ask the Board, you need more information. Your boss has told you that there have been problems in the past in Mexico. You request a summary on Mexico's oil history from the company library.

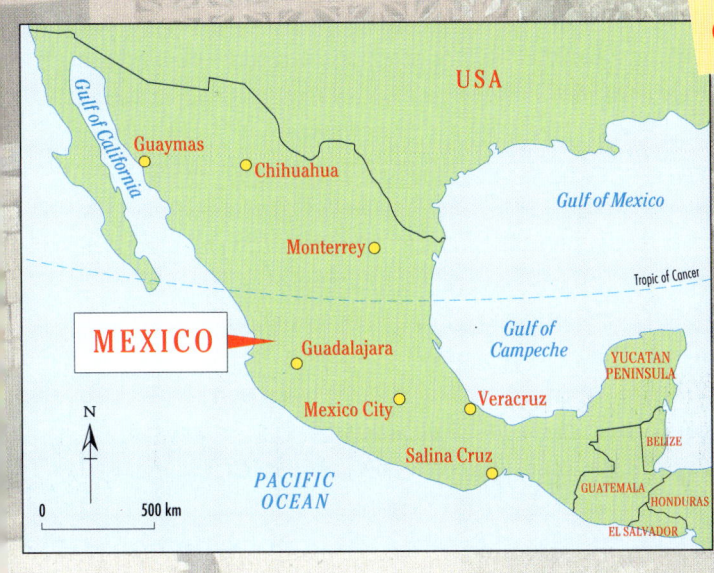

Mexico.

CASE STUDY M

The Mexican Oil Industry

Key Question 1
Why is the past important in planning the future?

Resource A

MEMO

REF: History of Mexican oil industry
From: Librarian

The first oil well was drilled in Mexico in 1869 and the first commercial find made in 1904. Since then Mexico's oil industry has passed through three phases: a boom-and-bust cycle in the first third of the century; a period of recovery and modest growth between 1940 and 1972; and since 1972 an oil bonanza which has catapulted Mexico into fourth place in the world league of **petroleum** producers.

In 1910 large British and American companies moved into Mexico. They bought out many of the pioneers, acquired their wells and concessions, and co-ordinated exploration: they found the famous Golden Lane field. Output soared as the First World War increased demand: almost all the production was exported. For a brief period in the 1920s Mexico was second only to the USA as a world oil producer. But by the beginning of the 1930s production had plummeted to a fifth of that a decade earlier. The British company El Aguila (managed by Shell) and the American Standard Oil of New Jersey, which between them accounted for over half Mexico's oil industry, became extremely unpopular and in 1938, on the urging of the oil workers' union, the revolutionary government seized the assets of all the oil companies and created Petroleos Mexicanos (shortened to Pemex) to run the industry. This almost brought joint British and American military intervention; instead, an international boycott of Mexican oil was organised. The turmoil of the Second World War and its aftermath and an agreement to pay compensation helped return Mexico to international respectability. Oil production gradually rose but output failed to keep up with the growing demands of industry and of a population growing at over 3% per annum; Mexico had to increasingly rely upon imported oil. Then came 1972.

1972 was a turning point in the development of the Mexican oil industry. It was in that year that the first of a whole family of new oil fields was discovered in the southern state of Chiapas. Almost every well drilled subsequently found oil and soon it was apparent that the reservoirs of oil extended for over 200 km north-eastwards under the southern end of the Gulf of Mexico – the Bay of Campeche – and southwards towards Guatemala. Higher oil prices made the new discoveries economical to exploit and transformed the prospects of the petroleum industry and the country at large.

The impact of these discoveries was rapid. In 1973 production surpassed the peak, achieved half a century earlier; in 1975 Mexico once again was producing more than she consumed. In 1977 the decision was taken to boost the export of crude oil to provide some of the capital needed to develop the new oil and gas **reserves** more fully. A lot of effort went into proving new reserves: with the price of oil during the 1970s continuing to rise – at times dramatically – proven reserves were translated by overseas bankers into assets on which they were prepared to lend money. Mexico borrowed heavily. Between 1977 and 1980 alone, Pemex obtained loans of over £12,600 million; by the end of 1980 these accounted for 37% of all Mexico's foreign debt. Within ten years, 70% of Mexico's oil was coming from under the Gulf waters. Some of the borrowed capital was used to create new pipelines and refining plants onshore; some to begin the building of giant petrochemicals complexes. In 1984 Mexico produced a record 1,024 million barrels of crude oil of which a little over a half was exported and the rest piped to Mexican refineries. Refined and manufactured products are many times more valuable, and if they are exported can bring in a much higher income for the country than crude oil. Since 1984 the proportion of oil refined at home has increased slightly and Mexico is close to becoming self-sufficient in some of the basic petrochemicals which underpin many of the modern products we now take for granted; but overall output has fallen a little. By 1990 Mexico had declared oil reserves of about 66,450 million barrels, enough to keep current production continuing for another 60 years.

Resource B

Mexican oil production 1904 – 72

CASE STUDY M

The Mexican Oil Industry

Resource D

Resource C

Reserves at 1st July 1968 (millions of barrels)
- △ 4,500 – 17,000
- △ 900 – 4,500
- △ 350 – 900
- △ 100 – 350
- ▲ under 100

Producing areas
- Major (red)
- Minor (pink)

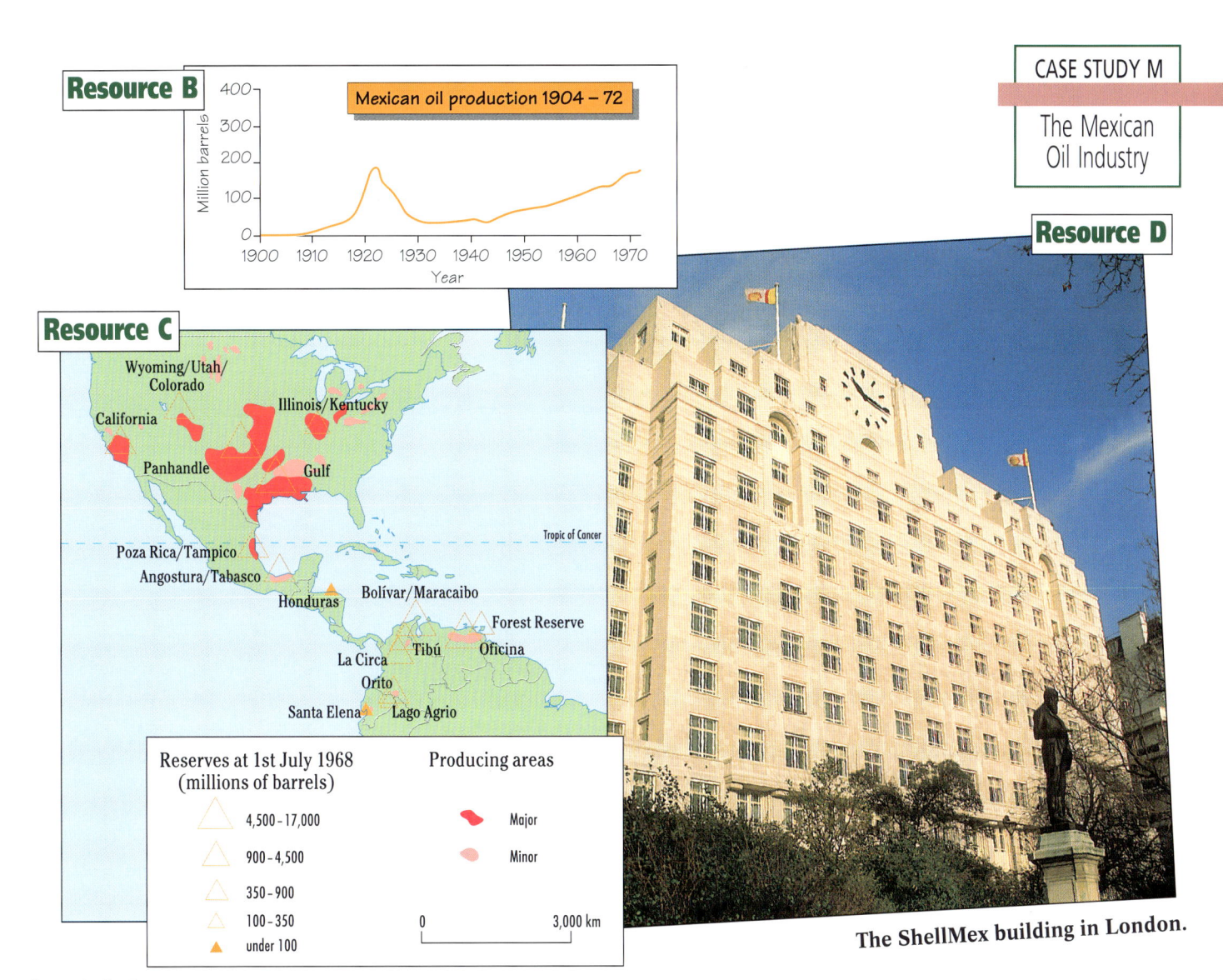

The ShellMex building in London.

Activities

Before you write your proposal to the Board, answer the following questions, to make sure you understand the information in the resources on these two pages.

1 How would you describe the change in oil production in the 30 years before 1972: declining, stable, slightly increasing, expanding rapidly?

2 What parts of the USA do you associate with oil? What other Latin American country is an important oil producer?

3 What is the origin of the name 'ShellMex'?

4 Draw a table like the one below:

1900–1940	1940–72	Post-1972

Write up to five statements in each column to describe the state of the Mexican oil industry during these periods.

5 Look at Resources B and C. Write a short introduction to your summary report to the Board, describing the location of Mexican oilfields and the trend of oil production this century.

6 What is different in the boom of 1972 onwards from that of the 1920s? You need to argue to the Board that this new boom will not 'go bust' and that your company should be 'part of the action'.

Now write a proposal to your oil company's Board, asking them to become involved in developing Mexico's oil reserves. Explain the benefits that you think are likely for the company.

CASE STUDY M

The Mexican Oil Industry

Key Question 2
Has oil been a good or a bad thing for Mexico?

Judging from the history of Mexico's oil industry, you feel excited, but also confused. Excited, because there is a lot of oil in Mexico and your company could possibly earn big profits. Confused, because on the face of it Mexico has huge resources: why should Mexico want to seek help from foreign companies? You seek more advice, this time from your company's department of economic analysis.

Resource E

MEMO

REF: Oil and the economic situation of Mexico
From: Economic Analysis Department

The new-found oil wealth has proved a mixed blessing: some regions of Mexico and some Mexicans have benefited but others have suffered. Clearly, that Mexico is a leading oil producer cannot be a bad thing! And it is certainly true that the new oil of the 1970s led to industrial developments and new economic opportunities and, at a time when the price of oil was rising and other exports were flagging, this boosted Mexico's fortunes dramatically.

For example, oil exports rose from virtually nothing in 1972 to be worth $10 billion in 1980, and between $14 and $16 billion in each of the years 1982 to 1985: over two-thirds of the country's export income. But it can be dangerous to be so dependent on just one commodity.

Just as the price of oil soared in the 1970s, so it began to slacken in the first half of the 1980s and then tumbled in 1986: in real terms (after adjusting for inflation and the changing value of the dollar, the currency in which international oil prices are measured), the price of oil at the end of 1988 was no more than it had been at the beginning of 1974: at the end of the 1980s a barrel of oil was worth less than a quarter, in real terms, what it had been in 1980.

In 1989, oil and natural gas exports brought in only about $7.3 billion. By now Mexico was importing large quantities of goods. Now, suddenly, oil earnings met the cost of only one-third of the total import bill; five years previously the entire costs of the country's imports had been covered by just two-thirds of the income from her exports of oil.

Such violent swings in price helped create economic instability and had an impact on Mexico's international reputation. Whereas in the 1970s international banks had bent over backwards to lend Mexico money, they got cold feet in the 1980s. In 1982, when Mexico found she had over-stretched herself and couldn't meet immediate interest repayments, she lost the confidence of her creditor banks and precipitated what became the international debt crisis and a world recession. The crisis produced fundamental changes in Mexico: the peso fell in value, investments dried up, and, for the average person, growing prosperity was replaced by belt-tightening austerity.

Eventually Mexico had to get help from the International Monetary Fund. The Fund required Mexico to adopt free-market principles, to float the peso, remove subsidies and restrictive practices, reduce government expenditure and expose industry to international competition. Now, many of the reforms have been put into effect and international confidence is beginning to return. The rights of foreign enterprises entering joint ventures with state or private corporations have been safeguarded.

Many believe that without the oil discoveries, Mexico would have borrowed less and her current debt problems would not be so serious. Some believe that the windfall of the oil bonanza was largely frittered away – used partly to delay difficult decisions which should have been taken earlier. But those decisions have now been taken and Mexico looks an interesting area for the company to consider.

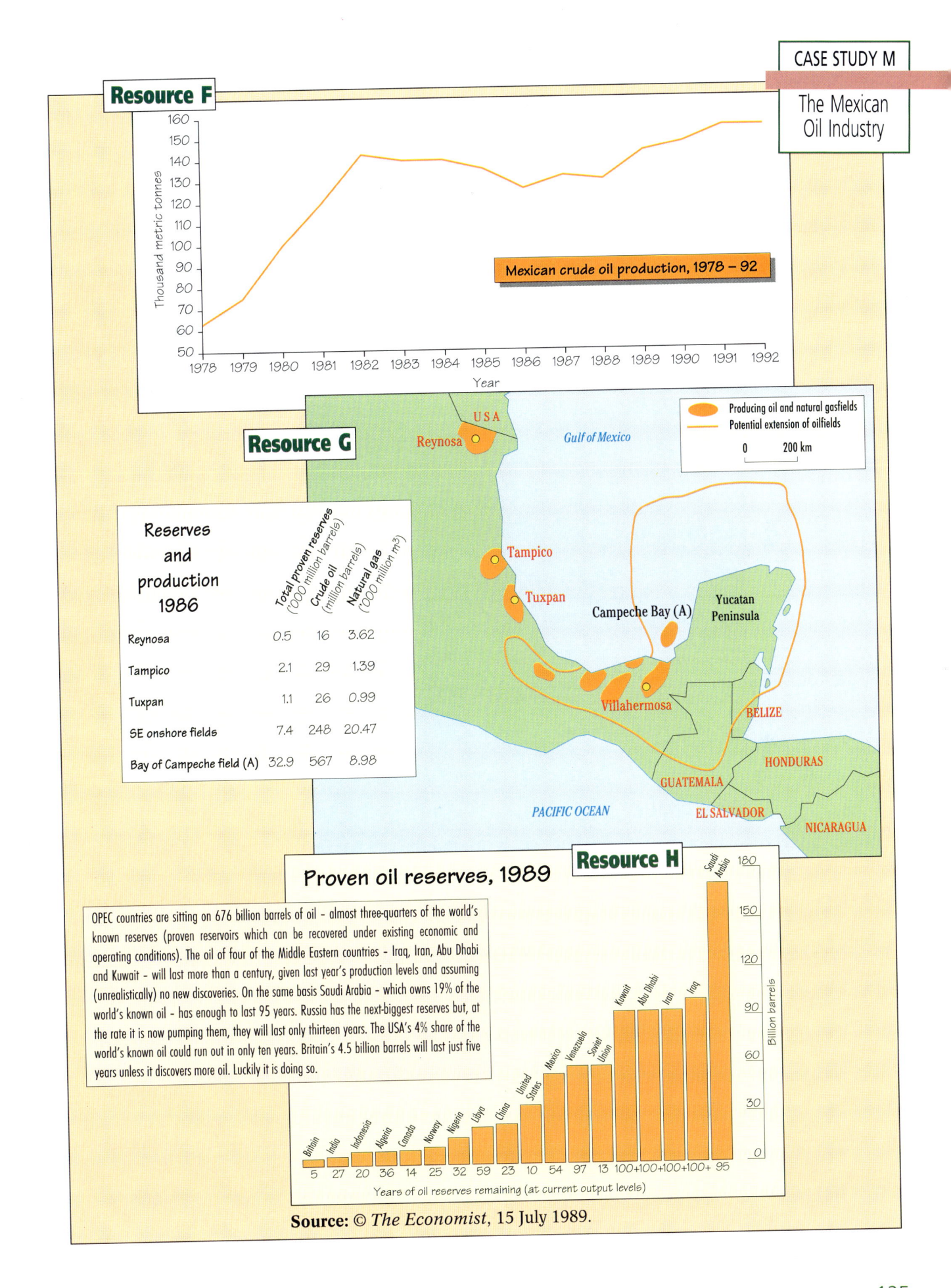

CASE STUDY M
The Mexican Oil Industry

Resource F

Mexican crude oil production, 1978 – 92

(Line graph: Thousand metric tonnes vs Year 1978–1992; values rising from ~63 in 1978 to ~143 in 1982, dipping to ~128 in 1986, then rising to ~160 by 1991–92.)

Resource G

Reserves and production 1986	Total proven reserves ('000 million barrels)	Crude oil (million barrels)	Natural gas ('000 million m³)
Reynosa	0.5	16	3.62
Tampico	2.1	29	1.39
Tuxpan	1.1	26	0.99
SE onshore fields	7.4	248	20.47
Bay of Campeche field (A)	32.9	567	8.98

Map legend: Producing oil and natural gasfields; Potential extension of oilfields. Locations shown: Reynosa, Tampico, Tuxpan, Villahermosa, Campeche Bay (A), Yucatan Peninsula, USA, Gulf of Mexico, Belize, Guatemala, Honduras, El Salvador, Nicaragua, Pacific Ocean.

Resource H

Proven oil reserves, 1989

OPEC countries are sitting on 676 billion barrels of oil - almost three-quarters of the world's known reserves (proven reservoirs which can be recovered under existing economic and operating conditions). The oil of four of the Middle Eastern countries - Iraq, Iran, Abu Dhabi and Kuwait - will last more than a century, given last year's production levels and assuming (unrealistically) no new discoveries. On the same basis Saudi Arabia - which owns 19% of the world's known oil - has enough to last 95 years. Russia has the next-biggest reserves but, at the rate it is now pumping them, they will last only thirteen years. The USA's 4% share of the world's known oil could run out in only ten years. Britain's 4.5 billion barrels will last just five years unless it discovers more oil. Luckily it is doing so.

Years of oil reserves remaining (at current output levels):

Country	Years
Britain	5
India	27
Indonesia	20
Algeria	36
Canada	14
Norway	25
Nigeria	32
Libya	59
China	23
United States	10
Mexico	54
Venezuela	97
Soviet Union	13
Kuwait	100+
Abu Dhabi	100+
Iran	100+
Iraq	100+
Saudi Arabia	95

Source: © *The Economist*, 15 July 1989.

CASE STUDY M

The Mexican Oil Industry

Resource I

A petrochemical plant in Mexico.

Activities

You need to prepare an answer for the Board to the question, 'Why does Mexico need our help?' Answer the following questions, then write your summary.

1 Compare the graph in Resource F with the one in Resource B. How does production in the 1980s compare with that 50 years earlier? When did Mexico resume oil exports?

2 What is the relationship between the geographical pattern of reserves and crude oil production (Resource G)? Estimate the proportions of Mexico's crude oil and natural gas which comes from under the Gulf of Mexico.

3 Examine the information in Resource H. Use it to calculate the production of oil in Mexico, the United Kingdom, and Saudi Arabia. In what way could the reserve figures change?

4 What advantages are there to Mexico in producing petrochemicals from crude oil?

5 Make a list of the benefits brought by the 'new oil' of the 1970s.

6 Explain why it is dangerous for a country to rely on one main export.

7a Why did Mexico have to turn to the International Monetary Fund for help?
b What did Mexico have to agree to in order to receive IMF help?

8 Who or what do you think is to blame for Mexico's huge debt?

Key Question 3
Should we be concerned about environmental impacts?

CASE STUDY M

The Mexican Oil Industry

It looks as though with the oil industry's proven potential your company could easily be persuaded to invest once again in Mexico's development. But there are other aspects of development that need consideration. Your partner shows you a newspaper article which you read with some concern.

Resource J

Why not leave well alone?

A growing concern of the Mexican oil industry is pollution – and not before time! The pace of change has been such that Mexico has adopted a careless attitude towards the ecological consequences when collecting her new oil bonanza. In the new oil fields of the south almost everything has been sacrificed to harvesting the new black gold: large tracts of primeval rainforest have been wantonly felled as new access roads have been cut, spillages have polluted farmlands and rivers, pipelines have been driven through virgin lands and Indian peasant communities trampled roughshod in the drive for oil. Once quiet towns, such as Villahermosa, have become cities of footloose workers, ramshackle housing, and disorder as the oil boom transformed their position in the national economy. The Gulf has been polluted by huge oil leakages from offshore platforms while the thousands of deaths in the 1984 explosion at the Mexico City refinery may be attributed to insufficient care and attention to safety and maintenance.

The pressure to exploit the new wealth as rapidly as possible means that too many corners have been cut and environmental concerns have taken a back seat. And the growing concern with the greenhouse effect – the warming of the earth's surface by adding to the carbon dioxide in the atmosphere, caused partly by the burning of fossil fuels such as petroleum products – makes one wonder if it wouldn't be best for everyone to leave Mexico's oil in the ground.

CASE STUDY M

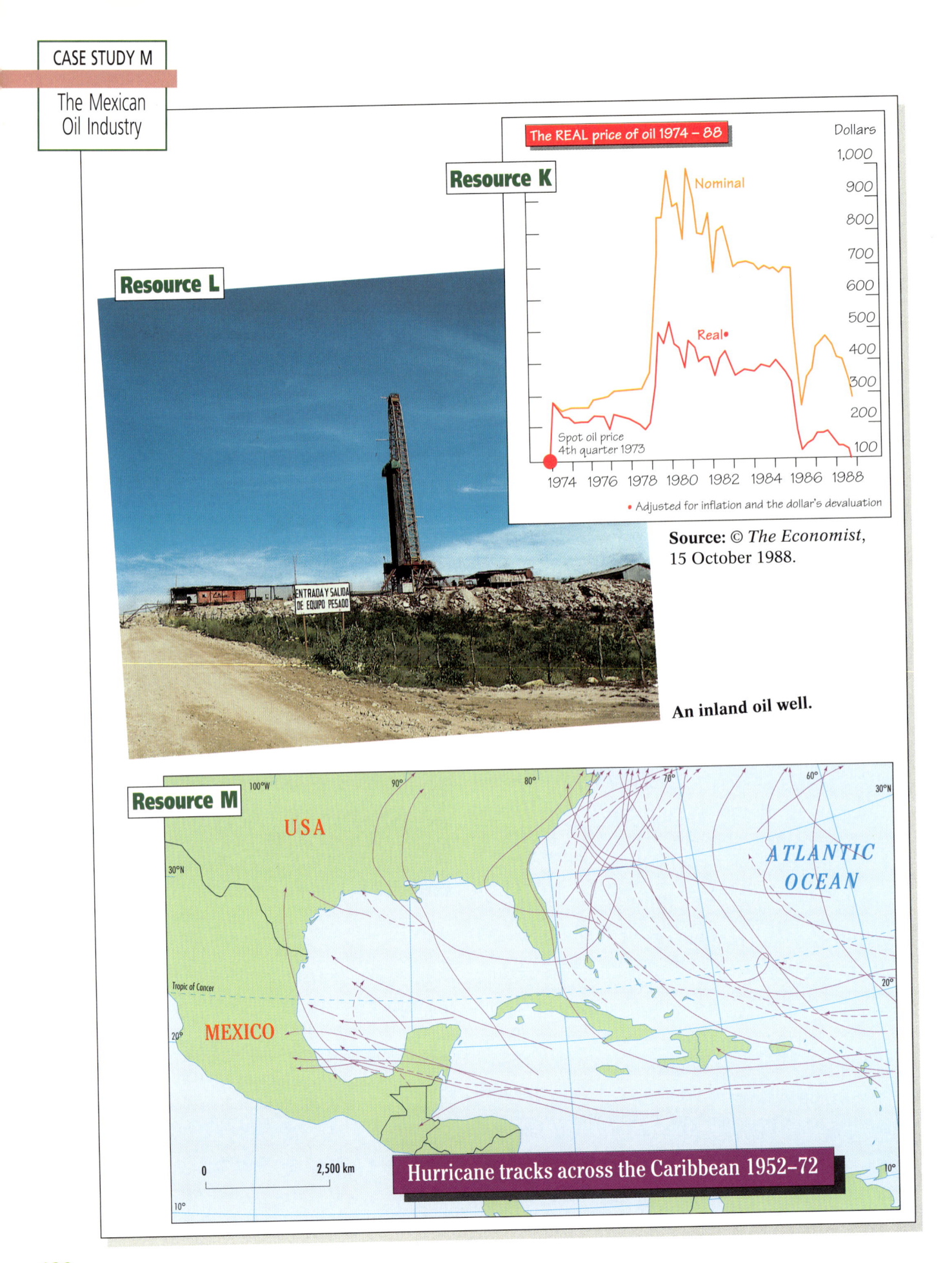

The Mexican Oil Industry

Resource K

The REAL price of oil 1974 – 88

Spot oil price 4th quarter 1973

• Adjusted for inflation and the dollar's devaluation

Source: © *The Economist*, 15 October 1988.

Resource L

An inland oil well.

Resource M

Hurricane tracks across the Caribbean 1952–72

Resource N

CASE STUDY M

The Mexican Oil Industry

An oil rig in the Gulf of Mexico.

Activities

Before you go on to present your case to the Board, answer the following questions using the information on pages 127–129.

1 What is meant by the term 'real price' (Resource K)? How does it compare with the dollar price? Is there a difference?

2 Study the map of hurricane tracks (Resource M). What is a hurricane? What do you think it would be like to be on an offshore drilling platform during a hurricane?

Now you must present your case to the Board, in favour of investing in Mexico. You know your boss will vote in favour, but some people will argue against the idea. The two most likely to disagree are Patrick Olando, the company's publicity officer who is worried about a 'looking after the environment' image, and Alice Pitts, whose father was bankrupted in Mexico back in the 1930s.

3 Organise your case using your answers to the activities on pages 123 and 126. Make a list of the main points of Patrick Olando's and Alice Pitts' likely arguments (you have to predict these).

4 For this activity work in groups of three or more.
a Act out a role-play of the Board meeting, which includes your boss, Patrick Olando and Alice Pitts. It is the job of your boss to persuade the others on the Board to invest.
b Was your boss successful? Record the outcome of your Board meeting, giving reasons why you all arrived at your decision.

5 There has been a protest in Mexico. Imagine you lived in the river port of Villahermosa between 1970 (when the population was 100,000) and 1990 (when the population was 500,000). Write a newspaper article explaining the changes you have seen, your opinion of them, and why you are concerned for the future. (You may find Resource N helpful.)

CASE STUDY M
The Mexican Oil Industry

Further activities

Short-answer tasks

1 Find out how oil is formed. Include a diagram in your explanation.

2 What do we use that comes from oil? Make a list of different types of products.

Library and research tasks

1 What international companies are involved in Mexico? What do they do?

2 How else is Mexico developing? Find out about the sorts of industry and standard of living in Mexico. Would you classify it as an economically developing country? Can you classify Mexico as a newly industrialising country (NIC)? Give reasons for your answer.

3 Find out all you can about the North American Free Trade Area (NAFTA). Which countries are members? Why was it formed? What will the benefits be for Mexico? Will there be disadvantages for Mexico?

4 What are some of the dangers of oil extraction? Try to find information on the *Piper Alpha* disaster in the North Sea.

5 What about transportation problems? Try to find out about the *Exxon Valdez* spillage.

Key Terms

hydrocarbon any organic compound consisting of only hydrogen and carbon, including oil, natural gas and coal.

mineral rights the ownership of sub-surface minerals. In Mexico minerals were reserved by the state until 1884 but after that could be privately owned. In 1916 the revolutionary government declared all petroleum reserves the property of the state, but awarded concessions to existing oil companies.

oil often used to mean petroleum, but when used in relation to natural gas, refers only to the liquid fraction.

petroleum usually gaseous or liquid hydrocarbons.

reserves oil or natural gas that is known to exist and which can be extracted under current economic and technological conditions. There are *proven* reserves, and also *probable* and *potential* reserves.

Key Understandings

- Resources development in economically developing countries usually requires foreign skills, techniques and money (capital).

- Exporting primary products (raw materials) is a precarious way to earn money because the price often fluctuates, and is low in comparison with finished products. This is true even in the case of oil, on which transport and industry all over the world depends.

- During the 1970s large sums of money were earned by the banks – partly because of the oil price rise in 1974 (when oil quadrupled in price). The banks were keen to lend this money to countries like Mexico (and Brazil, Venezuela, Nigeria and many others that looked like good, 'safe' customers). But when the oil price fell, these countries were left with huge debts and no way to pay the interest.

- Most major developments are given an environmental impact assessment before the final go-ahead is agreed. The results of such assessments often conflict with economic reasons for going ahead, and are often ignored by the rich and powerful.

Case Study N

A Multinational Company: Tate & Lyle

Stratford is a district in the east London borough of Newham. Newham has a population of 208,000 and is located north of the River Thames. The area once relied heavily on the London docks and historically most people were employed in the docks and in dock-related industries such as sugar refining. Today the docks have all closed down and many of the old industries have disappeared. The Tate & Lyle sugar refinery remains in the borough, within sight of the Canary Wharf office development, using its own jetty for importing raw cane from Jamaica and other sugar growing countries.

Tate & Lyle is a large **multinational company** operating in over 50 countries around the world. How does such a company operate and what is its impact upon the local community – both in Newham and in other countries where it operates?

You work in your spare time for your local community paper Stratford Voices. Your parents came originally from Jamaica. Your grandparents and several other relatives still live there. Whilst at school you found out that Tate & Lyle have a large factory near where you live. Now you decide to write a series of articles on the subject, especially because you know there are links between the factory and Jamaica. You have much to investigate. Your research begins with Key Question 1.

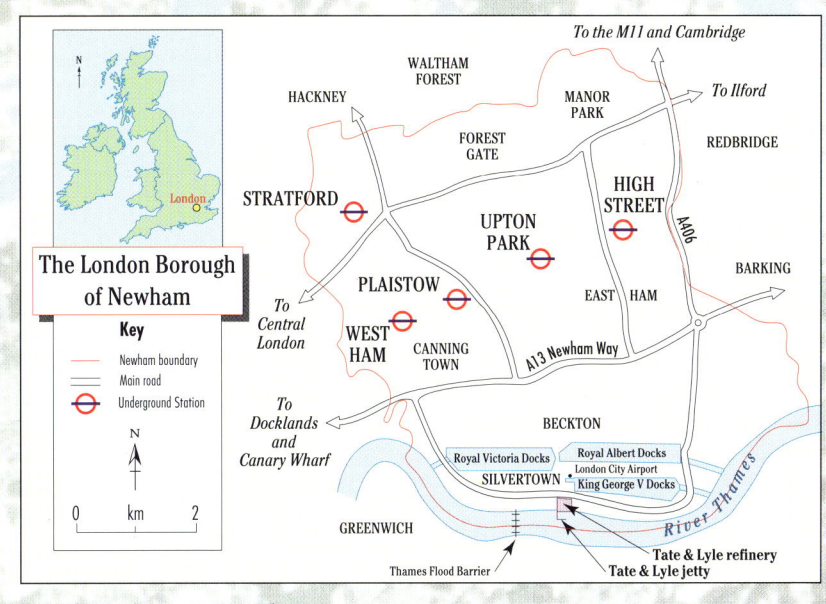

Newham in east London.

CASE STUDY N
Tate & Lyle Multinational

Key Question 1
(a) What is a multinational company?

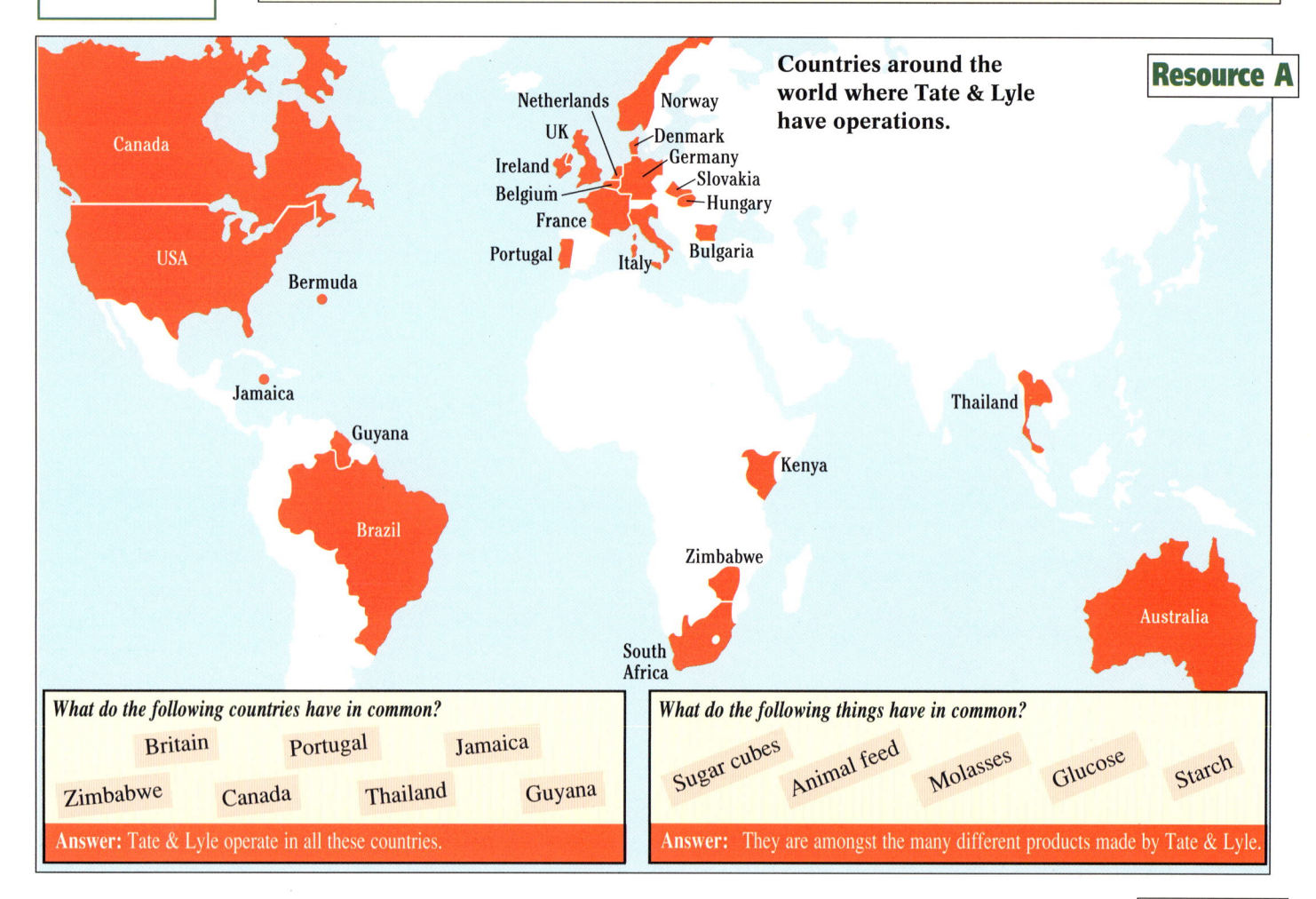

Resource A

Countries around the world where Tate & Lyle have operations.

Countries labelled on map: Canada, USA, Bermuda, Jamaica, Guyana, Brazil, Netherlands, Norway, UK, Denmark, Ireland, Germany, Belgium, Slovakia, France, Hungary, Portugal, Italy, Bulgaria, Kenya, Zimbabwe, South Africa, Thailand, Australia.

What do the following countries have in common?

Britain   Portugal   Jamaica   Zimbabwe   Canada   Thailand   Guyana

Answer: Tate & Lyle operate in all these countries.

What do the following things have in common?

Sugar cubes   Animal feed   Molasses   Glucose   Starch

Answer: They are amongst the many different products made by Tate & Lyle.

Resource B

Tate & Lyle Multinational Project

Although Tate & Lyle makes many different things and operates in countries around the world, it is still small compared with some multinational companies. Table 1 lists companies and their **annual turnover**, whilst Table 2 lists countries and their **gross national product**. Tate & Lyle specialises in sugar, sweetener and starch products. Through a subsidiary Booker Tate it is involved in the management of plantations in Jamaica where sugar cane is grown. Raw sugar is shipped to London and is refined into sugar at the Tate & Lyle refinery in east London. Once the sugar has been refined it is distributed in the UK by the company's fleet of lorries.

Table 1

Company	Annual turnover ($ million)
Mitsui (Japan)	117,027
General Motors (USA)	110,000
C. Itoh (Japan)	108,508
Sumitumo Corporation (Japan)	103,620
Marubeni (Japan)	96,093
Mitsubishi (Japan)	93,321
Ford (USA)	92,500
Exxon (USA)	87,300
Shell (UK/Netherlands)	78,394
Nissho Iwai (Japan)	72,876

Figures from *Business Week*, July 1989

Table 2

Country	Gross national product ($ million)
USA	5,446,000
UK	924,000
Mexico	214,500
Sweden	202,000
Belgium	155,000
Poland	64,000
Nigeria	31,300
Pakistan	42,600
Ethiopia	6,000
Burkina Faso	3,000

UNHDR 1993 (figures for 1990)

Resource C

At the start of the production process: a cane cutter.

CASE STUDY N

Tate & Lyle Multinational

Resource D

Multinational companies have three main features:

1 They operate in many different countries and are usually profitable. Some have annual sales that exceed the GNP of some quite large countries.

2 Some control many of the stages of the production, from raw material to finished product.

3 They are often involved in making a number of different products, though these tend to be in one sector, eg food, oil, chemicals, etc.

AND THEY PRODUCE ANYTHING FROM SUGAR TO SHIPS: Ship, Syrup, Oil Terminal, Plastic Pipe, Nuclear Components, Car Components, Spark plug, Tea, Artificial Sweeteners, Animal Feed

Towards the end of the production process: the sugar refinery at Newham, east London.

Key Question 1
(b) How does a multinational company operate?

Each year Tate & Lyle directors analyse the company's performance. They look at areas making the greatest profit and decide where they will invest in the future. If you were a Tate & Lyle director, what decisions would you make?

Resource E

Tate & Lyle made its name refining cane sugar in Britain. The company was formed in 1921 and in the early days made all its money from sugar refining. Its refineries were based in London, Liverpool and Greenock. Each was on a river estuary but close to a major city which provided a market for the sugar. By the 1930s Tate & Lyle was investing in sugar **plantations** which grew the sugar in Jamaica. Already it could be described as a 'multinational company'. Since then it has expanded and operates in over 50 countries.

Worldwide sugar consumption grows at a rate of 2 million tonnes per annum. In its desire to grow, Tate & Lyle now refines sugar in many other countries including the USA, Canada, Europe and Australia. It has also entered the market for sweetener and starch products made from maize and wheat. By expanding geographically and extending its product range, though remaining firmly in the food sector it has reduced the risk of exposure to one market and one product.

There are advantages for a multinational company that diversifies in this way. When one market becomes less profitable, the company can rely on its other markets. And when problems arise in one country the company can switch its investment to another area of the world.

CASE STUDY N
Tate & Lyle Multinational

Resource F

Tate & Lyle: profit and employees by sector

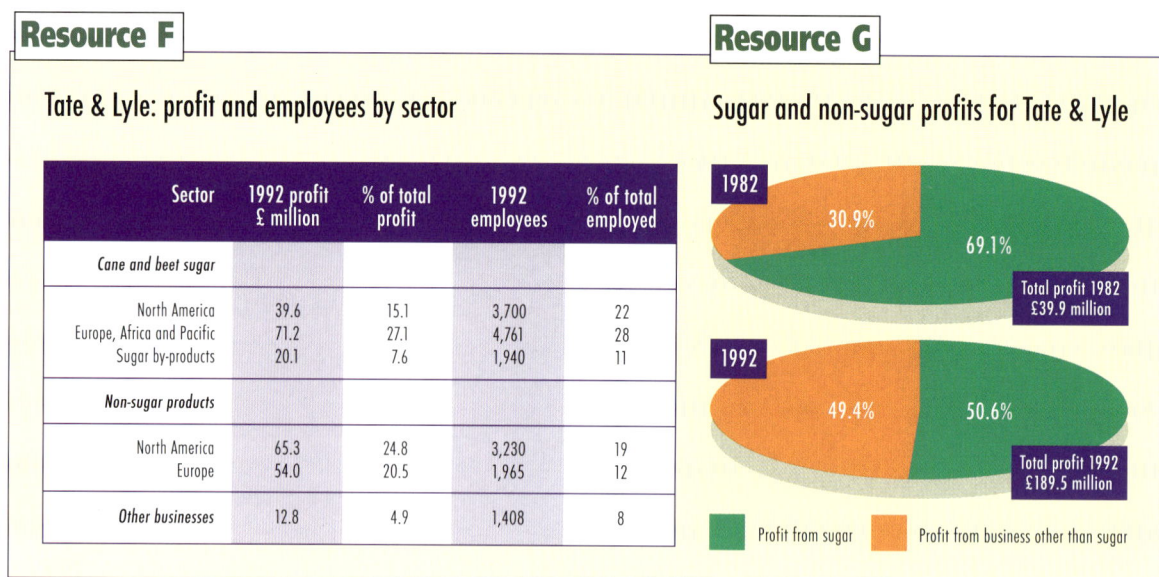

Sector	1992 profit £ million	% of total profit	1992 employees	% of total employed
Cane and beet sugar				
North America	39.6	15.1	3,700	22
Europe, Africa and Pacific	71.2	27.1	4,761	28
Sugar by-products	20.1	7.6	1,940	11
Non-sugar products				
North America	65.3	24.8	3,230	19
Europe	54.0	20.5	1,965	12
Other businesses	12.8	4.9	1,408	8

Source: *Tate & Lyle Annual Reports.*

Resource G

Sugar and non-sugar profits for Tate & Lyle

1982: 30.9% / 69.1% — Total profit 1982 £39.9 million

1992: 49.4% / 50.6% — Total profit 1992 £189.5 million

■ Profit from sugar   ■ Profit from business other than sugar

Activities

1 For this activity, work with a partner. Using the figures in Table 1, Resource B, draw a graph to show the annual turnover of individual companies, using a vertical scale of 1 cm to $10,000 million. Mark on this graph those countries that have a GNP that is less than the turnover of the largest company.

2 How is Tate & Lyle involved in the primary, secondary, tertiary and quaternary sectors of industry? Give examples to support your answer (see page 140 for definitions).

3 The two pictures in Resource C show different ends of the same business. Describe what happens in between.

4a Study Resource F. Complete the passage below using the information in the pie-charts. You need only use figures, and the words *rose* and *fell*.

Between 1982 and 1992 Tate & Lyle's profit _____ from _____ m to _____ m. At the same time the proportion of the profit from sugar refining _____ from 66.5% to 55.1% of the total. The proportion of the total from business other than sugar _____.

b Still in your role as the young journalist on the *Stratford Voices*, try to imagine the point of view of a Tate & Lyle director, thinking about the best investment for the future: what do the figures tell you?

5 Study the table of profit and employment (Resource G).

a Complete two pie-charts to illustrate the information in the table. Show the percentage figures on each chart. Shade each sector in a different colour, using the same colours on both charts for easy comparison. Divide the sugar refining sector into three parts showing the three areas where it is refined.

b Compare the two charts. Where percentage profit is greater than percentage employment, there is high profit per employee. Companies can use profit per employee as a measure of their success.
(i) Which sectors have high profit per employee?
(ii) Which sectors have low profit per employee?
(iii) In which areas does sugar refining make most profit per employee?
(iv) In which areas does sugar refining make least profit per employee?

c As a Tate & Lyle director thinking about the best investment for the future, what do the figures tell you? Why do you think a company director would see profit per employee as a good measure of success?

Now write your first article under the headline 'Tate & Lyle: multinational giant'. Remember that readers will want to know what a multinational company is.

Key Question 2
What effect have Tate & Lyle had on Jamaica?

CASE STUDY N
Tate & Lyle Multinational

Your grandmother lives in Jamaica and once wrote a book on the history of Jamaica. She also wrote many letters to the family in Newham, all of which were kept. On looking through her letters you discover some information relating to working conditions in earlier years.

Resource H

Sugar has been grown in Jamaica since 1655 when the British colonised the island. For the next 200 years rich landowners exploited slave labour for the British market. The slaves rebelled many times and finally won their freedom in 1833. The sugar plantations, which are large farms growing only one crop (sugar), began to decline as the former slaves left to find their own land, and by the 1930s 75% of the sugar cane was grown by independent tenant farmers.

Some sugar growing survived on the island. Although the workers were 'free', they still had low pay and poor conditions. In 1937, Tate & Lyle bought two of the largest Jamaican plantations and began building a new factory to handle the cane from seven old factories.

Jamaica won its independence from Britain in 1962. In 1972 the People's National Party won the election. The plantations became co-operatives which were to be organised by the workers, managed by the workers, for the benefit of the workers. Tate & Lyle sold its factories to a new state-owned National Sugar Company. The entry of the UK into the European Community in 1973 resulted in higher payments to producing countries like Jamaica for raw sugar. Consequently this helped wages to rise, and literacy schemes were started on the plantations.

However, the Jamaican economy was hit by the low world price for sugar and the increased price of oil, which it had to import. In the 1980 elections the People's National Party lost power and within a year the new government had closed down the co-operatives. In the second half of the 1980s, Tate & Lyle was asked back to Jamaica, not as an owner but to provide technical management of the sugar industry, to halt the decline in production and to introduce training and development programmes to advance the process of Jamaicanisation.

Today my friend Nelsetta Johnson is a cultivator on the Frome Estate, one of the oldest sugar plantations in Jamaica. Nelsetta lives in a one-room wooden house in the middle of the estate. The houses are provided free but Nelsetta has no running water or electricity. Nelsetta has two daughters and a 3-year-old son. Nelsetta's mother, a retired sugar worker, also lives in the house. For her week's work of 40 hours, Nelsetta takes home J$ 22.06. (I have sent you her wage slip to prove it!)

CASE STUDY N

Tate & Lyle Multinational

Resource 1 The wage slip of a woman who worked in a Jamaican cane field. **Source:** B. Coote, *The Hunger Crop*, 1987.

FROME   DATE 29.01.86   PAY STATION   MAN

SOURCE CODE	MAIN ACC.	SUBSIDIARY ACCOUNT	RATE CODE	DESCRIPTION OF WORK	RATE $ DECIMAL	QUANTITY OF UNITS DECIMAL	TIME CODE	GANG SIZE	EARNINGS $
131	23500	03032	1317	APPLY MANURE	0.1275	40.0000	ORD	0	63.77

PREV OVERPAY	NIS 1.45	INCOME TAX 7.16	CO PENSION	GOV BONDS 1.27	SAVING SCHEME	HOUSING SCHEME	CREDIT UNION 10.00	ADV. 20.00	STORES CLUB	UNION 1.20
EARNING 325.21	NIS 7.50	INCOME TAX 37.62	CO PENSION	DAYS 26 WKS 5	SICK DAYS VAC DAYS	TO DATE	S1 S5 2 1	COIN AGE 1.1		NAME
NIS NO		INCOME TAX REF	CODE	DAYS 5 WKS	NORMAL PAY 63.16	UT PAY SUN PAY	OTHER	GROSS 63.77	TOTAL DEDUCTIONS 41.71	NET PAY 22.06

At work in the cane fields.

Activities

1 The cost of the following food in Jamaica in January 1986 (when your grandmother wrote her letter) was:
- 3lb potatoes   J$3.60
- ½lb salt fish   J$3.50
- 1lb bread   J$1.90

How many hours would Nelsetta have to work to be able to buy this meal?

2 In order to survive on her wages, Nelsetta needs to make difficult choices. Each choice has *costs* (problems) and *benefits* (advantages). For each choice Nelsetta can do a simple *cost/benefit analysis* to work out the best option. Below are five choices that Nelsetta might have to make. With a partner, study each choice and think of as many costs and benefits as you can. The first one has been started as an example.

Make a list of any other choices that you think could be open to Nelsetta.

3 We have seen three different ways of running a sugar plantation: by slavery, capitalism and co-operatives. For each way of running the plantation answer the following questions:
a Who provides the work?
b Who does the work?
c Who gets the profit?
d Who is paid wages?
e Who owns the land?
f Who owns the capital?
g Who is in control?

Now write your second article, which should answer Key Question 2 on page 135. The choice of headline is up to you.

- Grow her own food
- Do without new shoes or clothes
- Stop paying trade-union fees
- Look for a different job
- Send her children out to work

Choice – grow her own food

Costs	Benefits
It is very hard work, especially after a day in the canefields	Would save some money on food bills

Key Question 3
How do multinational decisions affect a local community in Britain?

CASE STUDY N — Tate & Lyle Multinational

Resource J

Multinational companies increase their operations by investing in countries where they can make profits for their shareholders. They can do this by expanding existing businesses, building new factories or by taking over other companies. At the same time it may be necessary to reduce investments in certain countries by closing down or selling businesses because of the changing circumstances. Tate & Lyle has achieved growth in these ways.

When the UK joined the European Economic Community (now the EU) in 1973, circumstances changed for its UK cane sugar refining activity. Because the EU encourages European farmers to grow sugar beet, the quantity of cane sugar allowed into the EU for refining by Tate & Lyle was reduced. This meant that Tate & Lyle had excess refining capacity which it was unable to use. Earnings declined and to preserve the rest of its business, Tate & Lyle had to close down four of its refineries by 1981. It now has two refineries in Britain, at Greenock in Scotland and the one in east London. Elsewhere Tate & Lyle has been able to invest in sugar: in Portugal, now a member of the EU, in North America and more recently in Australia. Maybe more importantly, Tate & Lyle changed its strategy. It decided to become a worldwide sweetener and starch company, selling off most of its non-core businesses, eg Unitank and Ridgeways Tea, and investing in companies making sweeteners and starches from cereals (maize and wheat) in addition to cane and beet sugar.

Each decision a multinational company makes can affect a local community and its economy. When Tate & Lyle closed its Liverpool refinery in 1981, 1,500 people lost their jobs in an area which already had a high level of unemployment. Tate & Lyle had tried to lessen the blow. Firstly it attempted to influence the European Community (as did its workers - see Resource K), then it tried to operate the refinery at nearly half of its former capacity. When this failed it created jobs in new businesses such as tea blending and packing (packing cube sugar, making furniture and even skateboards). Inevitably this could not help all the workers at the Liverpool refinery. When a major employer such as a large factory closes, it has a knock-on effect on the local community. Engineering companies, cleaners, printers and shops that depend on the factory for business lose trade and may be forced to close.

The larger of Tate & Lyle's two remaining refineries is the Thames refinery at Silvertown in Newham, east London. This refinery produces most of the 1.1 million tonnes of refined sugar produced by Tate & Lyle each year. Newham is a deprived area. Its problems stem from the decline in traditional industries since the 1960s. The once thriving docks have closed and with them have gone big companies like Harland & Wolff (shipbuilders), Crosse & Blackwell (food manufacturers) and Standard Telephone and Cables. Over 30,000 jobs have been lost since 1971.

Tate & Lyle is Newham's largest industrial employer with over 1,400 employees. Twenty years ago the company employed more than twice as many people as it does today. This is a result of improving efficiency, new technology and investment. Although numbers employed have decreased, the company is involved in an active community programme in Newham, targeted on long-term schemes to improve education and training and thus employment prospects for local people. It also pays a large proportion of local industrial rates - an important source of income for the borough.

The future of the Thames refinery should be secure with the import of raw sugar guaranteed by the EU Treaty of Lomé, but to remain competitive Tate & Lyle will have to continue to improve its efficiency. In 1993 a number of jobs were lost by voluntary redundancy. As Tate & Lyle spreads its interests around the world, it depends less on refining in the UK but still values its position in that market.

Resource K

Workers set for battle
by Colin Wright

A mass meeting of Tate and Lyle workers later today will be urged to "resist at all costs" the closure of the Love Lane refinery.

Union leaders representing the 1,570 men and women under the cloud of redundancy look certain to recommend a campaign of industrial action although no details have yet been released.

Meanwhile plans are being made for national employees representatives to hold talks with EEC Food Committee Members to discuss the shut down at an emergency meeting in Brussels next week.

The delegation organised by the General and Municipal Workers Union will be headed by Liverpool-born general secretary Mr David Basnett.

At an emotional news conference called following yesterday's shut down announcement by the group, members of the workforce action committee and district officials from shop floor and white collar unions pledged unanimous support for any action the 11 a.m. mass meeting many decided on.

Divisional officer from the staff union ASTMS Mr David Bird, said the closure of the 112-year-old Tate and Lyle business in Liverpool symbolised the decline of Merseyside.

"This refinery is a symbol of the industry in this area and our task is not only to save the refinery but to save Merseyside as well."

"The closure decision by this company is completely anti-social." Mr Albert Sloane, elected Chairman of the Tate and Lyle Action Committee, vowed that unions would start an immediate fight against the closure.

"We will fight until we drop. We will resist any moves to close down this factory," he told yesterday's Press conference.

Mr Sloane will meet with other leading union officials before today's mass meeting of workers.

Item from a Liverpool newspaper, 1981.

CASE STUDY N

Tate & Lyle Multinational

Activities

1 To begin this activity, look at the facts on the Tate & Lyle refinery in Liverpool (Resource J), which closed down completely in the early 1980s. Now work with a partner. One of you should play the role of a company director, the other the role of an employee. You need to examine the same information, but look at it from a different point of view.

Read Resource K. Answer the questions by setting them out on a chart like the one below. Do any of the answers help you to argue for or against closure of the refinery? Tick the boxes depending on your view as a director or as an employee.

	Arguments for closure	Arguments against closure
A What is the reason for closing the refinery?		
B How many jobs would be lost?		
C How much profit did Tate & Lyle make that year?		
D How long had the refinery been open?		
E How much would closure cost the company?		
F What effect would closure have on other jobs in the area?		
G How much money would Tate & Lyle lose if the refinery stayed open?		

2 Now look at more recent events. You have been granted an interview with a director and an employee of Tate & Lyle, who have agreed to answer questions on the future of the Newham refinery.

a Make a list of questions to ask each person.

b With a partner take it in turns to interview each other and listen to the arguments for and against further job losses.

3 Study the information in Resource J. Make a list of the benefits that the refinery brings to the area. Then select information which shows the costs to the area. Put your information into a table like the one shown below.

Cost of Tate & Lyle to Newham	Benefits that Tate & Lyle bring to Newham

You are now ready to write your third and final report for *Stratford Voices*. Your report should be a general one on all the activities of Tate & Lyle, but with a focus on the costs and benefits to your borough – Newham.

Further activities

For discussion

Organise a formal debate in your class, to consider the motion:

> This class believes that multinational companies are beyond the control of national governments.

You need two people to make speeches to propose this motion and two people to make speeches to oppose the motion.

Some ideas to consider are:
- Where do multinational companies have their headquarters?
- Who owns them?
- Why do they operate in many countries?
- Can a company be everywhere – and nowhere – at the same time?
- Do countries benefit from the presence of multinational companies?
- If so, which kinds of countries benefit the most?

CASE STUDY N

Tate & Lyle Multinational

Assessment activity

Unilever: a multinational company
Unilever is the world's biggest producer of food and household goods. You may not recognise the name Unilever, but you will probably recognise Unilever products.

Task 1: Make your own survey of a multinational company *(4 marks)*

The best place to start is probably at a local supermarket, or by looking at recent newspapers and magazines. Many have advertisements for the products of multinational companies. You may find that the name of the multinational company is not always displayed on packets or tins. The names of some of the smaller companies owned by Unilever are listed on the right to help you.

Design a poster or an advertisement to display the results of your research. You should attempt to show a wide range of products produced by Unilever. Use the following background information.

PRODUCT	BRAND NAME
frozen peas	Birds Eye
margarine	Blue Band
toothpaste	Gibbs
packet soup	Batchelors

UNILEVER
- Owns over 70 companies
- Trades in 80 countries
- Employs 306,000 people
- Has its head offices in London and Rotterdam

Task 2: Why do many economically developing countries encourage multinational companies to establish new industries? *(6)*

> We need foreign capital and technological skills. We need to attract foreign companies because they will bring capital and technology. We need to become an industrial nation. We can offer a much cheaper labour force than they can find at home.

Imagine you are the Minister of Employment in an economically developing country where there is a great deal of unemployment and many people live in poverty. A large multinational company wants to build a new car factory in your country.

Prepare a short report outlining the benefits that investment by the multinational company will bring to your country.

CASE STUDY N
Tate & Lyle Multinational

Task 3: Is this the right sort of development? (6)

Much of the evidence so far indicates that economically developing countries have not wholly benefited from the activities of multinational companies.

A group of workers in the capital city have organised a campaign to try to prevent the new car factory being built. Design a leaflet to be distributed by the campaign which outlines the main arguments against the proposal.

Task 4: What do *you* think? (4)

Write a short conclusion to this piece of work. In your conclusion you should
- describe the characteristics of a multinational company
- state whether or not you are in favour of the new car factory being built, giving reasons for your answer.

Total 20 marks

Key Terms

annual turnover the amount of money that comes into a company in one year.

co-operatives businesses in which everyone is treated equally. Everyone is a 'worker' and everyone is a 'boss'.

gross national product (GNP) the amount of money (measured in goods and services) made by one country in one year.

invest put money into a company, eg buying shares; or when a company buys something that is useful to it, eg land or machines.

multinational companies very large businesses which work in more than one country.

plantations large farms growing just one crop year after year.

sectors of industry industry is usually divided into four sectors:
  primary: raw materials
  secondary: manufacturing
  tertiary: services
  quaternary: research and development.

Key Understandings

- Multinational companies are very wealthy and powerful parts of the global economy. They often have an annual turnover exceeding the GNP of whole countries.

- Multinational companies control a surprisingly large number of different industries. For example, Tate & Lyle refines sugar and builds ships.

- Although the refining of cane sugar depends upon the source of raw materials, the people employed in producing the cane in Jamaica have a very low income.

- Multinational companies are large and powerful and can exert a huge influence on the prosperity and economic development of local communities.

Case Study 0

Subsistence Farming in Burkina Faso

Burkina Faso is the world's third poorest country. It is landlocked, slightly larger than the United Kingdom, and situated in the dry savanna-Sahel zone of West Africa. Until 1960 Burkina was a colony of France, known as Upper Volta. In August 1984 the country was renamed 'Burkina Faso', which means 'land of noble people'. Inhabitants of Burkina are called Burkinabe.

You are working with a firm called ECODEV which specialises in giving advice on environmental development. Your first job involves a one-month visit to Burkina Faso in West Africa where the government has asked for your suggestions for the future development of the department of Yatenga. Before you fly out to Burkina it is essential that you find out as much as possible about the country.

Burkina Faso in West Africa.

CASE STUDY O
Subsistence Farming

Key Question 1
Why is Burkina Faso so poor?

Your supervisor passes you a report written by an expert who was working in Burkina in 1990 for a charity called Africaid. The report gives a good introduction to the country.

Burkina Faso: Report, June 1991 — Resource A

Burkina Faso has little rainfall, poor soil and, with much soil erosion, the country and its people are very **vulnerable**. Savanna vegetation, with trees scattered amongst grassland and farms, is common in the south. Moving north, rainfall is less reliable, trees are fewer and smaller, and savanna gives way to the Sahel zone. Being on the edge of the desert, Burkina suffered badly from droughts in 1968–74 and 1979–84.

When Burkina was a French colony, taxes were introduced. The only way to get money was either to grow cash crops, such as cotton, or leave your village and find work in a town or a more prosperous agricultural area. Many people, particularly young men, left Burkina to work in wealthier countries such as Ivory Coast and Ghana. This **migration** still goes on today. Although migrants can send money back home, their wives and families must continue growing food crops and may have to manage without the men for up to four years. Even today some 3 million Burkinabe live in Ivory Coast, when the total population of Burkina is only 7.9 million.

More than 90% of Burkinabe live in rural villages where the majority are farmers or herders. There are few mineral resources and little modern industry. Most industry – bakeries, bottling factories, soap making, tanneries, textiles and bicycle assembly – is located in the capital, Ouagadougou (pop. 441,514) in the centre of the country, or in the second city, Bobo Dioulasso (pop. 228,668) in the south-west. Most imported goods come through Ivory Coast along the only railway which goes to Ouagadougou and Kaya. Roads are poor, few are surfaced and many become impassable in the rainy season, making movement difficult. The country relies heavily on overseas aid, and Ouagadougou has been called 'the aid capital of West Africa'.

The French encouraged a small, wealthy educated **elite** living in the towns, but there was little benefit for the majority of rural poor people. Over 90% of adults cannot read or write, only 4% of children attend secondary school, and many children die before they reach the age of 4. Many Burkinabe eat far less food than people in the UK, and during drought years they depend on food aid. **Life expectancy** is only 45 years compared with 75 in the UK.

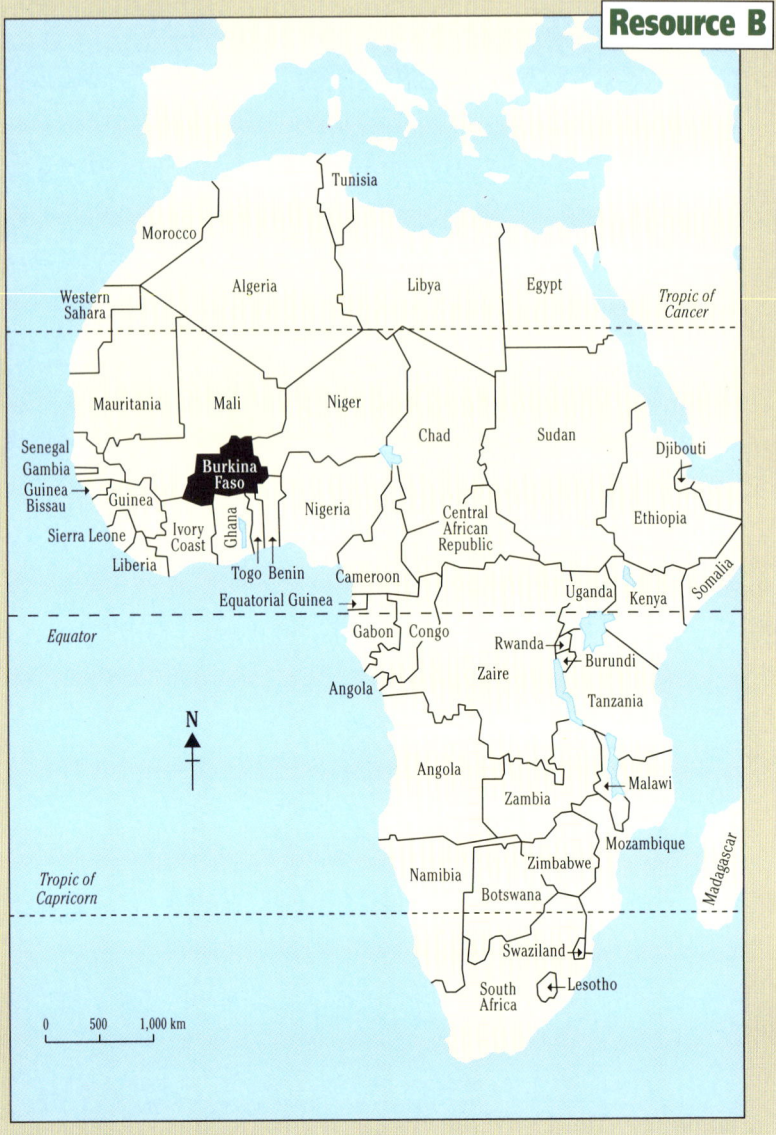

Resource B

The countries of Africa.

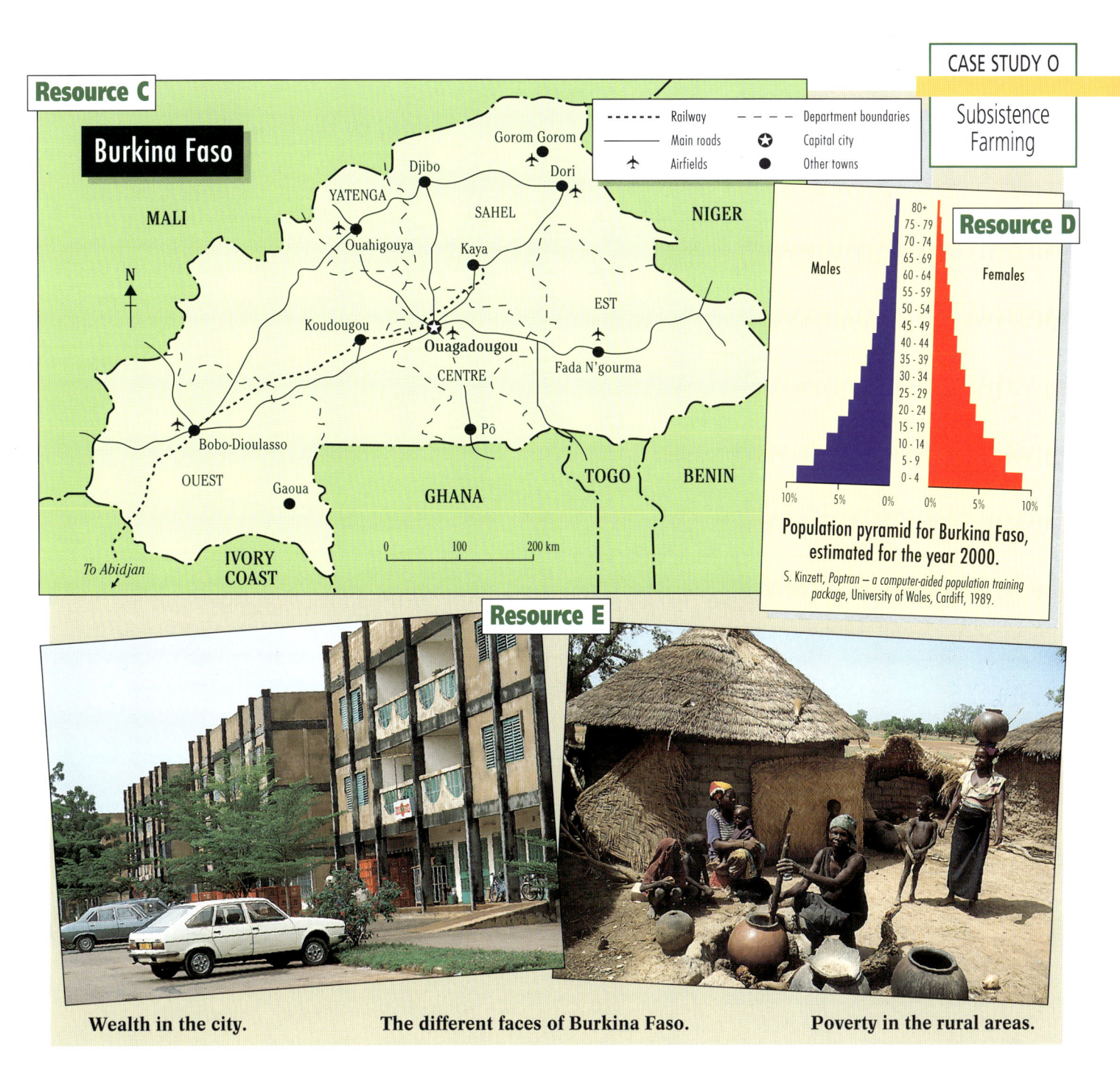

Resource C

Burkina Faso

Map legend: Railway; Main roads; Airfields; Department boundaries; Capital city; Other towns

Map shows: MALI, NIGER, BENIN, TOGO, GHANA, IVORY COAST (To Abidjan). Towns: Gorom Gorom, Djibo, Dori, Ouahigouya (YATENGA), Kaya, Koudougou, Ouagadougou (CENTRE), Fada N'gourma (EST), Bobo-Dioulasso (OUEST), Gaoua, Pô. Region: SAHEL. Scale 0–200 km.

CASE STUDY O

Subsistence Farming

Resource D

Population pyramid for Burkina Faso, estimated for the year 2000.

Males / Females; age bands 0-4 through 80+; scale 10% – 5% – 0% – 5% – 10%.

S. Kinzett, *Poptran – a computer-aided population training package*, University of Wales, Cardiff, 1989.

Resource E

The different faces of Burkina Faso.

Wealth in the city. — Poverty in the rural areas.

Activities

You need to prepare a background file on Burkina Faso. Answer these questions to help you do this.

1 Using Resource B:
a identify the countries that have a common border with Burkina Faso
b name those countries bordering Burkina Faso which are also landlocked – that is, they do not have a coastline.

2 Describe the location of the main towns and communications in Burkina Faso (Resource C).

3 List the main reasons for poverty in Burkina Faso under the following headings: Environmental/ Geographical/Historical/Economic/Social.

4 Describe the characteristics of the population of Burkina Faso as shown in the population pyramid for the year 2000 (Resource D).

5 Compare and contrast the photographs (Resource E). What are the most striking features in the photographs?

CASE STUDY O
Subsistence Farming

Key Question 2
What are the main problems for people farming on the fringe?

With the background information you now have, it is time to set off for Burkina Faso. After three days meeting officials in Ouagadougou, you travel by Land Rover to the department of Yatenga in the north-west corner of the country, near to the border with Mali.

Arriving in Ouahigouya, the main town, after a six-hour journey from the capital, you are taken to meet the Regional Development Officer who gives you an introduction to Yatenga.

You keep a diary as you travel around the country.

Resource F

July 20th
Yatenga is one of the poorest areas in Burkina Faso. The region is heavily populated and its population more than doubled between 1925 and 1984. Population densities reach 70–100 per km² in central Yatenga, and densities of above 50 per km² are common elsewhere. This is the homeland of the Mossi people who make up 48% of Burkina's population. The other main group living here are the Fulani, who make up 10% of the country's population and are well known throughout West Africa for their skills as herdsmen of cattle, sheep and goats.

Yatenga has a harsh climate with no rain from November to March and an average of 720 mm falling between June and September. Soils are poor, apart from in a few river valleys. Much of the natural vegetation has been cleared to grow crops, and rapid runoff and erosion can occur during heavy, often isolated, downpours.

You spend the next week travelling through Yatenga visiting farms and talking to farm families.

July 23rd
Mossi farmers grow millet, sorghum (guinea corn) and a small amount of maize. During the colonial period, the French insisted that all farmers should grow cotton and groundnuts, and new land was cleared for this purpose. Around their huts Mossi have small vegetable gardens fertilised with kitchen waste. There are fewer trees than there used to be, but important ones such as tamarind and baobab are carefully tended and harvested. Unlike the Fulani, the Mossi used to keep few animals – perhaps one or two sheep, goats and chickens. Now, though, the Mossi see cattle as a form of investment and insurance against disaster. After harvest, cattle graze the stubble and add manure to the soil which otherwise receives no fertilisation. The Mossi cannot afford to buy chemical fertilisers.

Many Mossi have left Yatenga for other parts of Burkina or neighbouring countries. In the colonial period, Yatenga was always seen as a problem area, but little help was given. In October 1984, after four bad harvests, Yatenga had a **cereal deficit** of 149 kg per inhabitant per year (assuming that 190 kg of cereal per year is accepted as each person's minimum food needs).

You are taken to the village of Say.

July 25th
Say is a typical Mossi hillside settlement with villagers' strips of land extending up and down the slope covering different soil types. Those who have lived in the village longest have the best land. Out of the total surface area of 1,300 hectares in Say, 950 hectares are cultivated. Large blocks of farmland are split into household units, and sorghum and millet are alternately grown on the same land for five or six years. The severe pressure of people on the land means the soil has little time to recover. Yields of food crops have declined whilst farmland is devoted to more valuable cash crops, mainly cotton and groundnuts.

Resource G

1925	250,000
1960	415,000
1973	500,000
1984	620,692

Population figures for Yatenga, 1925–84.

Resource H

Burkina Faso: population density

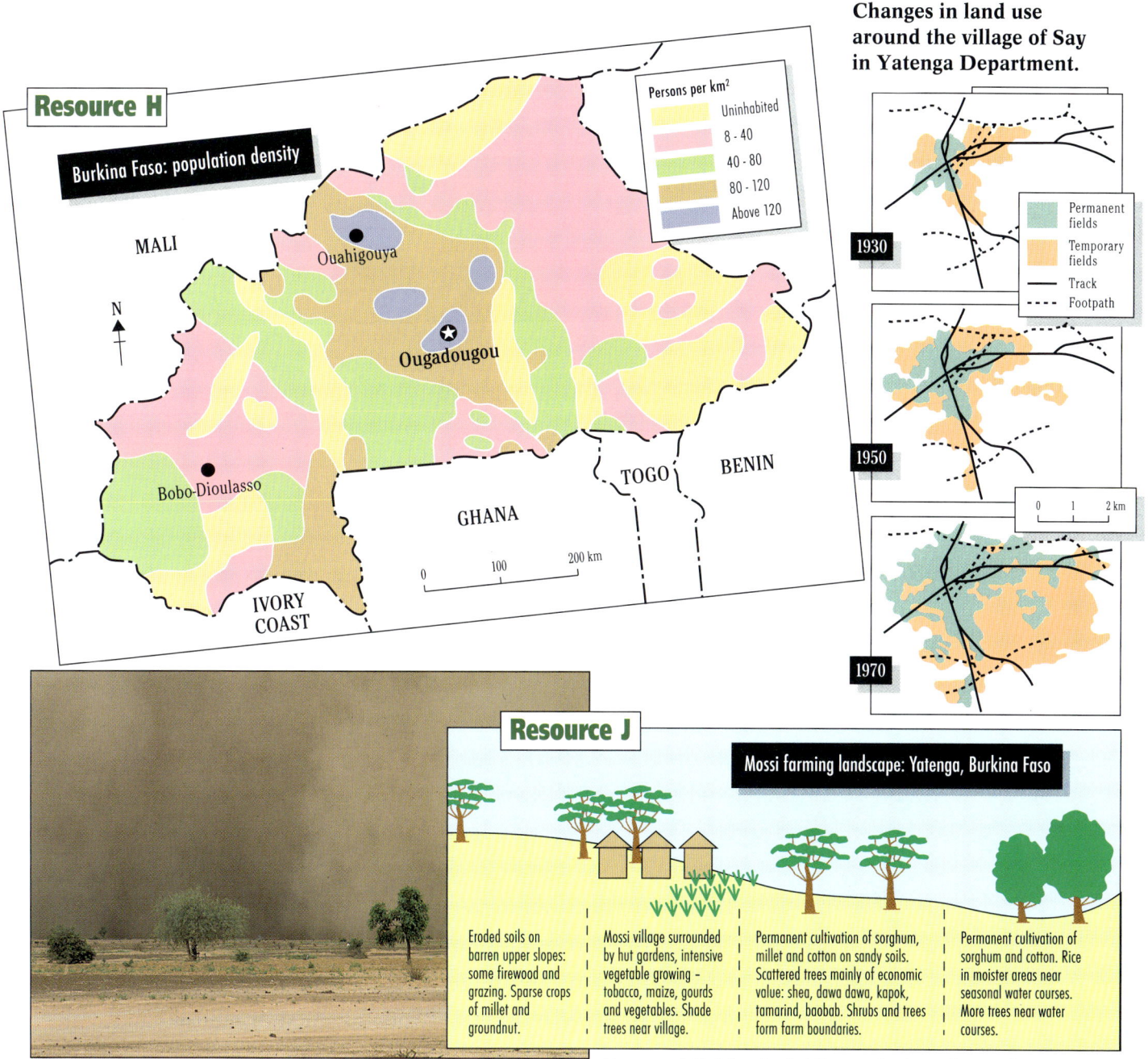

Persons per km²
- Uninhabited
- 8 - 40
- 40 - 80
- 80 - 120
- Above 120

Changes in land use around the village of Say in Yatenga Department.

- Permanent fields
- Temporary fields
- Track
- Footpath

1930

1950

1970

Erosion and land degradation.

Resource J

Mossi farming landscape: Yatenga, Burkina Faso

Eroded soils on barren upper slopes: some firewood and grazing. Sparse crops of millet and groundnut.

Mossi village surrounded by hut gardens, intensive vegetable growing – tobacco, maize, gourds and vegetables. Shade trees near village.

Permanent cultivation of sorghum, millet and cotton on sandy soils. Scattered trees mainly of economic value: shea, dawa dawa, kapok, tamarind, baobab. Shrubs and trees form farm boundaries.

Permanent cultivation of sorghum and cotton. Rice in moister areas near seasonal water courses. More trees near water courses.

Source: J.Y. Marchal, 'The evolution of agrarian systems: the example of Yatenga (Upper Volta)', *African Environment* 2(4) and 3(1) Nov. 1977, pp.73–85.

Activities

Answering questions 1–4 will help you analyse the farming problems in Yatenga. Then, you can start your ECODEV report (question 5).

1 How did the population of Yatenga change between 1925 and 1984 (Resource G)?

2 From the map of population density in Burkina Faso (Resource H), which parts of the country are most densely settled and which are most sparsely settled?

3 Describe the landscape of Yatenga as shown in the photograph (Resource I).

4 With the help of the diagram and map of the village of Say (Resource J), explain how Mossi farmers use their land.

5 Write a short report for ECODEV, stating what you feel are the main problems facing the people of Yatenga. Try to identify the most urgent priorities for help from overseas.

CASE STUDY O

Subsistence Farming

Key Question 3
What are the priorities for development in Burkina Faso?

After a week in Yatenga you return to Ouagadougou to draw together information on Burkina's development policies. You interview the Minister of Development, who tells you about the country's recent approaches to development. Here is an extract from your notes.

Resource K

Notes on interview with Minister of Development, Ouagadougou

Since independence in 1960, Burkina has been unstable politically, with many **coups** and attempted coups. Before 1983, much of the nation's trade was with France, the former colonial power. Many countries gave aid to Burkina, but little progress was made. A small wealthy **elite** grew richer whilst the living standards of most people got worse.

Since 1983, however, there has been a major change in direction. On 4 August 1983, Captain Thomas Sankara, a young army officer, seized power with his National Revolutionary Council (CNR). He was a practical man and a good speaker who impressed many in Burkina and throughout Africa. It was a shock to everyone when he was killed on 15 October 1987 and Captain Blaise Compaore and the Popular Front came to power. Compaore was a good friend of Sankara and he has continued with many of the former leader's policies, though some would say not strongly enough.

Sankara was keen that power should go to the ordinary people. Some of his aims were:

* For Burkina to be self-sufficient in basic foodstuffs. He told people to grow food crops rather than cash crops.

* For agriculture and village life to become more attractive so that people would stop leaving Burkina.

* To encourage the building of reservoirs to provide water for drinking and for agriculture.

* For small industries like poultry farms to be set up in each province rather than just in the big cities.

* To value manual work. He got rid of expensive cars owned by civil servants and he himself cycled to work. He stressed the importance of physical fitness, and soldiers and civil servants could be seen jogging in Ouagadougou, the capital.

* To cut imports and to get rid of **corruption**.

✓ Early in 1985 he launched 'the battle for the railway', when he encouraged everyone to help build a railway from Ouagadougou to Tambao in the north of Burkina. He hoped to develop the poor Sahel zone and mine valuable manganese ore.

✓ A programme was introduced to plant trees and prevent soil erosion.

✓ Much emphasis was placed on women's rights, and in 1988 an intensive literacy campaign taught 10,000 women to read and write.

✓ Sankara introduced a 'common approach' to better rural health. In 15 days nearly 3 million children were vaccinated against three killer diseases: measles, meningitis and yellow fever. Two thousand **primary health care** posts were set up in the rural areas.

✓ Houses and schools were built.

During your visit to Yatenga you saw two Oxfam-sponsored development projects which were helping to improve rural living standards. Both are typical of the new approach to development in Burkina. From talking to farmers and development workers you put together the following notes.

CASE STUDY O
Subsistence Farming

Resource L

Project A: Village cereal banks

Cereal banks are being set up to enable villagers to buy grain when prices are low and store it until the **hungry season** before the next harvest, when it can be sold at a better price. Farmers also save time and money spent on long trips in search of food. In the first year, village group committees receive a loan from Oxfam to buy grain (sorghum, millet, rice and maize) which is stored in village houses. Villagers learn how to run a cereal bank and then decide who will make the best leaders. In the second year the group receives a grant to build a simple one- or two-room grain store and a further loan to help them buy more grain. Oxfam arranges for spare parts so that two lorries could be repaired and grain could be taken to remote settlements that had suffered poor harvests. As loans are repaid, money can then be used to set up new banks. Villages are very keen to have a cereal bank to improve their **food security**.

Project B: Water harvesting

During heavy rain much of the water runs off the continuously cultivated land in Yatenga and erosion is a major problem. In 1979 Oxfam's field director started a tree-planting scheme to help provide firewood. There were meetings with village groups to discuss water harvesting. First, low earth walls were arranged in rectangular or crescent shapes to trap water where trees were planted. Farmers experimented by planting crops such as rice and sorghum in these basins, and manure was added.

Farmers had long-tested traditional methods of using rock barriers, bundles of stalks or branches placed across the direction of water flow. So emerged the idea of the diguette, a small dyke about 30–40 cm high and usually made of rocks. These are built along the contours, snaking across the fields for up to several hundred metres. In 1981 only 6–7 hectares were covered by diguettes, but by 1987 about 1,200 hectares were covered.

A simple water level was developed to determine contour lines accurately so that diguettes can be built. The level consists of several metres of transparent flexible tube, fixed at either end to pieces of wood with marks on. The tube is filled with water and is used in a similar way to a spirit level held vertically. One piece of wood is held at a fixed point and the other moved until the water in the tube is at equivalent marks. The exercise is repeated across the field to get a series of points along the same contour which are then joined by a diguette. Farmers can learn how to use these tube levels with 2–3 days' training. They are accurate and cheap to produce.

Oxfam has also helped to buy a tipper-lorry to transport stones. Crop yields have improved as a result of this project and serious erosion has been brought under control.

In both of the projects described in your notebook:
- Farmers are consulted at all stages and their local knowledge is valued.
- The projects are based in villages and managed by village groups.
- Tools and materials are cheap and usually available locally.
- Little training is needed.
- The people do the work themselves and can appreciate the benefits of this.

CASE STUDY O
Subsistence Farming

Resource M

'Our revolution is democratic and popular. It has set in motion a set of priorities for all our people; adequate food, clothing, shelter, medical care and education.'

'Right now, our No. 1 priority is agricultural self-sufficiency. We have our entire population geared to building dams in the countryside for irrigation so that we can grow food in every possible inch of available space. We have established a house-building programme – 500 units in three months. We plan to construct a network of clinics, schools and small stores throughout the countryside to supply villagers with basic necessities. We aim to use the strengths of the people of Burkina Faso to provide two meals a day and drinking water for all our people.'

'We have tightened our belt from the top. We have reduced the salaries of high officials and civil servants. Ministers will no longer travel first-class, they will get rid of their Mercedes-Benzes and Cadillacs and instead use Renaults without air-conditioning.'

'A woman in Burkina Faso wakes at 5am and walks for several kilometres daily to fetch water. She then cooks, cleans, farms, guards the sheep, and watches over her children. She goes to sleep after midnight. By the time she is 30, she looks like an old lady. Our revolution believes that a woman is equal to a man. We have women High Commissioners in charge of certain provinces. We have women Ministers in charge of the budget, sports and social affairs. Women make up our military establishment and defence system. We have gone further: we are forcing men to do what used to be considered women's chores: to go out to the market, and to look after the family from time to time.'

Captain Thomas Sankara.

Source: Interview with Captain Thomas Sankara, *Newsweek*, 19 November 1984.

A women's group working together in Yatenga.

Resource N

A village cereal bank

Resource O

Tree planting in Yatenga.

Water harvesting.

CASE STUDY O

Subsistence Farming

Activities

You can now start writing your final report for ECODEV. Answer questions 1–4 first.

1 From the information provided in this section and the quotations from Thomas Sankara (Resource M), what do you think are the three most important aims of the government in Burkina Faso?

2 Why are women's groups important? What do you feel about Sankara's statement on the position of women in Burkina Faso (Resource M)?

3 Explain the purpose of village cereal banks and how they might help poor farmers in Yatenga (Resources L and N).

4 Why do you think the water harvesting project has been so popular amongst the people of Yatenga (Resource O)?

5 As part of your final report for ECODEV, write a short piece about how the work of Oxfam in Yatenga fits in with the development policies outlined by Thomas Sankara.

6 Design a poster showing some of the main issues in the future development of Burkina Faso.

Further activities

Short-answer tasks

1 Examine the table showing the main products traded by Burkina Faso (right), and comment on the types and values of various imports and exports. How did these change between 1985 and 1989?

2 Look at the table below showing the production of millet and sorghum (the main food crops) and cotton (an important export crop) and comment on the figures. Bear in mind what you already know about the problems faced by the people of Burkina Faso.

3 Why do so many young people, particularly men, migrate from Burkina Faso to neighbouring countries?

Burkina Faso: Main products traded (million CFA* francs).

	1985	1986	1987	1988	1989
Exports					
Cotton	11,660	10,633	20,138	19,011	14,356
Gold	5,884	7,666	13,059	12,307	6,893
Hides and skins	1,891	1,408	1,654	2,205	2,809
Live animals	3,490	2,725	2,537	1,702	1,681
Karite (sheanut)	2,190	737	243	72	111
Others	6,042	5,496	8,962	6,650	4,419
TOTAL	**31,157**	**28,665**	**46,593**	**41,947**	**30,269**
Imports					
Manufactures	25,725	33,564	34,109	35,814	31,127
Foodstuffs	43,921	25,166	24,326	28,067	29,222
Chemicals	14,825	15,749	17,583	15,767	15,252
Road vehicles and transport equipment	13,327	17,703	13,691	14,823	11,549
Refined petroleum products	18,643	15,413	10,073	9,836	10,801
Others	29,802	32,045	30,745	30,637	27,401
TOTAL	**146,243**	**139,640**	**130,527**	**134,944**	**125,352**

* CFA = Communauté Financière Africaine
Source: Economist Intelligence Unit, *Niger, Burkina Faso: Country Profile 1993/94*, 1993.

	1960	1976
Cotton	2,379	56,143
Millet/sorghum	1,051,968	1,001,875

Production of cotton and millet/sorghum in Burkina Faso (tonnes).

CASE STUDY O

Subsistence Farming

Find out about . . .

1 Try to obtain some more information about the work of Oxfam and other British charities in Burkina Faso.

2 Make a water level as used in the Yatenga water harvesting project, and try it out on a slope in the grounds of your school. Mark a line on the ground to show where you would actually place the stones. If you have some stones available, you could actually build a 'diguette' and see what effects it has during and after a period of rainfall. Write up your notes after the experiment, explaining what materials you used, how much they cost, how easy it was to work out a line for the stones and (if you actually use stones) what effect they had on the movement of water, soil and vegetation. You could repeat the experiment on different slopes and different areas of vegetation and compare your results.

3 Find out more about the causes and effects of erosion in arid and semi-arid areas. Look at some different ways of preventing erosion.

Library and research tasks

1 With the help of atlases, encyclopaedias and other library books, look at other landlocked states in Africa and see if they have similar problems to Burkina Faso. How are they trying to cope with their problems?

2 Try to obtain some information of British overseas aid to poor countries. How much aid do we give and for what sort of projects? Does Britain give aid to Burkina Faso? If so, give some details. Do you think governments should give aid as well as charities like Oxfam? Explain your reasons for and against.

3 Find out about the history of Burkina Faso and some other countries in West Africa, for example Nigeria and Ghana. We often fail to realise that these, and many other countries, have a fascinating history stretching back many thousands of years. The colonial period was only a short phase in their history, from the late 19th century to around the 1960s, when they obtained independence. How far do you think the problems faced by these countries today were caused by events and policies which happened in the past?

Key Terms

cereal deficit the total amount of cereals (grain) available to an area, population or an individual *below* what is needed.

corruption dishonest behaviour.

coup the overthrow, often violent, of a government or political regime.

elite a favoured, usually wealthy and powerful group of people.

food security having enough food to last from one harvest to the next without having to buy food or sell other things in exchange for food.

hungry season the period just before the harvest when food from the previous harvest may be in short supply – a common feature of many rural communities in tropical areas.

life expectancy the average number of years that people are likely to live.

migration movement, in this case of people, from one place to another.

primary health care basic health facilities, usually provided in a small clinic or dispensary by health workers who have often had only limited training.

vulnerable people likely to be affected badly, for example by drought, which may lead to starvation.

Key Understandings

- Burkina Faso is the third poorest country in the world. There are many different reasons for its poverty.

- Yatenga in the north-west of the country is densely populated and its people are very poor. Droughts have often led to famine and starvation, and erosion is a widespread problem.

- Since 1983, Burkina Faso has followed a rather different approach to development from many other poor countries, and Oxfam and other charities have introduced village-based projects. These have been popular with rural people because their living standards have improved.

Case Study P

The Rise and Rise of Taiwan and the East Asian NICs

NICs (newly industrialising countries) are countries where manufacturing industry has developed quickly over the last 30 years or so. Some are large countries like Brazil, but others like Hong Kong are much smaller. Four of the most successful and smallest NICs – Hong Kong, Singapore, South Korea and Taiwan – are located in East Asia. Most of us have at home goods made in these countries: radios from Singapore, watches from Hong Kong, sports equipment from Taiwan or cutlery from South Korea. We can make these items in the UK, so why do we buy them from Asia?

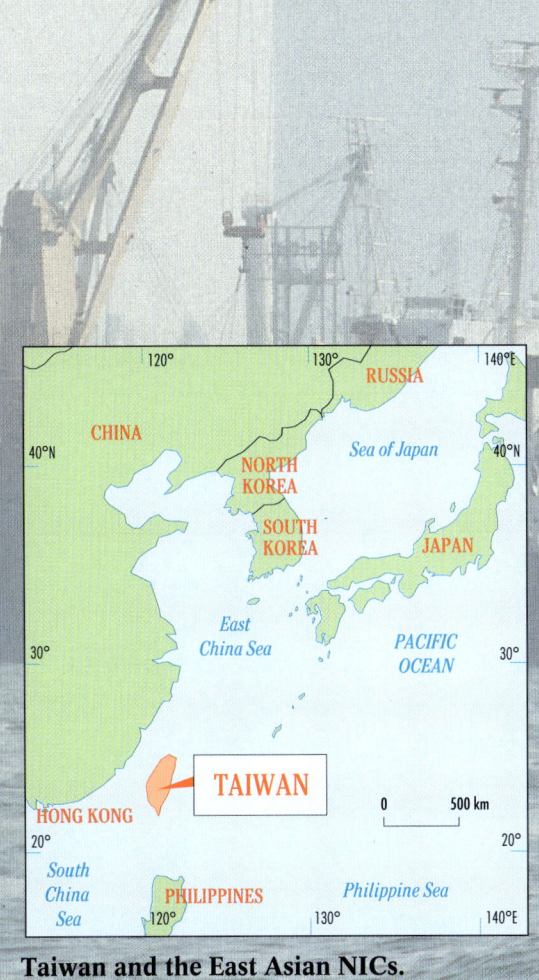

> You have been asked to lead a Department of Trade and Industry research team on an important overseas mission. The team will include economists, geographers and managers from British industry. The government wants to discover why some countries have become so successful in electronics manufacture. Your destination is Taiwan, one of the leading newly industrialising countries in East Asia. You will need to present your report to a meeting with ministers soon after your return.

Taiwan and the East Asian NICs.

CASE STUDY P
Taiwan and the East Asian NICs

Key Question 1
How have the NICs like Taiwan become so successful?

Resource A

MEMO

To: Research team
From: British High Commission in Hong Kong

There are four **newly industrialising countries** (NICs) in East Asia. All were poor after the Second World War with no capital to invest and little machinery available for factories. Natural resources were scarce and most had to be imported. What the NICs did have was plenty of people who were keen to work and satisfied with low wages. Many were immigrants after the war, including refugees from China.

At first, industries concentrated on processing, using simple machines to produce things which a poor population needed and could afford, like clothes. There was a limit to how much these countries could sell to their own people, especially in Hong Kong and Singapore which had small populations. For industry to prosper it had to export to other countries which already had their own clothing industry. It did so by making and selling goods more cheaply. Soon large multinational companies were setting up branch factories in the NICs to make popular products like jeans for export to the USA and Europe.

After success with clothes, the NICs cashed in on the 1960s boom in plastic goods like kitchen utensils and toys. Then they moved into the consumer market making electronic gadgets. Assembling these items is labour intensive, so it suited the large workforces available. It is relatively cheap to assemble such goods in Taiwan, even when the parts come from Tokyo and the finished products are exported worldwide. East Asia's NICs are ideally placed for trade: Hong Kong and Singapore are great ports because of their position, and ports quickly grew up in Taiwan and South Korea to export the growing volume of manufactured goods.

All of this has not happened by chance: governments played their part by encouraging education, keeping wages low in a non-unionised labour force and successfully attracting **transnational companies** from overseas with their vital capital to invest. Transnationals were most important in the industrial development of Hong Kong and Singapore but they have played a part in both Taiwan and South Korea. It is also true that all of these countries have had long periods of strong government dedicated to growth, although political freedom is less than in Western Europe.

Taiwan's changing industries.

Resource B

Assembling electronic components.

Clothes made in Taiwan are modelled in a shop window.

Assembly line at the Tatung Company factory.

Resource C

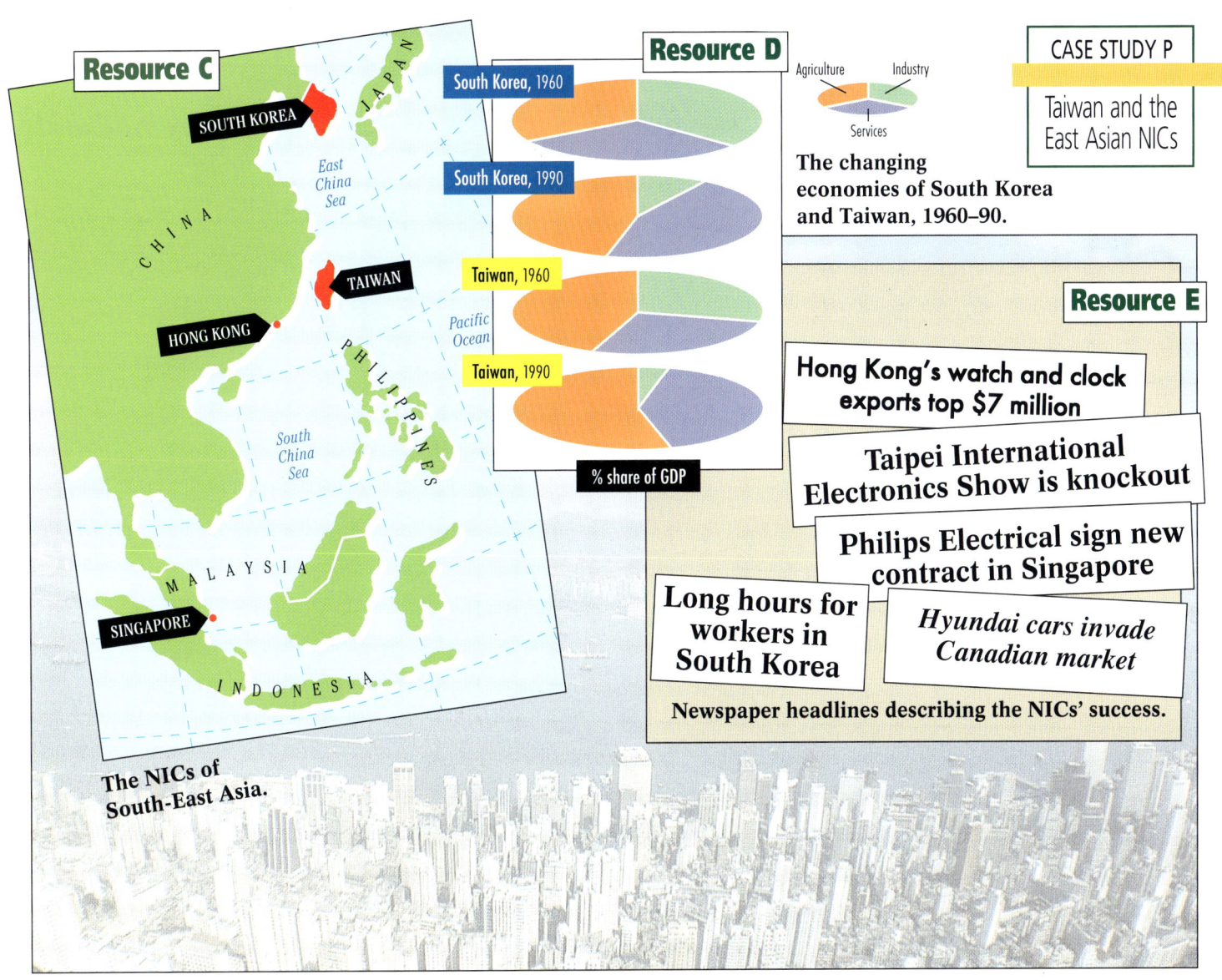

SOUTH KOREA
TAIWAN
HONG KONG
SINGAPORE

CHINA, JAPAN, East China Sea, Pacific Ocean, PHILIPPINES, South China Sea, MALAYSIA, INDONESIA

The NICs of South-East Asia.

Resource D

South Korea, 1960
South Korea, 1990
Taiwan, 1960
Taiwan, 1990

Agriculture · Industry · Services

% share of GDP

The changing economies of South Korea and Taiwan, 1960–90.

CASE STUDY P

Taiwan and the East Asian NICs

Resource E

Hong Kong's watch and clock exports top $7 million

Taipei International Electronics Show is knockout

Philips Electrical sign new contract in Singapore

Long hours for workers in South Korea

Hyundai cars invade Canadian market

Newspaper headlines describing the NICs' success.

Hong Kong harbour.

Activities

Among the documents provided before your visit to Taiwan are Resources A–E. You must write a short report which answers Key Question 1. This report will be the main document sent to all the members of your team. It should include the important facts, background information and any other impressions you gather from these resources. Try answering these questions to start you thinking.

1a Name the four East Asian NICs.
b Approximately what proportion of Taiwan's gross domestic product (GDP) was made up by industry in (i) 1960 and (ii) 1990?
c Name the three main industries which contributed to this increase in GDP.
d What information about working conditions is suggested by the newspaper headlines in Resource E?

2 Look around your home and list any products you can find that were made in the East Asian NICs.

3 Look carefully at the photographs of Taiwan's industries (Resource B).
a How would you describe the work being done?
b What do you notice about the workers in the factory?

4 Make a list of the contributions which you think each of the following has made to the success of industry in these NICs:
- the government
- raw materials
- the population
- capital
- transport
- location
- multinationals.

Now write your report.

153

CASE STUDY P
Taiwan and the East Asian NICs

Key Question 2
What factors have encouraged the location of the electronics industry in Taiwan?

Resource F

Taiwan is a small island about the size of Wales, 300 km off the east coast of China. In 1949 China was taken over by the Communists and over one million people fled to Taiwan. Here they began to build a capitalist economy. Taiwan is mountainous and has few raw materials, so industries had to import them. Since 1949, Taiwan has developed one of the largest steel industries in Asia in addition to major shipyards. However, exports of textiles and electronics goods bring in even more money.

Resource G

The Rise of Electronics Manufacturing

The output of the electronics industry is used in many different ways. Electronics can be found at the heart of everything, from space travel to video-recorders. The industry is an **assembly industry** like the motor industry, where the finished product is put together from individual parts. Assembly requires care but no high-level skills, so the workforce for these tasks can be easily trained.

Most electronics parts or gadgets are small in relation to their value, and although they may need to be transported to assembly points, they are not costly to move. The industry does not depend on large quantities of raw materials or fuels, unlike steel production. The electronics industry is one of a group of what are known as **footloose industries**, which can be sited in a wide range of locations. They are also able to change location if new circumstances make a location cheaper. This is how electronics came to Taiwan.

A footloose industry does not just locate anywhere. The key is *transport*, because parts need to be brought together and products need to be sent off to markets. Most of Taiwan's industries have grown up on the western lowlands. Fast railways and new motorways link the capital, Taipei, with the main ports and industrial cities of Keelung, Taichung and Kaohsiung. Special Export Processing Zones (EPZs) have been created in the ports to make it easier to export goods, and more attractive for foreign firms to establish factories. Here, factories can import machinery and raw materials without paying taxes, as long as they export what they produce.

The electronics explosion in Taiwan during the 1970s and '80s

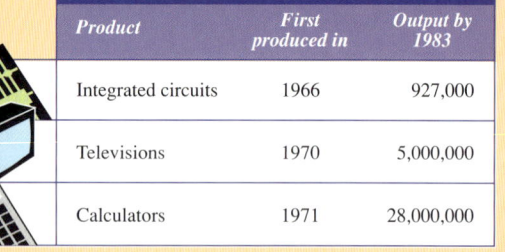

Product	First produced in	Output by 1983
Integrated circuits	1966	927,000
Televisions	1970	5,000,000
Calculators	1971	28,000,000

Taiwan builds for the future.

Container facilities help efficient exports.

Resource H

[Map of Taiwan showing industrial locations]

Locations marked: Keelung, Taipei, Hsinchu, Suao, Taichung, Hualien, Tainan, Nantze, Taitung, Kaohsiung

Features: Taiwan Strait, Pacific Ocean, South China Sea

Legend:
- Highland
- Main road
- Railway
- ■ Capital city
- ■ Major town
- ▲ Science Park/Export Processing Zone
- ● Industrial estate

Scale: 0, 50, 100 km

Resource I

My family live at Sun Moon Lake in the mountains about 150 km from here. It is beautiful there, but much of the land is unsuitable for farmers like my father, and the area is quite remote. When there are typhoons our water supplies, electricity and roads are cut. There is little work there although tourism is growing.

Before we left school we were told about opportunities for work in Taiwan's new industries, but we knew we would have to move to one of the country's large cities. I came to Taipei with three other girls from my village. It is very different here. There are 70 workers in our factory – most are girls in their twenties. We live in a hostel near the factory and sleep in dormitories. Taipei is an exciting city with many large shops, but the traffic is frightening and the air is polluted. Work in the factories is boring and repetitive, but it is a job, and I would have found it hard to get work back home.

Industries are growing so fast here that there are not enough people to work in the factories. Many companies send officers into the country to recruit workers like me. My younger sister says she would rather go to college than come to work here, and my brother says he never wants to leave Sun Moon Lake.

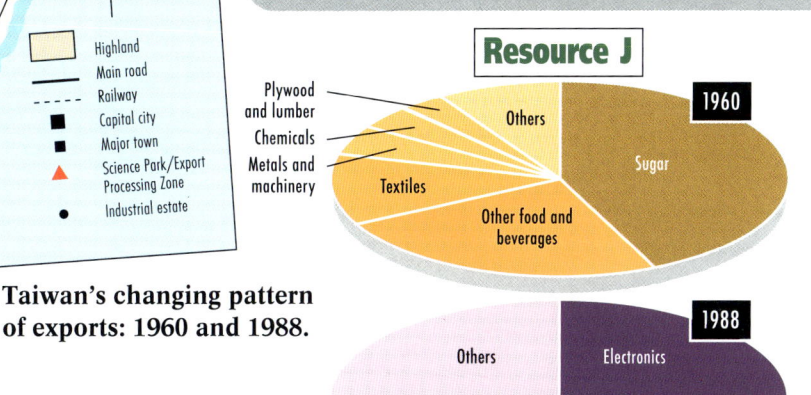

Resource J

[Pie chart 1960]: Sugar, Other food and beverages, Textiles, Metals and machinery, Chemicals, Plywood and lumber, Others

[Pie chart 1988]: Electronics, Textiles, clothing and footwear, Metals and machinery, Food and beverages, Toys and sports goods, Plastic products, Others

Taiwan's changing pattern of exports: 1960 and 1988.

Lan-Ting.

Activities

On your visit to Taiwan you collect the resources on pages 154–155. You should work in a small group to do these activities. Your task is to summarise the main reasons for the growth in the electronics industry in Taiwan. An urgent fax message is required, which must be no more than one page in length, so you must analyse the information here carefully before you draft a list of reasons.

1a Explain what an 'assembly industry' is.
b What advantages does Taiwan have for developing this type of industry?
c Which parts of Taiwan are most suitable for locating the electronics industry (Resource H)? Why do you think this is so?

2 During your visit to a factory in Taipei, you meet a young girl called Lan-Ting from Sun Moon Lake who moved to the city to work in the electronics factory. A member of your team interviews her and provides you with a summary of her comments (Resource I). In your group, study what Lan-Ting says.

a Why it is necessary for industries to bring in workers from over 100 km away?
b How does Lan-Ting feel about her new life in Taipei?
c Why are her brother and sister unlikely to follow Lan-Ting to the city?

3a Draw up a table with three columns, with these headings:

> Decline in share of exports since 1960
> Same as 1960
> Increase in share of exports since 1960

Using the data in Resource J, place each of the exports in one of the columns on your table according to the changes shown.

b Which export was most important in 1960? Which sector of the economy does it belong to?
c Which industry has expanded its exports most rapidly since 1960?

Now write your fax.

CASE STUDY P
Taiwan and the East Asian NICs

Key Question 3
Has technology influenced changes in industry in Taiwan?

During your visit to Taiwan you are able to interview various people. Here is a record of what some of them said.

Resource K

Minister responsible for industry

Interviewer What do you think has been the reason for Taiwan's success?
Minister Undoubtedly over the past 20 years it has been high productivity from low labour costs. But this will not always be the case.
I Why not?
M As the population produces more, so they want better living standards and higher wages. Also we have neglected our environment. So industry must spend more on wages and the environment.
I Is this a problem – surely this is true of other industrial countries?
M Yes, but less industrialised countries with very low wages are following us: Thailand, Malaysia and the Philippines.
I Will this mean a change in policy?
M Yes, we are already changing. Our people are well educated and they quickly learn new skills. So we are moving into higher technology to keep ahead of our rivals.

Minister of Technology

Technology is important for Taiwan. It allows us to keep our own industries up to date, and to sell better products overseas. The government plays an important part in encouraging the use of technology. Every 10 years it selects a programme of new projects which it will back, such as new ports, power stations and motorways. For the 1990s, it has selected eight industries with 'key technologies' for special support. These include biotechnology, opto-electronics, advanced sensing technology and industrial automation.

Chairman of the National Science Council

Our new Science Park was opened in Hsinchu in 1980. It's on the main highway, 80 km from Taipei. We have developed close links with universities and their research. Already by 1991 we have 116 factories in such fields as micro-computers, biotechnology and semi-conductors. The park employs 25,000 people, and this number is expected to grow.

Graduate technologist

After school, I studied at the Taiwan National Institute of Technology before taking a higher degree in the United States. I now work for an electronics company at Hsinchu Science Park where I earn US$877 a month. More and more graduates like me work in Taiwan's new industries, and the higher wages we earn and the taxes we pay help the economy.

Spokesperson for the opposition Democratic People's Party

Our **economic miracle** has been achieved at a price, and people are starting to realise what that price is. We have had a one-party government since 1949 and many of its members are old and out of touch. Only in the last few years has my party been allowed to exist. Wages are low and factory hours long. Most of our urban and industrial growth has occurred at the expense of the environment. We are campaigning for change.

Science parks might look clean and attractive, but rapid growth in Taipei has resulted in poor-quality housing with inadequate sanitation and garbage collection. Traffic and heavy industry pollute the air so that motor cyclists ride in the streets with face masks. Noise and safety standards in factories also need to be improved.

Spokesperson, Taiwan Investment Services

Co-operation is being encouraged with countries whose technology is more advanced. In the first seven months of 1989, there were 250 separate foreign investments in Taiwan, chiefly in electronics. Most investors were from Japan, the USA and Western Europe. Taiwan is already in the big league in computers. In the long run we have to invest in better technology. Many of the industries on which Taiwan built its success in the 1970s are footloose industries, and they will move on to other cheaper labour countries in Asia.

CASE STUDY P
Taiwan and the East Asian NICs

Resource L

Invest at Hsinchu, where Taiwan's hi-tech thrives

For hi-tech investment in Taiwan, the Science-Based Industrial Park (SIP) represents excellent opportunities, and with good reasons:

- **Phenomenal growth**
  Output of the Park has grown 109% annually for the past seven years, with an 88% increase to US$850 million in 1987 *(see graph)*. The number of companies increased 30% annually to 76 last year.
- **Skilful human resource**
  Abundant supply of well-trained scientists and engineers.
- **Low production costs**
  Costs of labour, engineering and management average only one-fourth of those in the USA.
- **Strong government supports**
  R&D grants, one-door service and tax holiday.
- **Idyllic community**
  Just 1-hour drive south of Taipei.

Come to where Taiwan's hi-tech thrives. Come to the Silicon Valley of Taiwan.

Advertisement for the Science Park at Hsinchu.

Resource M

	Microcomputers	Monitor screens
1st	USA	Japan
2nd	Japan	Taiwan
3rd	Taiwan	

World production league, 1987.

Activities

As you are part of an official party, you meet several key people in Taiwan, including two government ministers. Summaries of the main meetings you had are included on page 156. Also included here is an advertisement (Resource L) which you came across for the Science Park at Hsinchu.

1a Re-read your interviews with key leaders in Taiwan, then identify what you think are the five main items of government policy with regard to industry.
b List some of the problems which rapid industrialisation has brought to Taiwan.

2 Study Resource L.
a Suggest reasons why the Science Park was located at Hsinchu.
b Draw a sketch map to help you explain the geographical advantages of this location.

3 On a blank world map outline, produce a poster to attract new industries to Taiwan. Indicate the particular advantages which you think Taiwan has to offer.

4a In a small group discuss (i) how higher wages for many people will affect the shops in Taipei, and (ii) what the city might spend its higher tax revenue on.
b Discuss why Taiwan has gone in for high technology and how its success has been achieved.

Using the resources in this case study, write a short report for the British government's Minister for Trade and Industry, entitled *The Rise and Rise of Taiwan and its Electronics Industry*. In your report you should indicate:
- how and why the electronics industry has grown in Taiwan
- what steps were taken by the Taiwanese government to encourage this
- any disadvantages or difficulties caused by rapid industrialisation.

157

CASE STUDY P
Taiwan and the East Asian NICs

Further activities

Short-answer tasks

1 Study the data in the tables below.
a Which type of employment increased fastest between 1966 and 1982 in Taiwan?
b Did the number of workers or the value of exports increase the fastest? Explain your answer.

Number of employees in Taiwan by sector, 1966–82 (thousands).

	Agriculture	Services	Industry
1966	1,617	1,235	870
1972	1,632	1,726	1,590
1982	1,287	2,718	2,806

Value of exports from Taiwan, 1962–82 ($ US million).

	Agriculture	Processed agricultural goods	Industry
1962	26	82	218
1972	203	295	2,988
1982	420	1,260	22,204

2 Name four countries that would be likely to import Taiwan's products.

3a What is a container port (Resource G)?
b What advantages do container ports offer to exporters of electronics goods?

4 Can you explain the pattern of major roads in Taiwan shown in Resource H?

Find out about . . .

1 The four NICs described in this case study are part of a new economic region in the Pacific Ocean. Using your atlas and reference books, try to work out which Pacific countries are richer than the four NICs; which are poorer; and which are about the same. On an outline map, shade these three groups of countries using different colours.

2 Like the graduate technologist interviewed as part of Key Question 3 (Resource K on page 156), over 5,000 students each year leave Taiwan to study in the USA. Try to explain why, and suggest reasons why many do not come back to Taiwan.

3 Try to imagine what comments different people might make about industrial development in Taiwan. The statements should be like those in Resource K, but should be made by:
a a recently redundant textile worker in the UK
b a Japanese business tycoon
c the manager of a TV shop in the USA
d the British Minister for Trade and Industry (who has just read your report).

CASE STUDY P

Taiwan and the East Asian NICs

Library and research tasks

1 Find out about the location of the electronics industry in the UK. Things to look for:
- Is it concentrated in certain areas?
- Do major roads influence location?
- Are they involved with foreign technology?
- What is the level of wages compared with those in Taiwan?

You might look back at Case Study A, pages 5–14.

2 The following is a list of major projects undertaken by the Taiwan government in the 1970s which helped to lay the basis for massive industrial growth in the 1980s:

- Developing two new ports
- Electrifying the west coast railway
- Building a new international airport
- Developing nuclear power
- Establishing a petrochemicals industry
- Building a large shipyard
- Developing a new integrated steelworks
- Building a new expressway from Keelung to Kaohsiung.

Suggest the advantages and disadvantages which each of these national developments would give to Taiwan.

Key Terms

assembly industry enterprises whose products are manufactured by using a number of components (parts) which are gathered from a variety of locations and then put together (assembled).

economic miracle term used to describe the rapid improvement in economic circumstances of a country.

footloose industry industry that is not tied to the location of its raw materials or markets but which tends to locate where other costs are cheapest. Such industries can therefore change location easily.

newly industrialising countries (NICs) countries, mostly in the developing world, that experience rapid industrialisation.

transnational company a large firm which has branches in a number of countries, and which is also often involved in a range of economic activities (goods and services).

Key Understandings

- Some countries like the newly industrialising countries (NICs) of East Asia have managed to industrialise rapidly even though they have few raw materials and little capital.

- The NICs have a large labour force and have developed their industries by providing basic goods for the home market (clothes). Industries moved on to manufacture low-value goods (toys and plastics) and then progressed to the assembly of high-value goods (electronics) for export.

- Much of Taiwan's industrial development can be attributed to the government's policies which have emphasised the development of the country's infrastructure.

- Rapid industrialisation can cause problems for the environment, as well as increasing land prices, causing congestion and bringing about changes in the distribution of population.

Index

Bold numbers indicate definitions of **key terms**.

accessibility 20, **24**
Africa
　farming 141-50
　water 111-20
agriculture *see* farming
agro-industries 60, 61, **64**, 84, **90**
agronomist 87, **90**
algae 68, **72**
alluvium 102, **110**
annual turnover 132, **140**
arid areas and drought
　Burkina Faso 142, 144
　India 102, 105
　Nigeria 112, **120**
　and nuclear power 79-80
　Soviet Union, former 85, 86, **90**
　USA 91-100
Asia *see* India, Taiwan
assembly industry 152-4, **159**
balance of payments 74, **82**
biodegradable material 66, **72**
Burkina Faso
　farming 141-50
Cambridge science parks 5-14
CAP (Common Agricultural Policy) 36, 38, 40, **44**
car production in Spain 45-54
cereal deficit 144, **150**
C.I.S. 83-90
co-operatives 135, **140**
coal 66, 74-5
　decline 15-19
collective farms *see* kolkhoz
communist state 83, **90**
　see also Soviet Union
conservation 28-9, 31-2, **34**, 41
　water 94-6, **99**
consumer 45-54, **54**
co-operatives 56, **64**
corruption 146, **150**
coup 146, **150**
crofts 26-7, **34**
dams
　India 106-7, 109
　Nigeria 114, 116-17
　USA *see* water transfer
　see also hydro-electric power, irrigation
dependence 60, **64**
discharge of water 65, **72**
diversification
　farming 38, 39, 41, 43, **44**, 60-1, **64**
　industry 20, **24**, 60
drought/dry seasons *see* arid areas
economic miracle 156, **159**
ecosystem 94, **99**
　see also conservation, habitat
effluents 66, **72**
electricity 74-82, 106, 110
elite 142, **150**
employment structure 16-18, **24**
energy
　in France 73-82
　see also coal, natural gas, oil
England
　farming 35-44
　industry 5-14, 15-24, 131-40
enrichment, fuel 76, 77, **82**
entrepreneurs 8, **14**
Environmentally Sensitive Area (ESA) 40, **44**
ethical consumer 47, **54**
Europe *see* France, Rhine, Spain
European Community 137
　and farming 36, 38, 40, **44**, 55-64, **64**
European Social Rights 54
Europort (Wakefield) 23
fabrication 76, **82**
farming

Burkina Faso 141-50
England 35-44
France 55-64
India 101-10
Scotland 25-6, **34**
Soviet Union, former 83-90
　see also irrigation
fast-breeder reactor 79, **82**
Flow Country (Scotland) 25-34
food
　security 147, **150**
　see also farming
footloose industry 154, **159**
forestry 26, 29-32
France
　energy 73-82
　wine 55-64
gross national product (GNP) 132, **140**
groundwater 93, **99**, 103
habitat 28-9, **34**
high-technology industry 5-14, **14**, 152-7
Hong Kong 151-3
hungry season 147, **150**
hydro-electric power 74-5, 106, **110**
hydrocarbons 66, **72**, 130
　see also coal, natural gas, oil
hyv (high-yielding variety) 102, **110**
India
　irrigation 101-10
　industry
　　location 48, **54**, 154
　　manufacturing *see* secondary industry
　　see also pollution, sectors
infrastructure 84, **90**
intervention price 38, **44**
investment 133, 137, **140**
irrigation
　Burkina Faso 147, 148
　France 60, 61, **64**
　India 101-10
　Nigeria 114-17, **120**
　USA 92, **99**
kavalai 106, 107, **110**
kolkhoz 84, 88, **90**
Languedoc-Roussillon
　farming 55-64
life expectancy 142, **150**
location of industry 48, **54**, 154
marginal farming 36-8, **44**
Mexico
　oil industry 121-30
migration 26, **34**, 142, **150**
mineral rights **130**
Mono Lake 94-7, 100
monoculture 56, **64**
monsoon 102, 110
multinationals 131-40, **140**, 152, **159**
natural gas 74-5, 124, 125, **130**
NICs **159**
　see also Taiwan
Nigeria
　Sokoto River 111-20
non-renewable energy 74, **82**
　see also coal, natural gas, oil
nuclear power in France 74-82
　nuclear fuel cycle 76, 78, **82**
oil
　France 61, 74
　Mexico 121-30
　pollution 66, **72**, 127
overcapacity 79, **82**
perestroika 87, **90**
permafrost 84, **90**
Persian wheel 106, 107, **110**
pesticide 102, **110**
petroleum *see* oil
plantations 133, 135, **140**
pollution **130**
　oil 66, **72**, 127
　water 65-72, 79-80, 103, 110, 196

pressurised water reactor (PWR) 75, 76-8, **82**
primary health care 146, **150**
primary industry 16, **24**
　forestry 26, 29-32
　see also energy, farming
quaternary industry 16, **24**
quota 38, **44**
rainy season 112, 114, **120**
redundancy 16, 19, **24**
renewable energy 74-5, **82**
reprocessing, nuclear 76, 77, **82**
reserves, oil and gas 122, 125, **130**
Rhine River
　pollution 65-72
salinity, water 70, 103, 106, **110**
science parks 5-14, 157
Scotland
　rural land use 25-34
secondary industry
　agro-industries 60, 61, **64**
　Asian NICs 151-9
　Cambridge 5-14
　high-technology 5-14, **14**, 152-7
　Spain (cars) 45-54
　transnationals 131-40, **140**, 152, **159**
　Wakefield 16, 20, **24**
sectors of industry **140**
　quaternary and tertiary industry 16, **24**
　see also primary industry, secondary industry
security of tenure 26, **34**
set-aside scheme 40, **44**
silt 68, 69, **72**
Singapore 151-3
Sokoto River Project 111-20
South Korea 151-3
Soviet Union, former
　farming 83-90
sovkhoz 84, **90**
Spain
　car production 45-54
spiral decline 20, **24**
structure plan 11, **14**
subsidy 36, 38, **44**
subsistence farming 112-17, **120**, 141-50
sugar industry 131-40
surplus 38, 58-60, 61, **64**
Taiwan and Asian newly industrialising countries 151-60
tank 102, **110**
Tate & Lyle 131-40
terminal lake 94, **99**
tertiary industry 16, **24**
toxicity 66, **72**
　see also pollution
trade unions 50-1, **54**
tufa 94, **99**
tundra 84, **90**
United States
　water 91-100
unproductive land 116, **120**
uranium 76, 77
venture capital 8, **14**
viticulture 56, 58-60, 61, **64**
vulnerable people 142, **150**
Wakefield
　industries 15-24
water
　conservation 94-6, **99**
　pollution 65-72, 79-80, 103, 110, 196
　shortage in USA 91-100
　table 112, **120**
　transfer scheme 92, 93, 96, **99**, 100
　see also irrigation
waterlogged soil 106, **110**
wine lake 58-60, 61, **64**
yield, farming 114, 117, **120**
Yorkshire
　Dales farming 35-44
　Wakefield industries 15-24

160